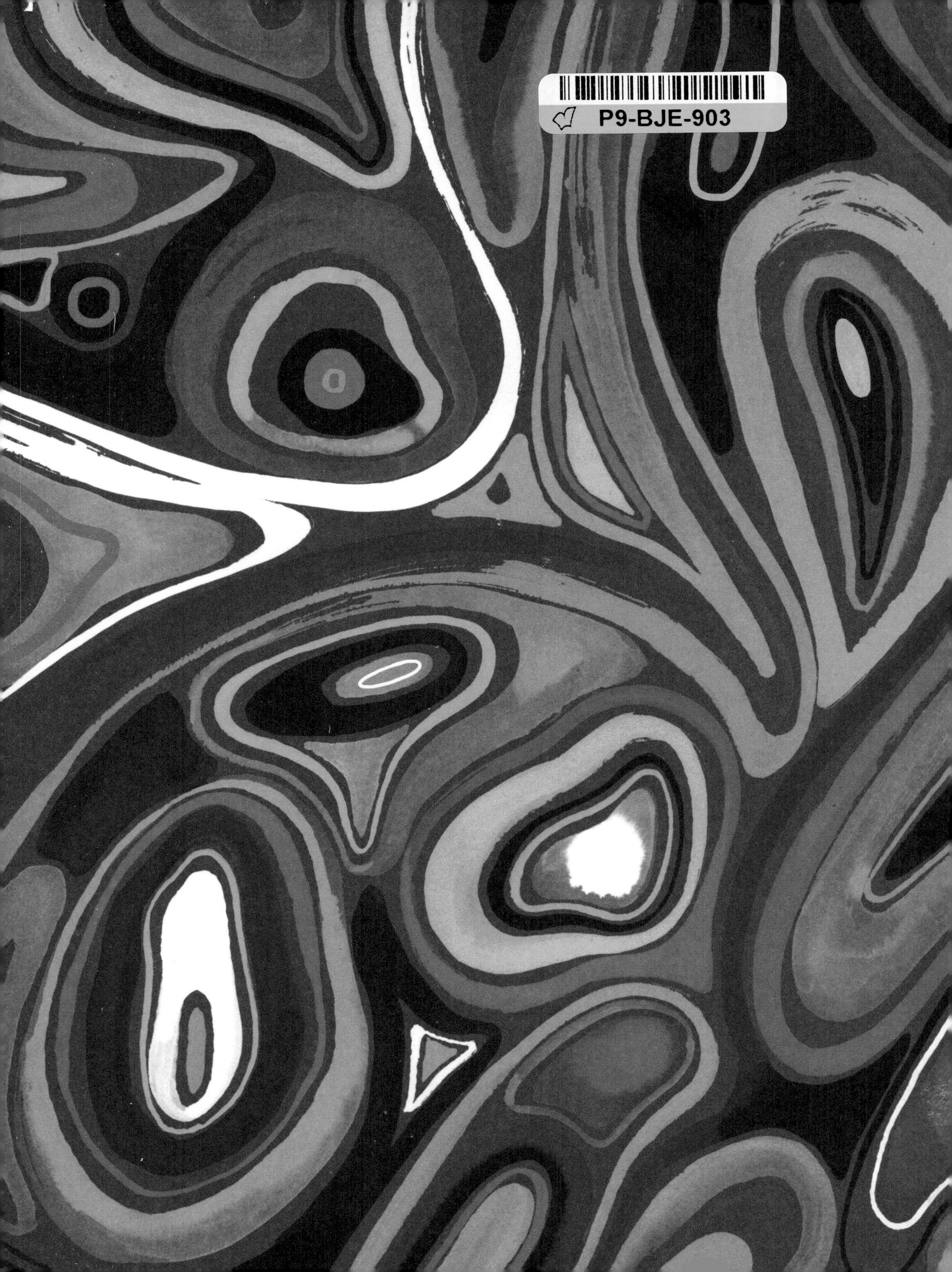

FOR THE ONES I LOVE.
THANK YOU FOR SUPPORTING ME
UNCONDITIONALLY, EVEN WHEN I STUMBLE.

FIRST PUBLISHED IN 2019 BY NOBROW LTD.
27 WESTGATE STREET, LONDON E8 3RL.

TEXT AND ILLUSTRATIONS © MOLLY MENDOZA 2019

1 3 5 7 9 10 8 6 4 2

PUBLISHED IN THE US BY NOBROW (US) INC.
PRINTED IN LATVIA ON FSC® CERTIFIED PAPER.

FSC
www.fsc.org
MIX
Paper from
responsible sources
FSC® C002795

ISBN: 978-1-910620-42-7

WWW.NOBROW.NET

MOLLY MENDOZA

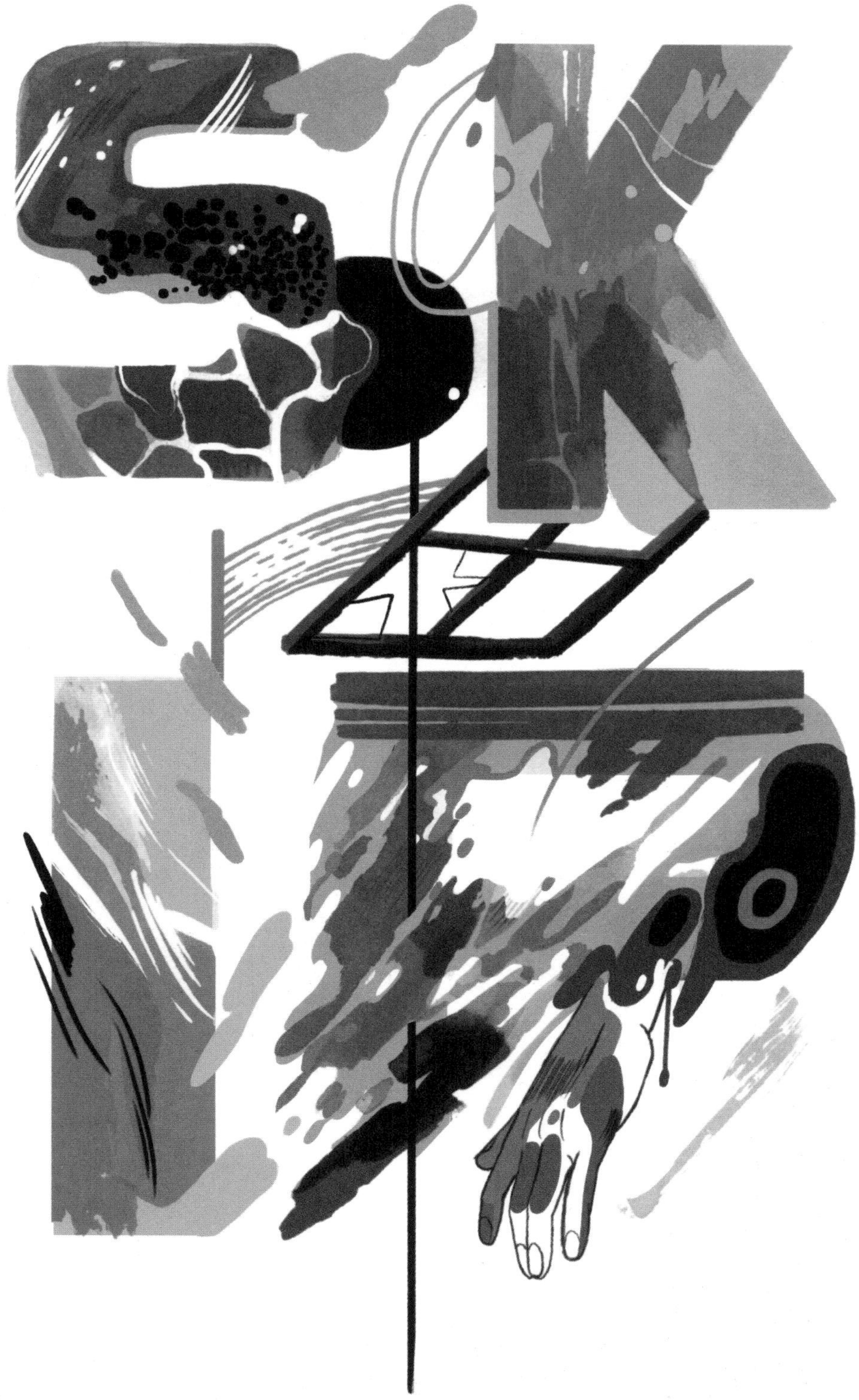
SKIP

NOBROW
LONDON | NEW YORK

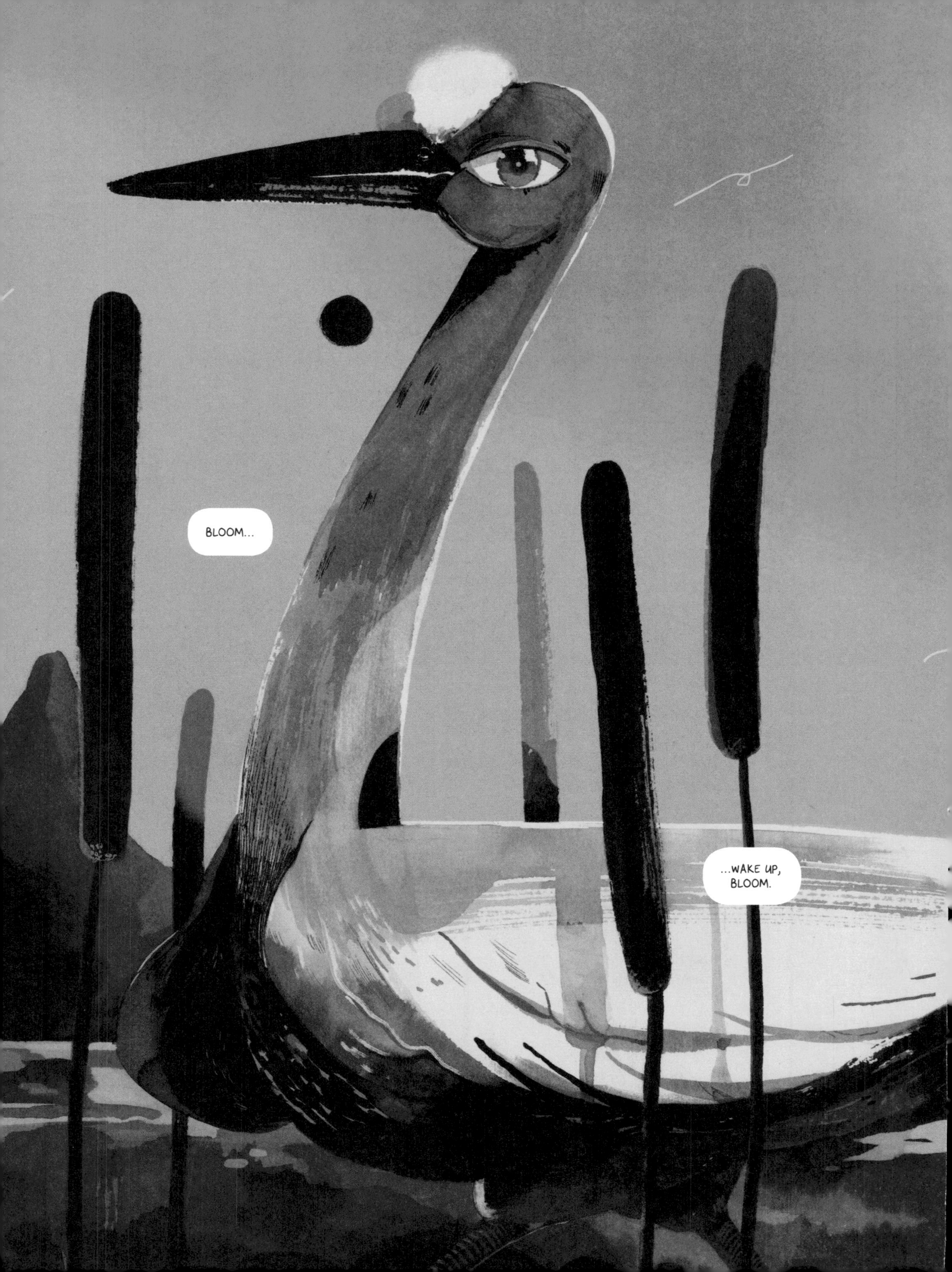
BLOOM...
...WAKE UP, BLOOM.

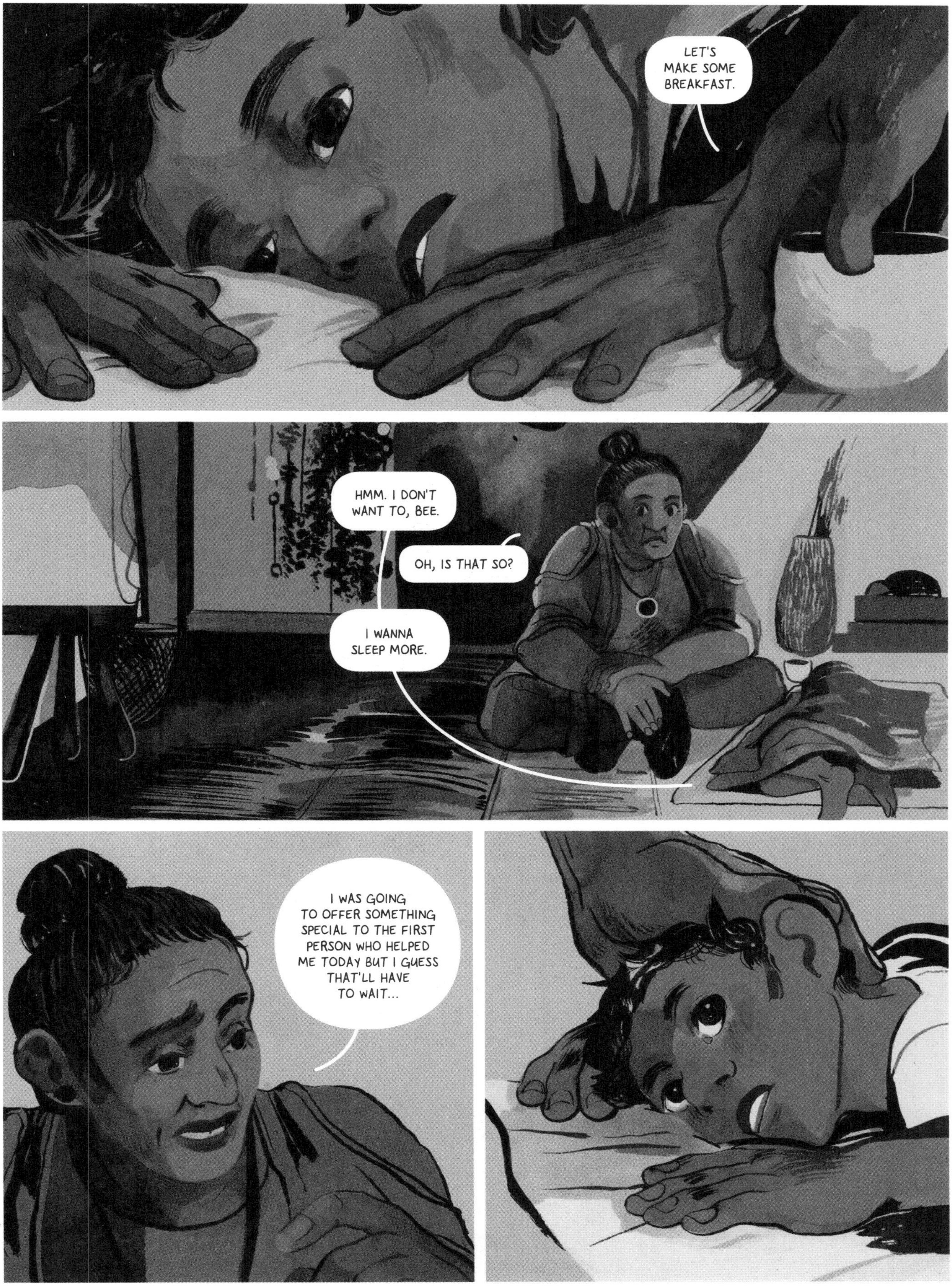
LET'S MAKE SOME BREAKFAST.
HMM. I DON'T WANT TO, BEE.
OH, IS THAT SO?
I WANNA SLEEP MORE.
I WAS GOING TO OFFER SOMETHING SPECIAL TO THE FIRST PERSON WHO HELPED ME TODAY BUT I GUESS THAT'LL HAVE TO WAIT...

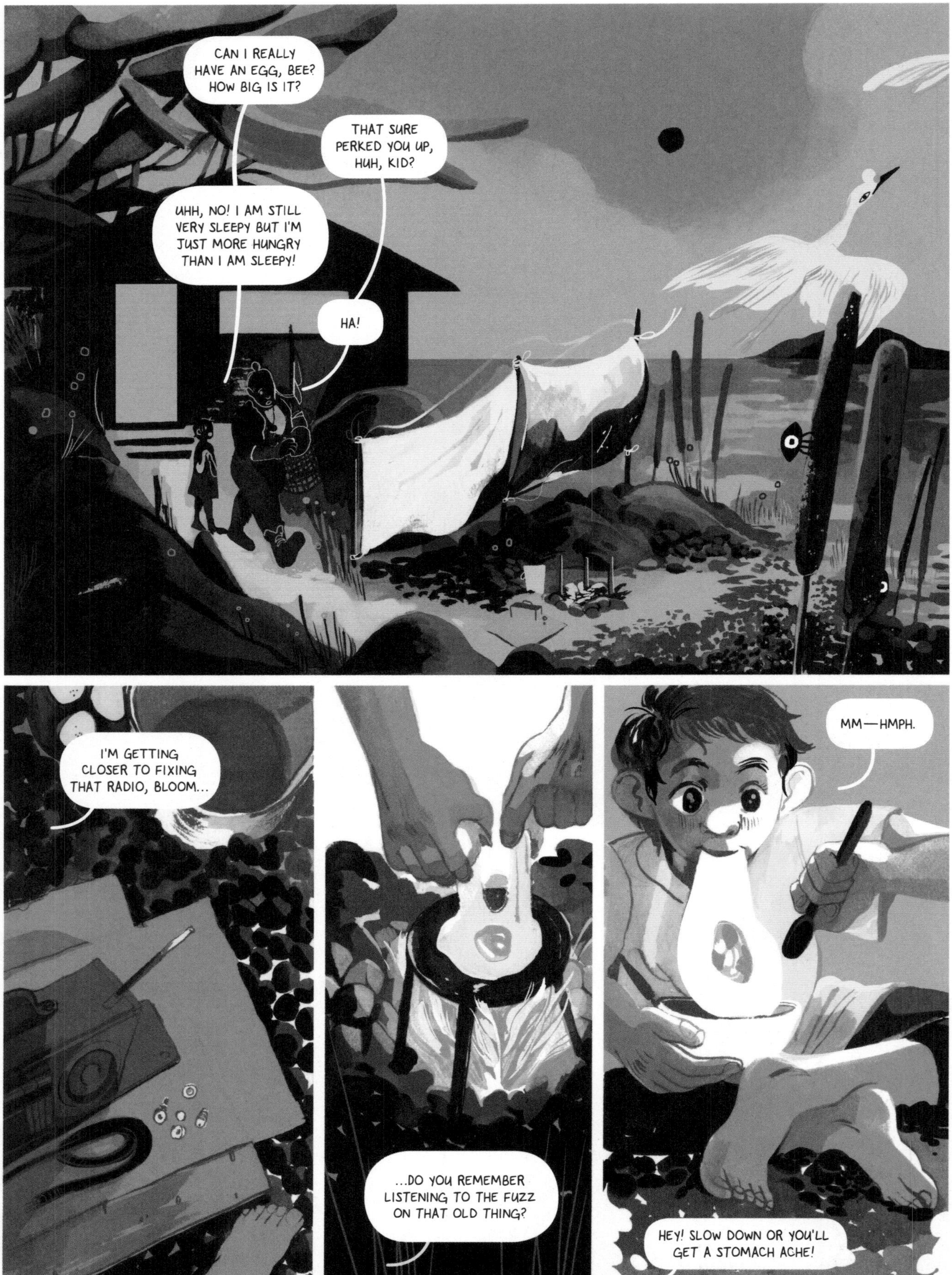
CAN I REALLY HAVE AN EGG, BEE? HOW BIG IS IT?
THAT SURE PERKED YOU UP, HUH, KID?
UHH, NO! I AM STILL VERY SLEEPY BUT I'M JUST MORE HUNGRY THAN I AM SLEEPY!
HA!
I'M GETTING CLOSER TO FIXING THAT RADIO, BLOOM...
...DO YOU REMEMBER LISTENING TO THE FUZZ ON THAT OLD THING?
MM—HMPH.
HEY! SLOW DOWN OR YOU'LL GET A STOMACH ACHE!

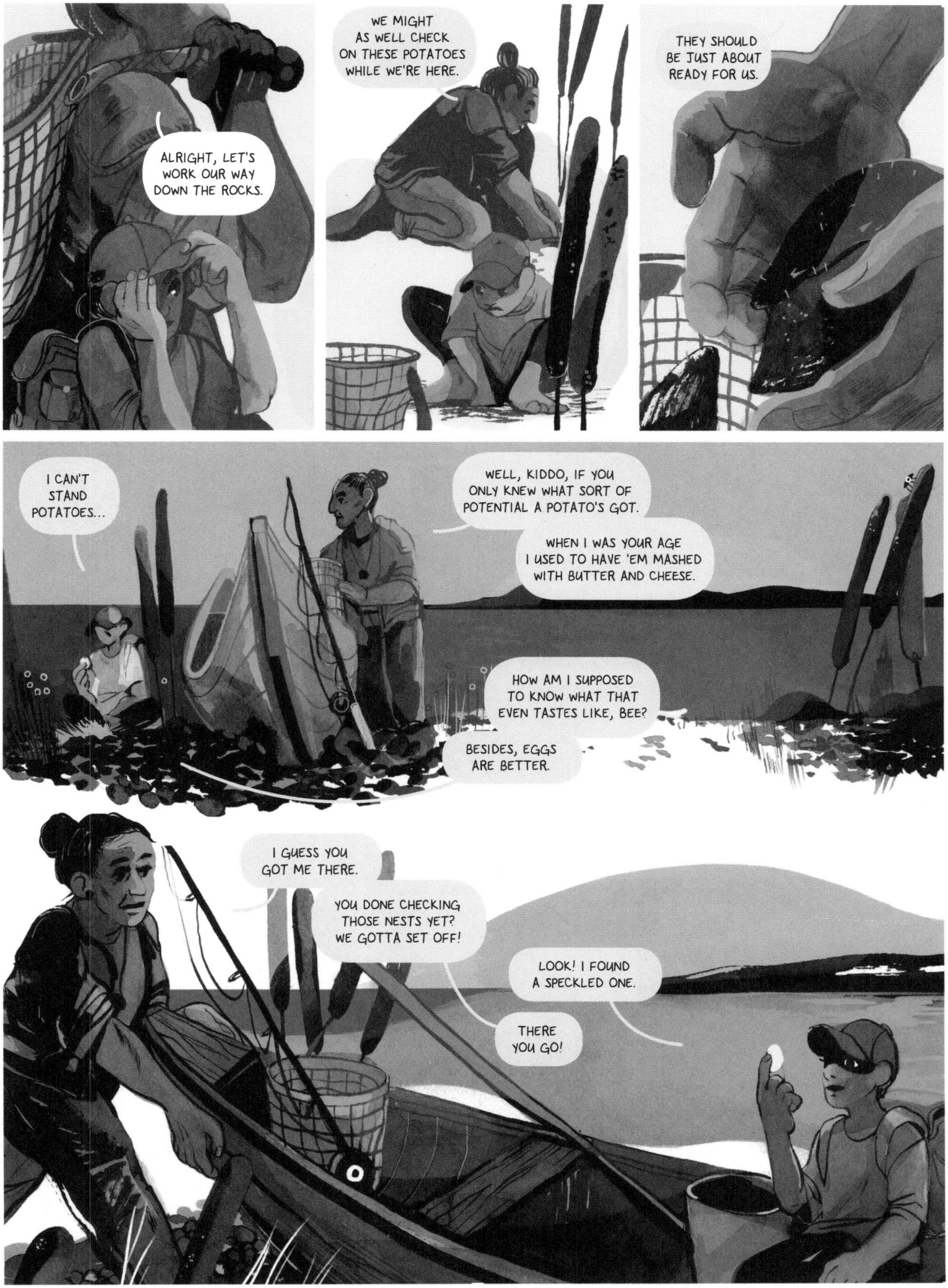

ALRIGHT, LET'S WORK OUR WAY DOWN THE ROCKS.
WE MIGHT AS WELL CHECK ON THESE POTATOES WHILE WE'RE HERE.
THEY SHOULD BE JUST ABOUT READY FOR US.
I CAN'T STAND POTATOES...
WELL, KIDDO, IF YOU ONLY KNEW WHAT SORT OF POTENTIAL A POTATO'S GOT.
WHEN I WAS YOUR AGE I USED TO HAVE 'EM MASHED WITH BUTTER AND CHEESE.
HOW AM I SUPPOSED TO KNOW WHAT THAT EVEN TASTES LIKE, BEE?
BESIDES, EGGS ARE BETTER.
I GUESS YOU GOT ME THERE.
YOU DONE CHECKING THOSE NESTS YET? WE GOTTA SET OFF!
LOOK! I FOUND A SPECKLED ONE.
THERE YOU GO!

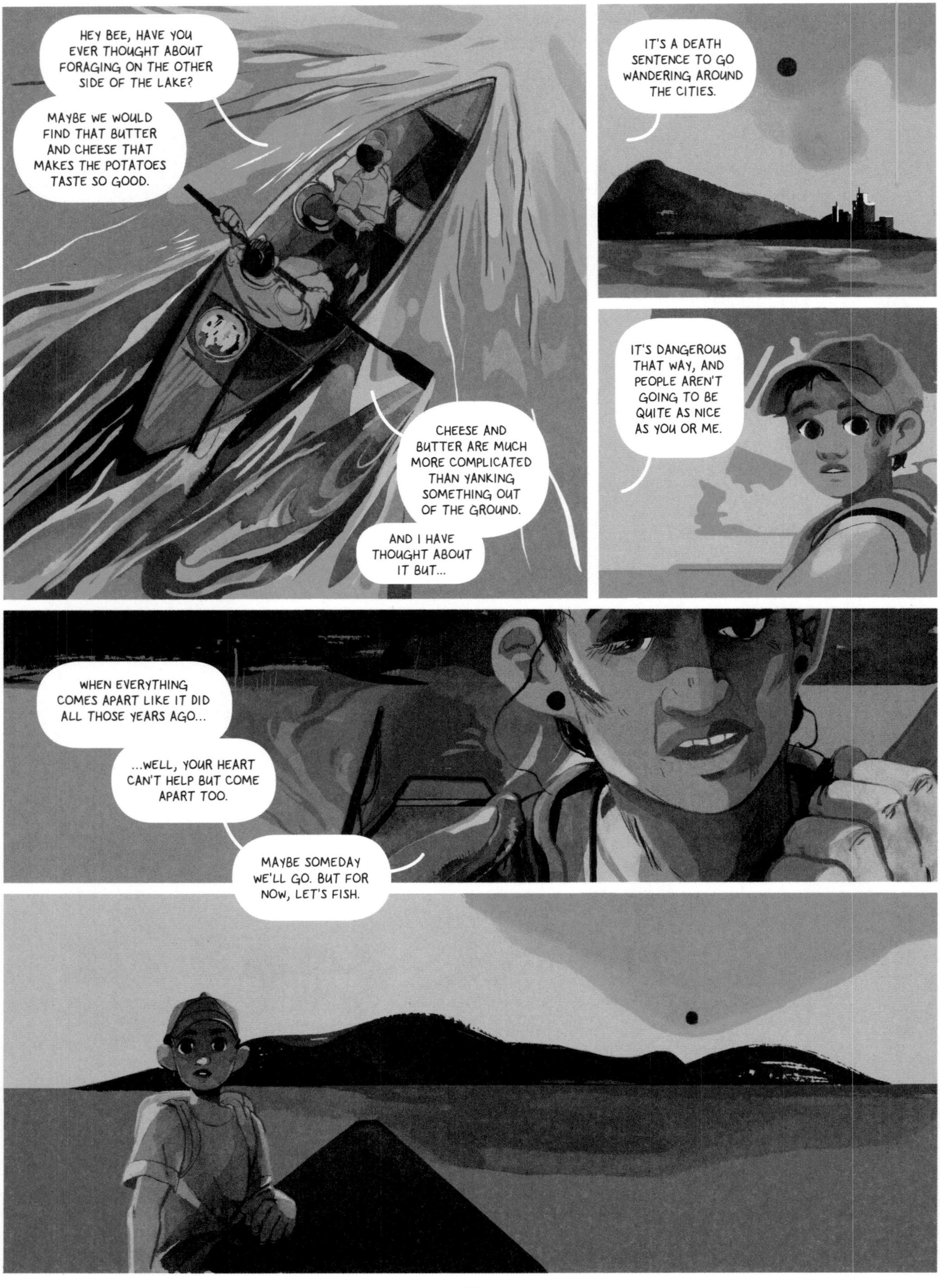
HEY BEE, HAVE YOU EVER THOUGHT ABOUT FORAGING ON THE OTHER SIDE OF THE LAKE?
MAYBE WE WOULD FIND THAT BUTTER AND CHEESE THAT MAKES THE POTATOES TASTE SO GOOD.
CHEESE AND BUTTER ARE MUCH MORE COMPLICATED THAN YANKING SOMETHING OUT OF THE GROUND.
AND I HAVE THOUGHT ABOUT IT BUT...
IT'S A DEATH SENTENCE TO GO WANDERING AROUND THE CITIES.
IT'S DANGEROUS THAT WAY, AND PEOPLE AREN'T GOING TO BE QUITE AS NICE AS YOU OR ME.
WHEN EVERYTHING COMES APART LIKE IT DID ALL THOSE YEARS AGO...
...WELL, YOUR HEART CAN'T HELP BUT COME APART TOO.
MAYBE SOMEDAY WE'LL GO. BUT FOR NOW, LET'S FISH.

I BET BUTTER AND CHEESE AREN'T EVEN REAL.

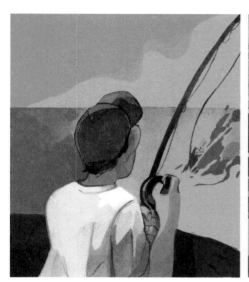

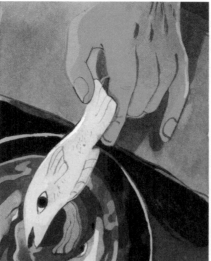

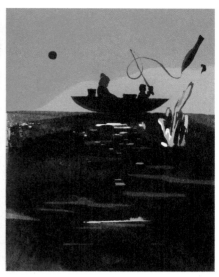

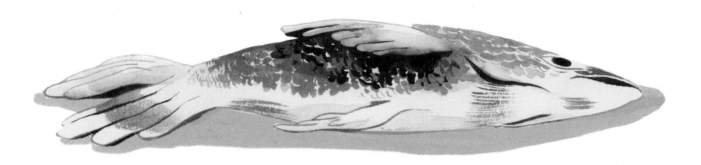

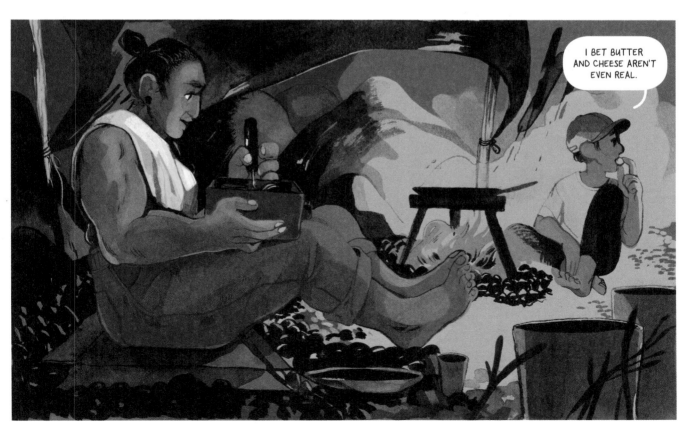

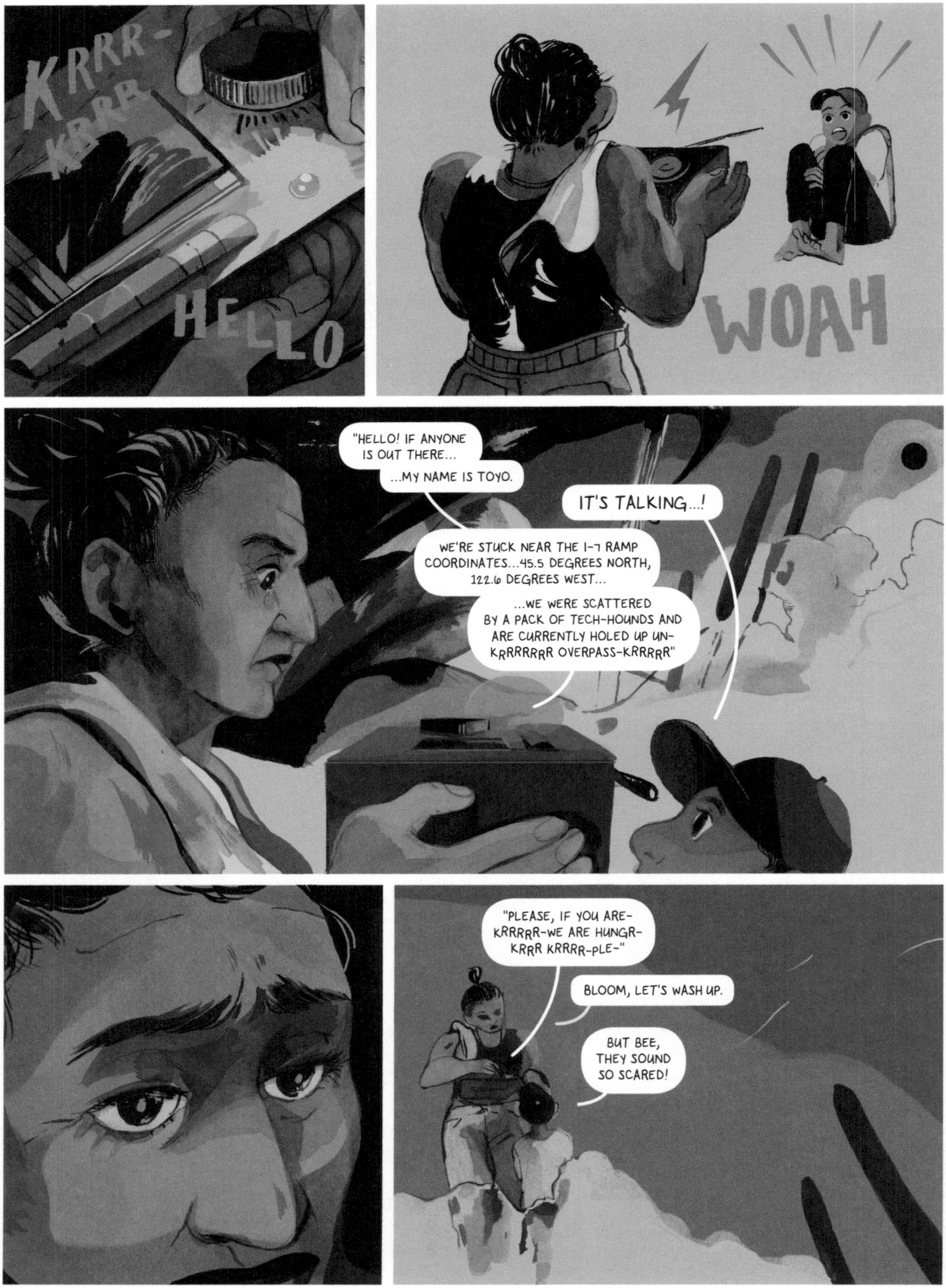
KRRR-KRRR
HELLO
WOAH
"HELLO! IF ANYONE IS OUT THERE...
...MY NAME IS TOYO.
IT'S TALKING...!
WE'RE STUCK NEAR THE I-7 RAMP COORDINATES...45.5 DEGREES NORTH, 122.6 DEGREES WEST...
...WE WERE SCATTERED BY A PACK OF TECH-HOUNDS AND ARE CURRENTLY HOLED UP UN-KRRRRRRR OVERPASS-KRRRRR"
"PLEASE, IF YOU ARE-KRRRRR-WE ARE HUNGR-KRRR KRRRR-PLE-"
BLOOM, LET'S WASH UP.
BUT BEE, THEY SOUND SO SCARED!

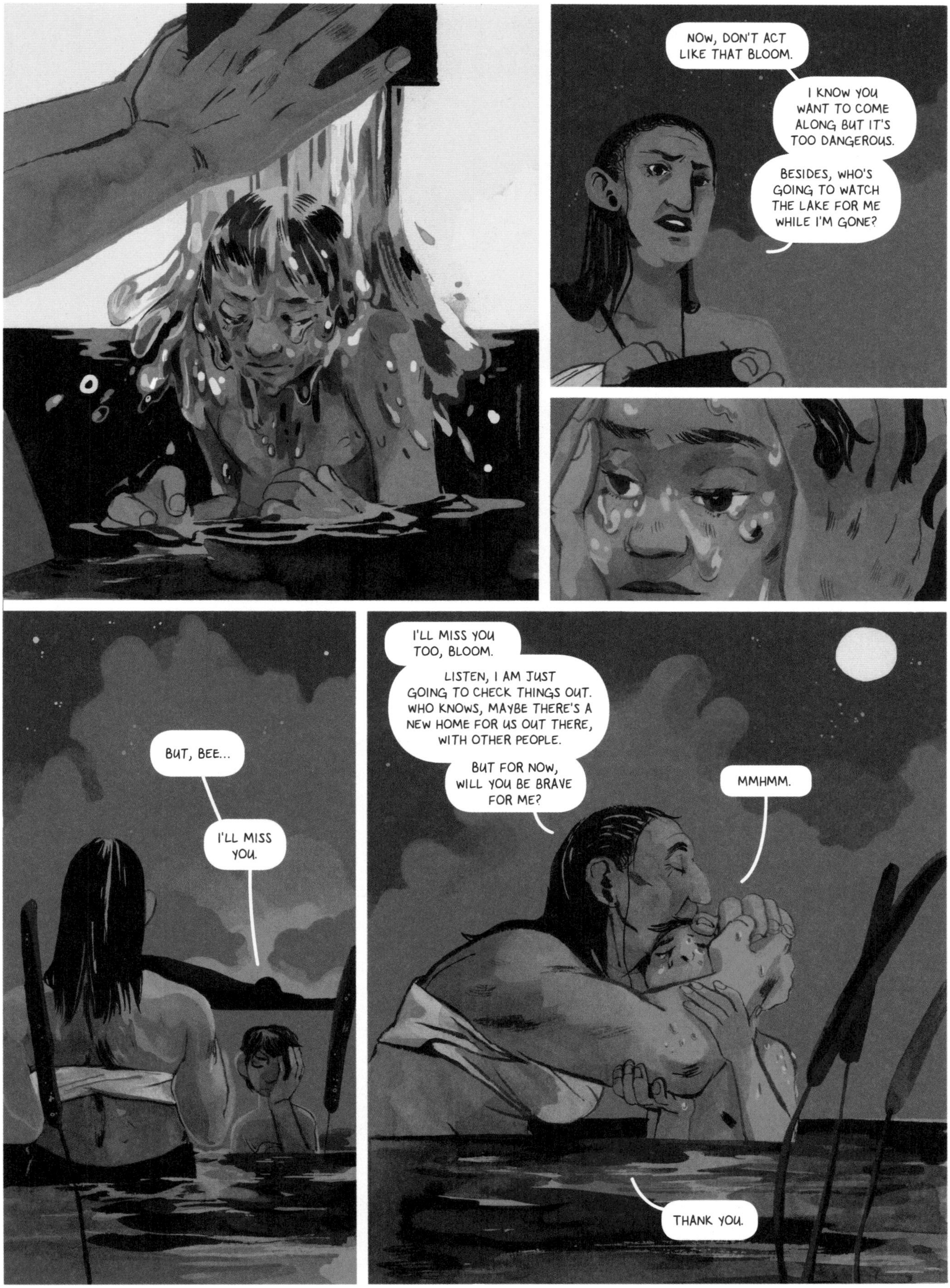
NOW, DON'T ACT LIKE THAT BLOOM.
I KNOW YOU WANT TO COME ALONG BUT IT'S TOO DANGEROUS.
BESIDES, WHO'S GOING TO WATCH THE LAKE FOR ME WHILE I'M GONE?
BUT, BEE...
I'LL MISS YOU.
I'LL MISS YOU TOO, BLOOM.
LISTEN, I AM JUST GOING TO CHECK THINGS OUT. WHO KNOWS, MAYBE THERE'S A NEW HOME FOR US OUT THERE, WITH OTHER PEOPLE.
BUT FOR NOW, WILL YOU BE BRAVE FOR ME?
MMHMM.
THANK YOU.

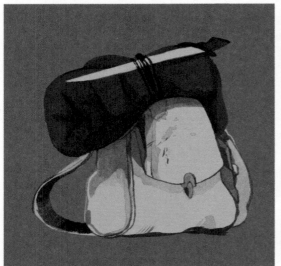

WILL YOU HOLD ON TO THIS FOR ME?

I'D HATE FOR IT TO GET LOST.

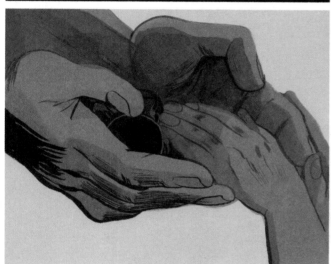

I'LL SEE YOU SOON, KIDDO.

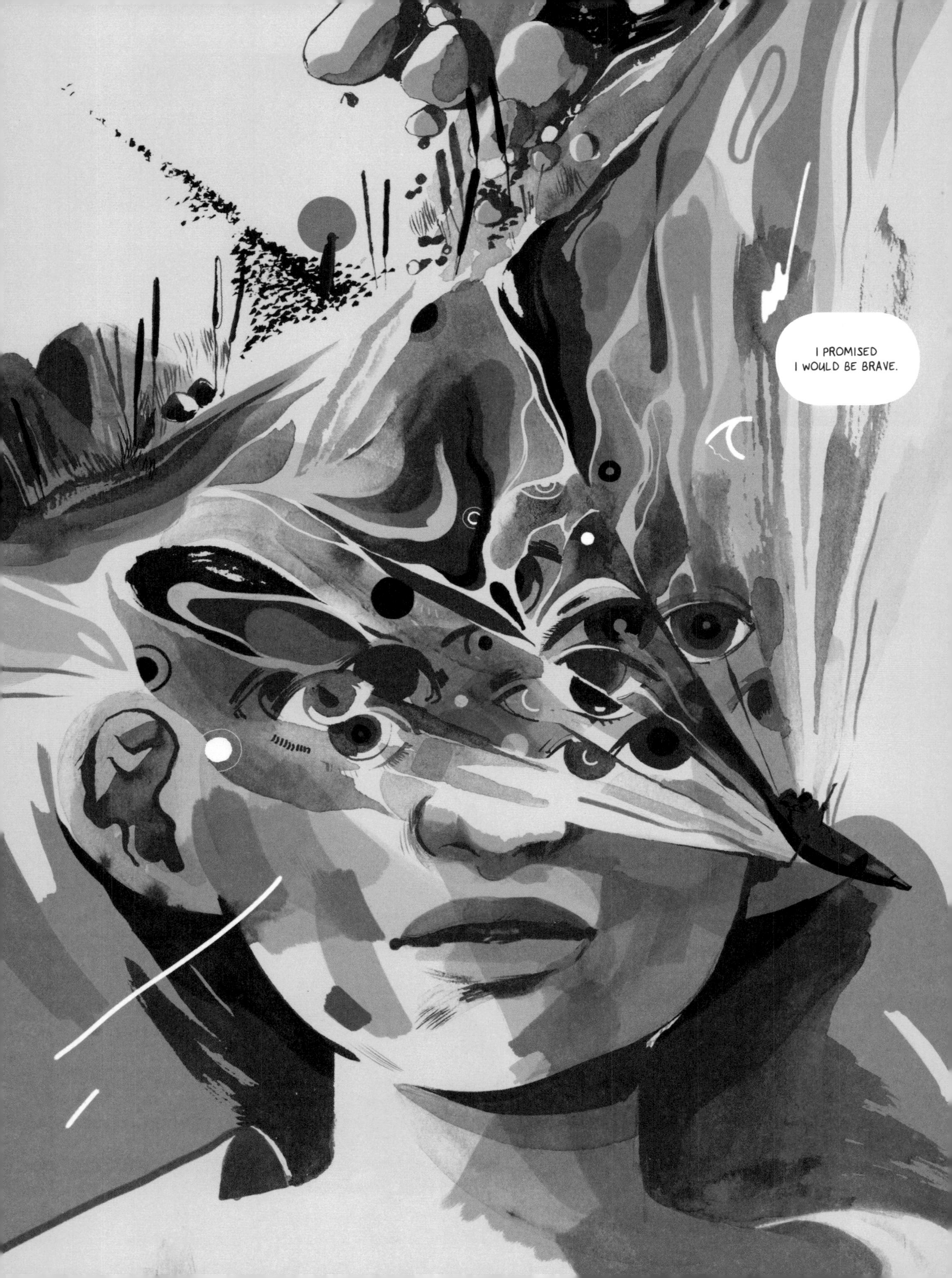
I PROMISED I WOULD BE BRAVE.

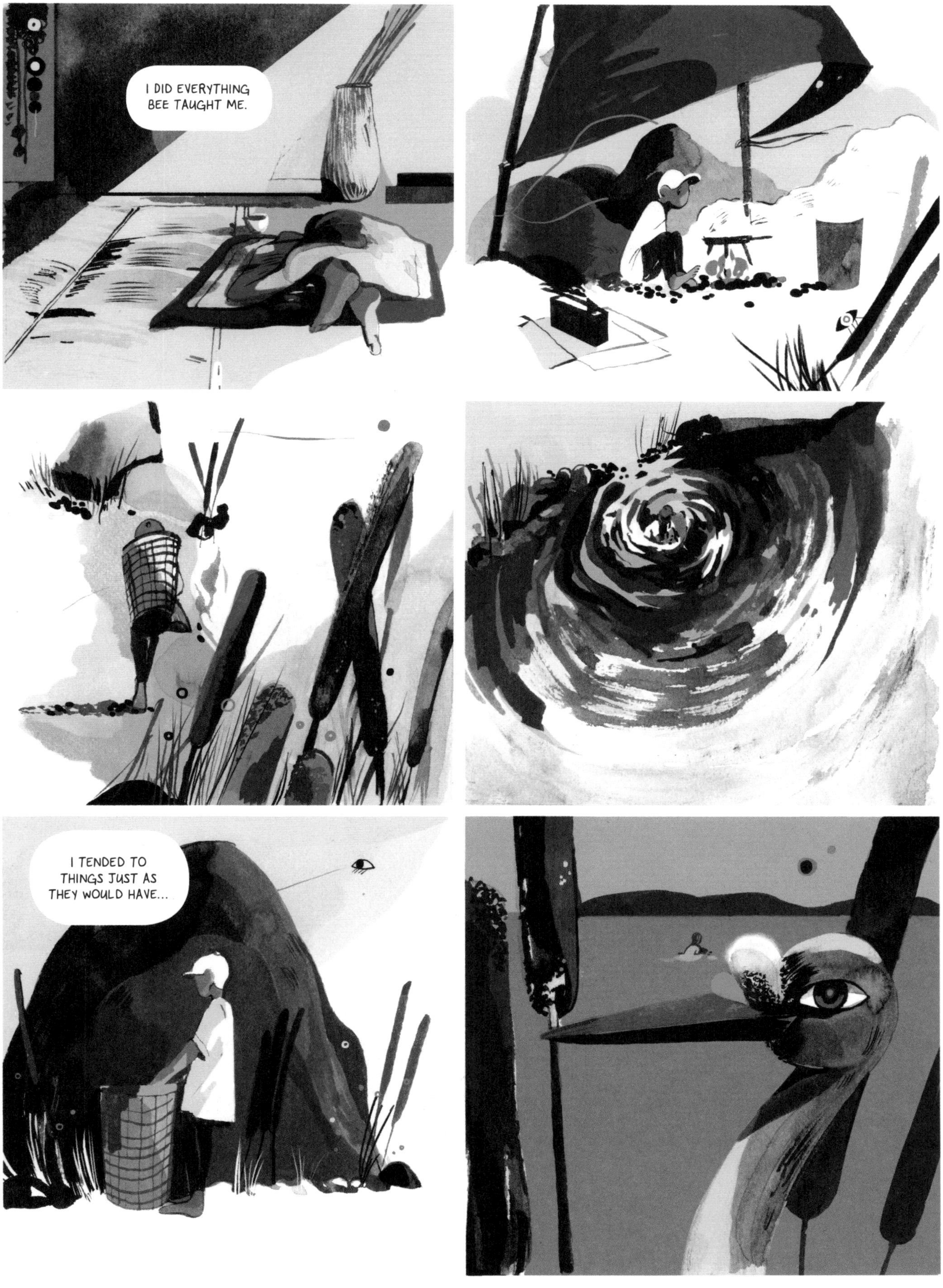
I DID EVERYTHING BEE TAUGHT ME.
I TENDED TO THINGS JUST AS THEY WOULD HAVE...

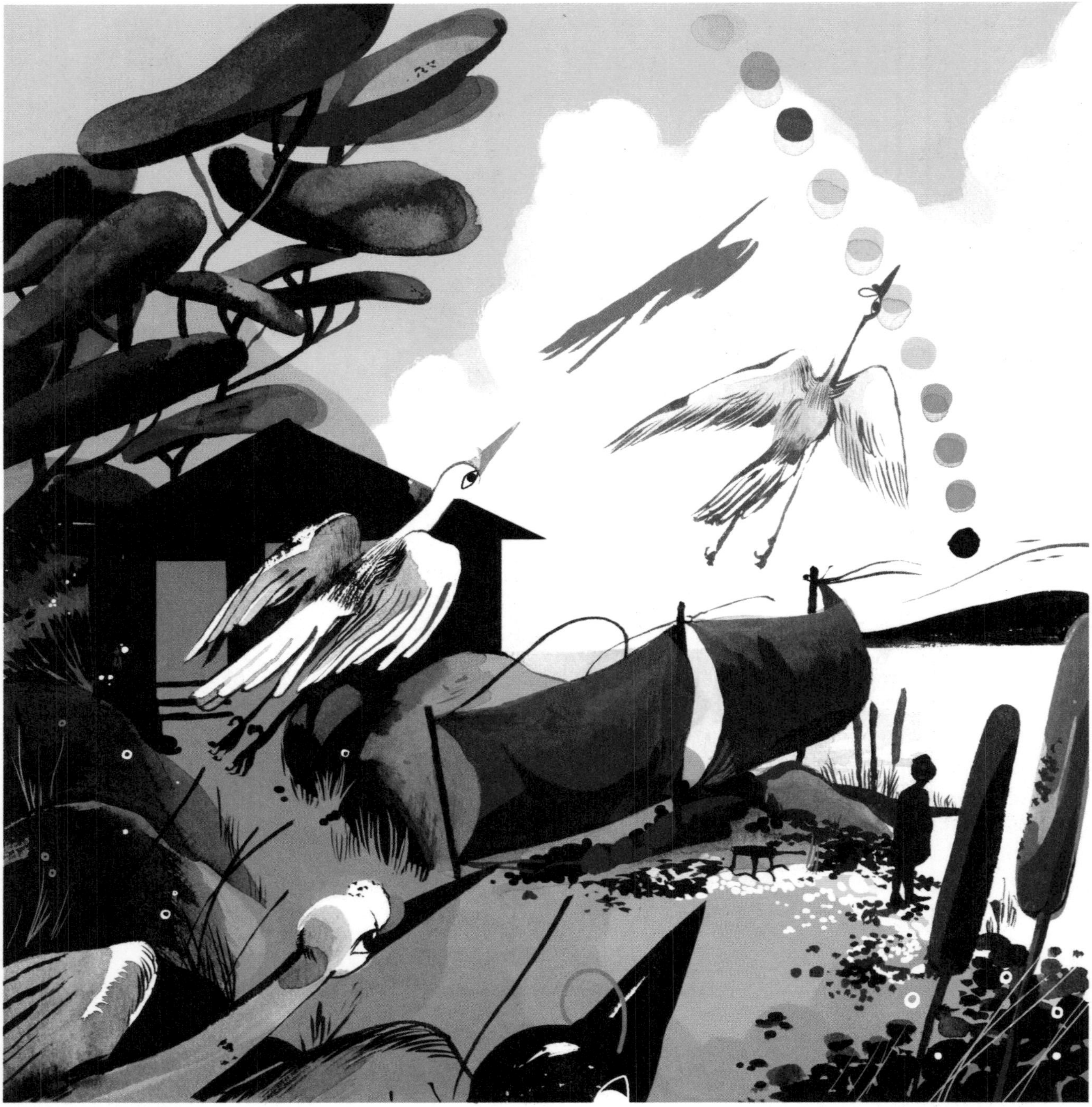

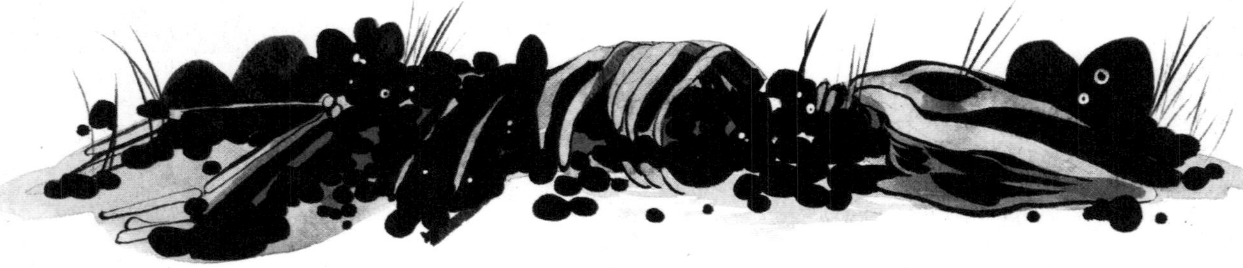

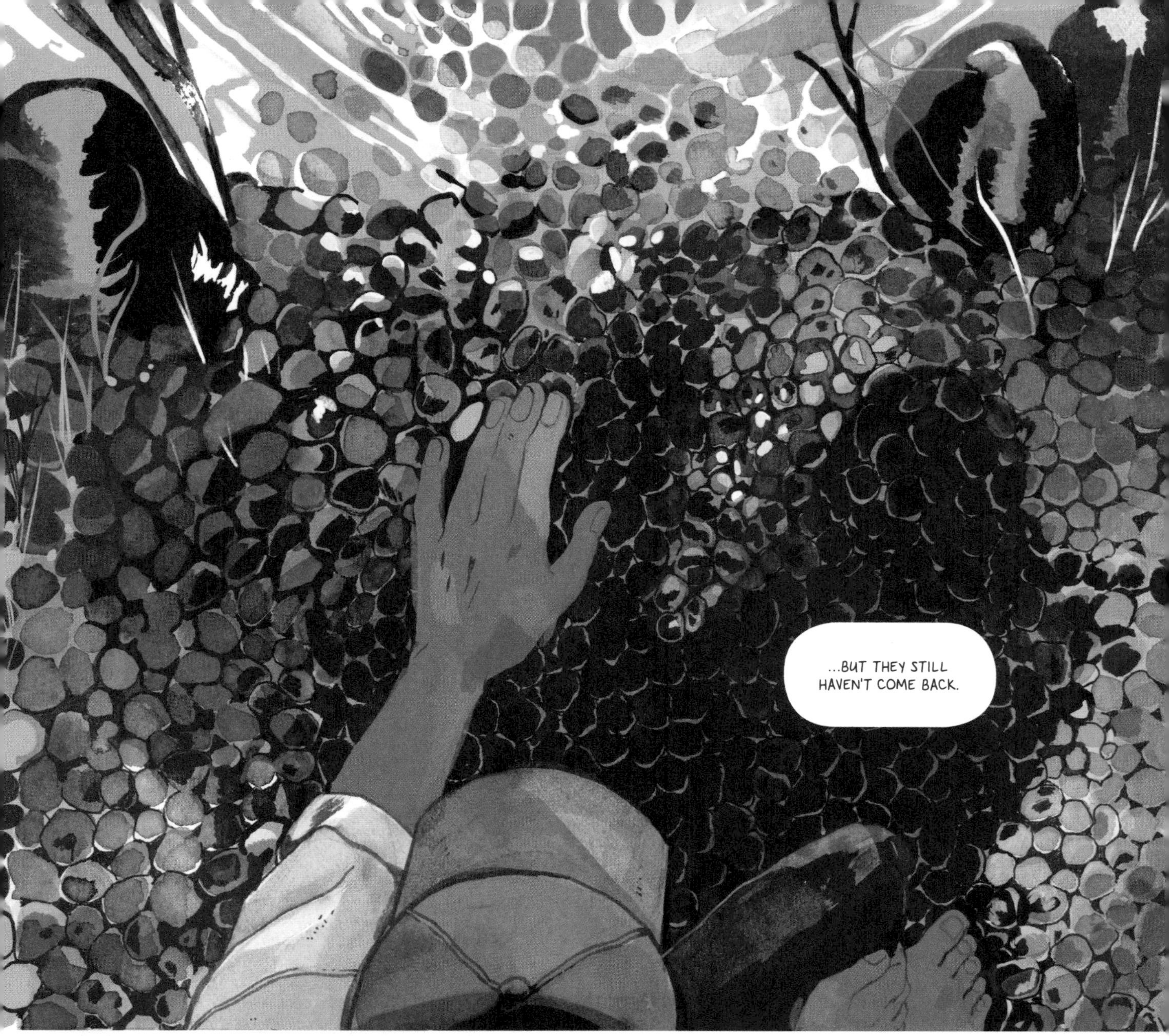
...BUT THEY STILL
HAVEN'T COME BACK.

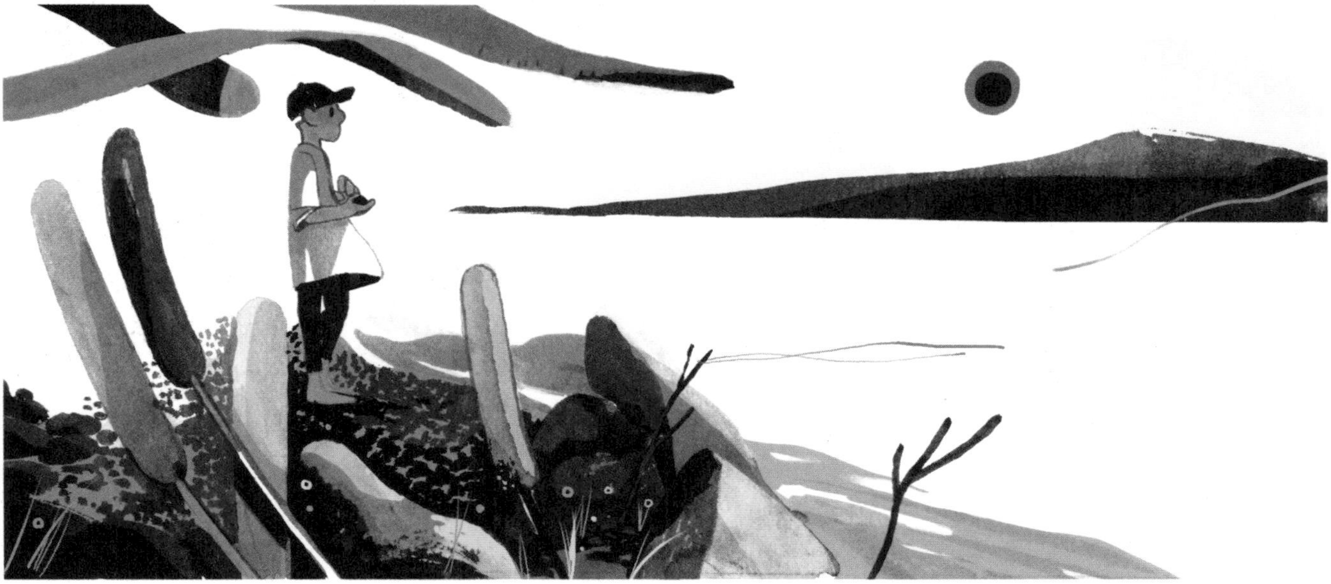

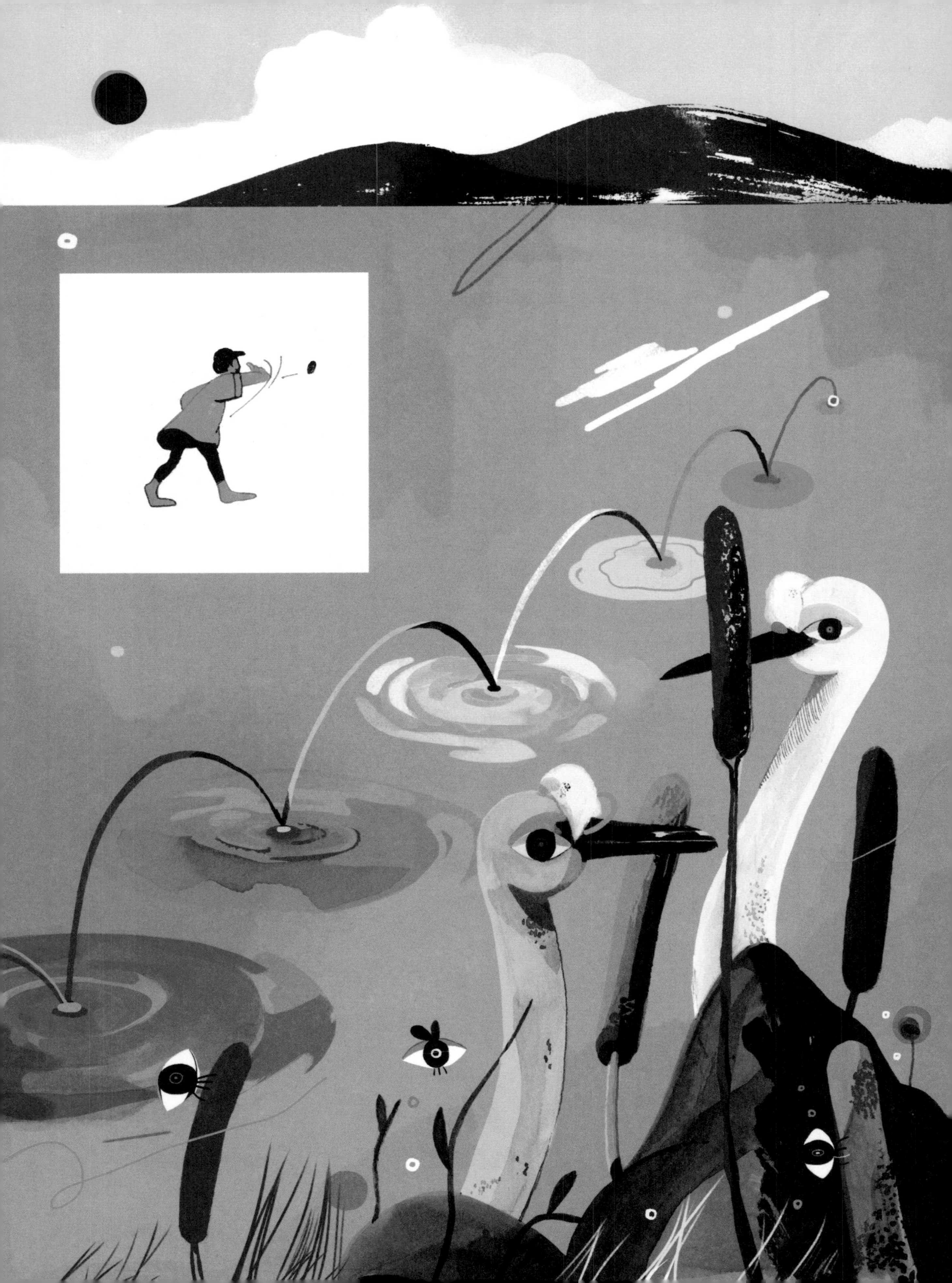

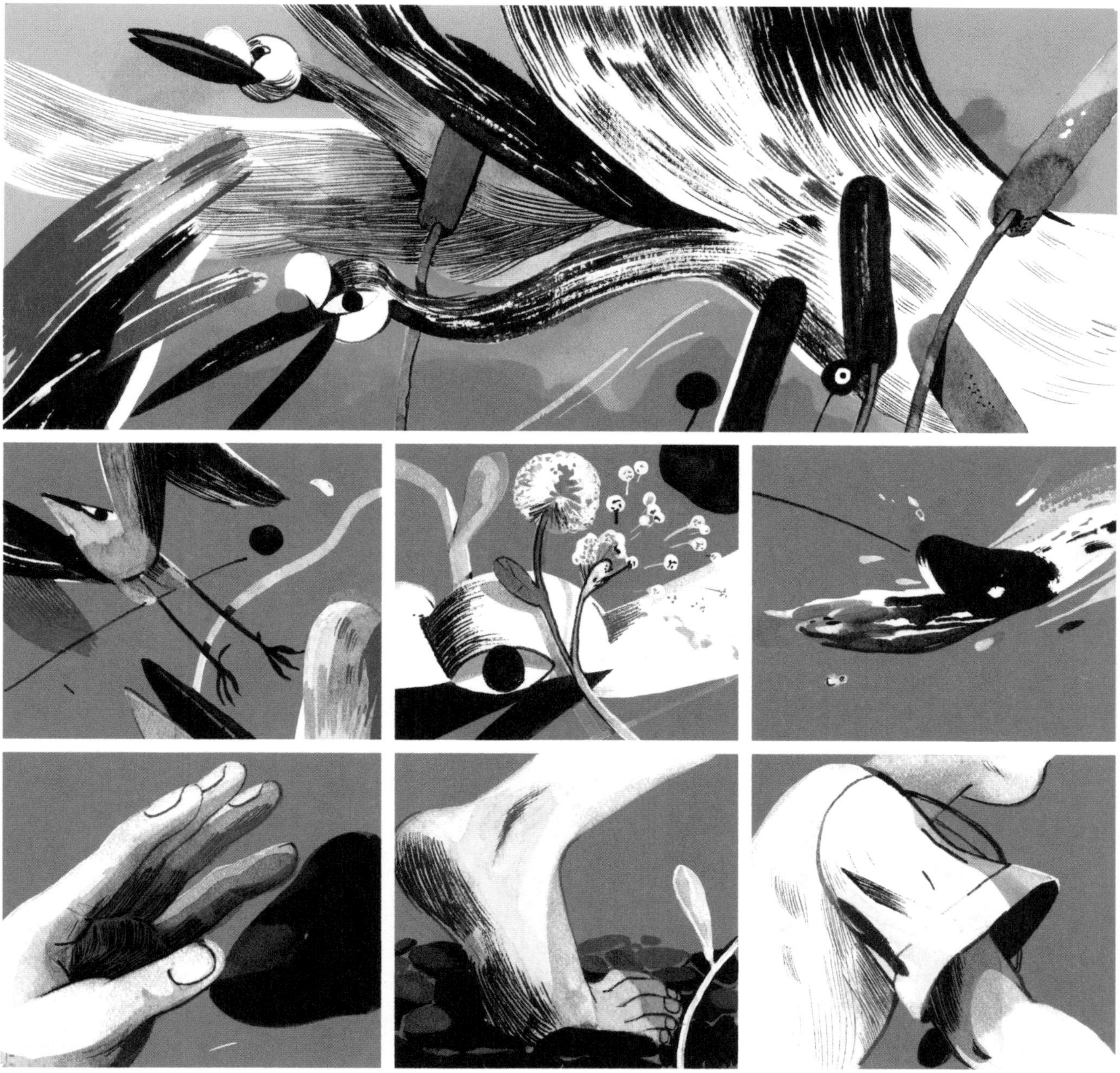

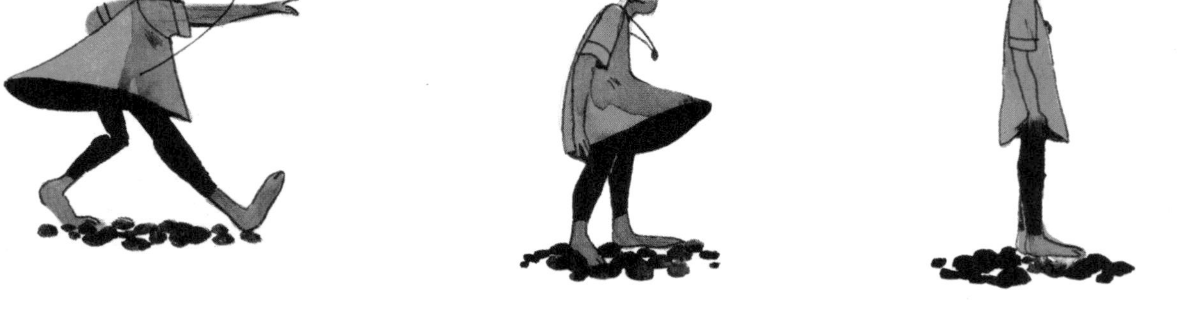

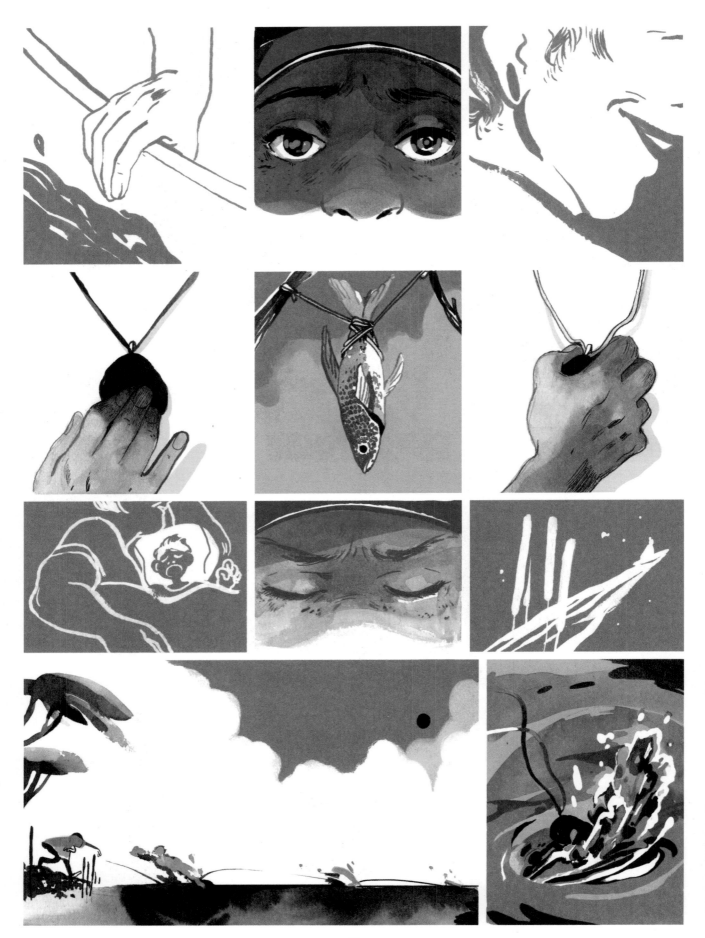

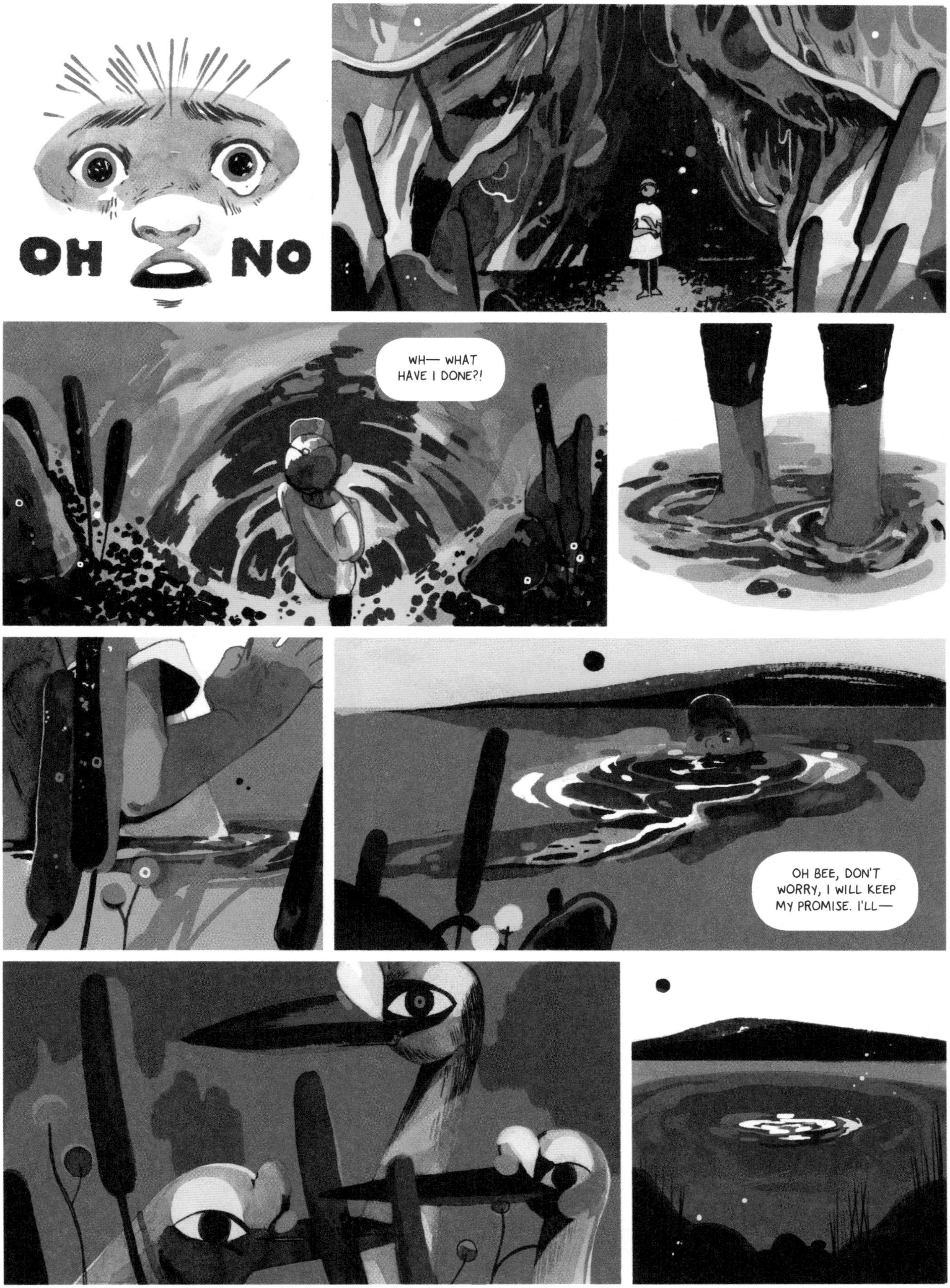
OH NO
WH— WHAT HAVE I DONE?!
OH BEE, DON'T WORRY, I WILL KEEP MY PROMISE. I'LL—

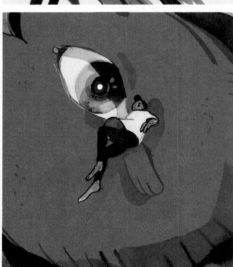

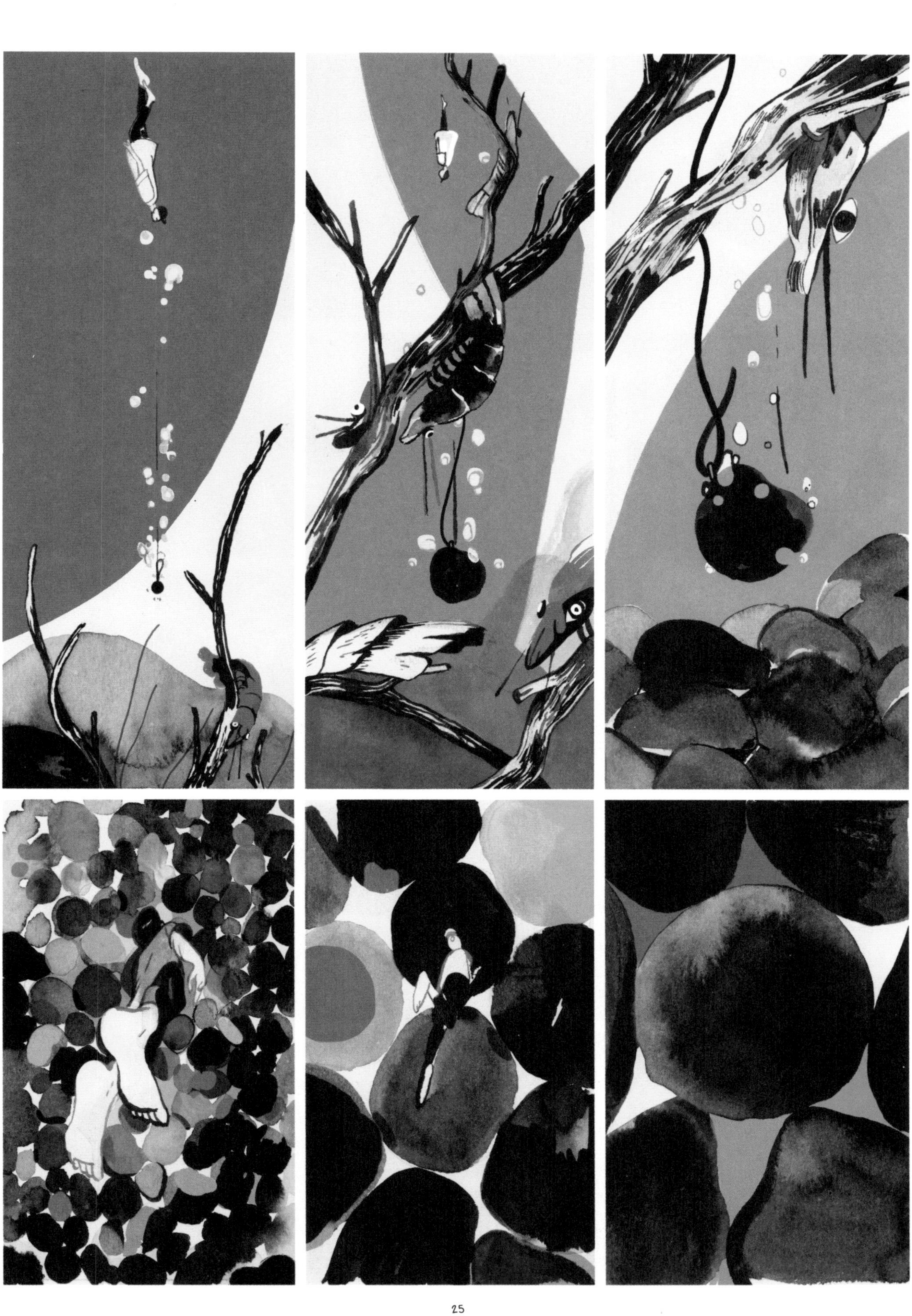

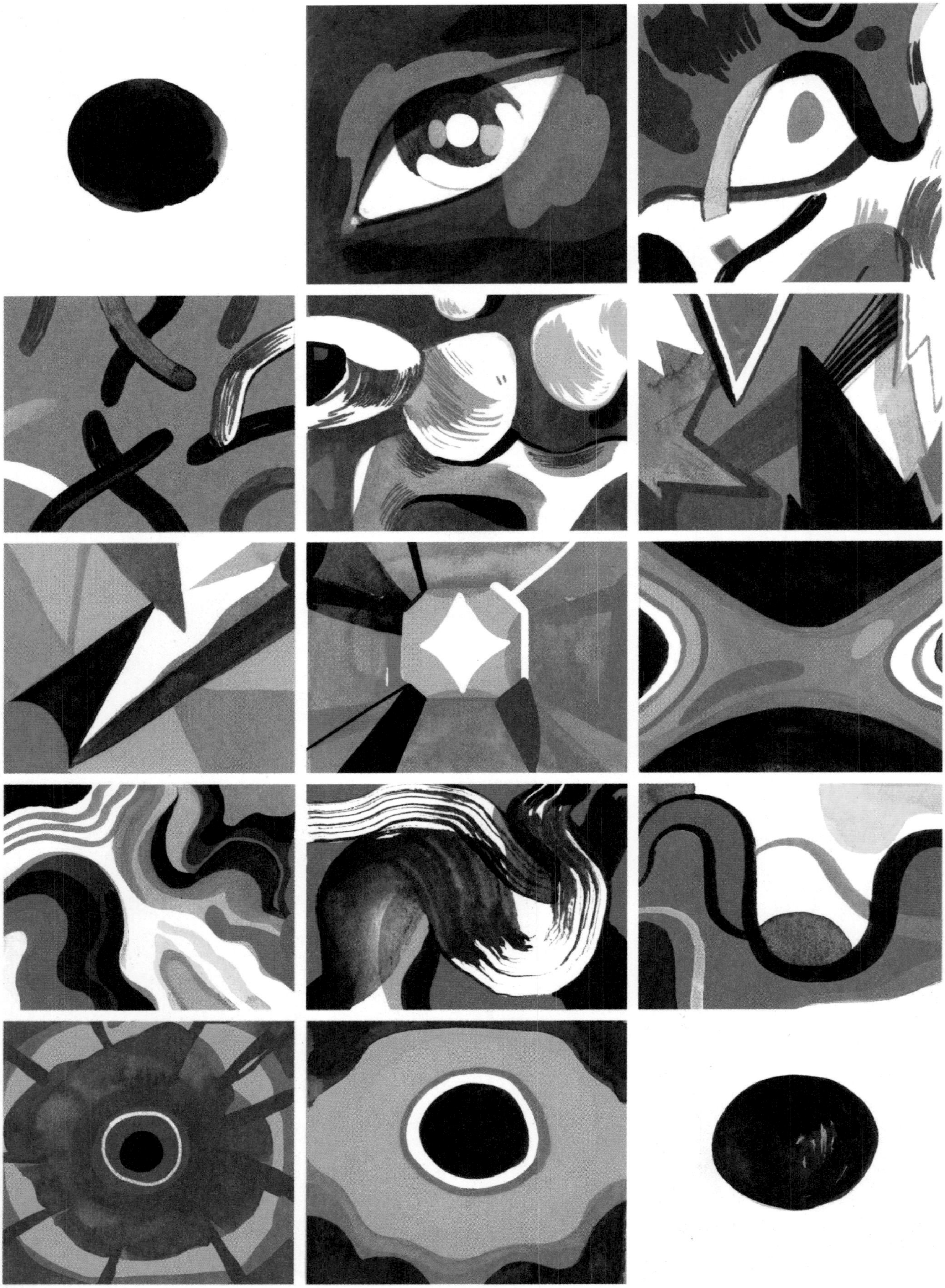

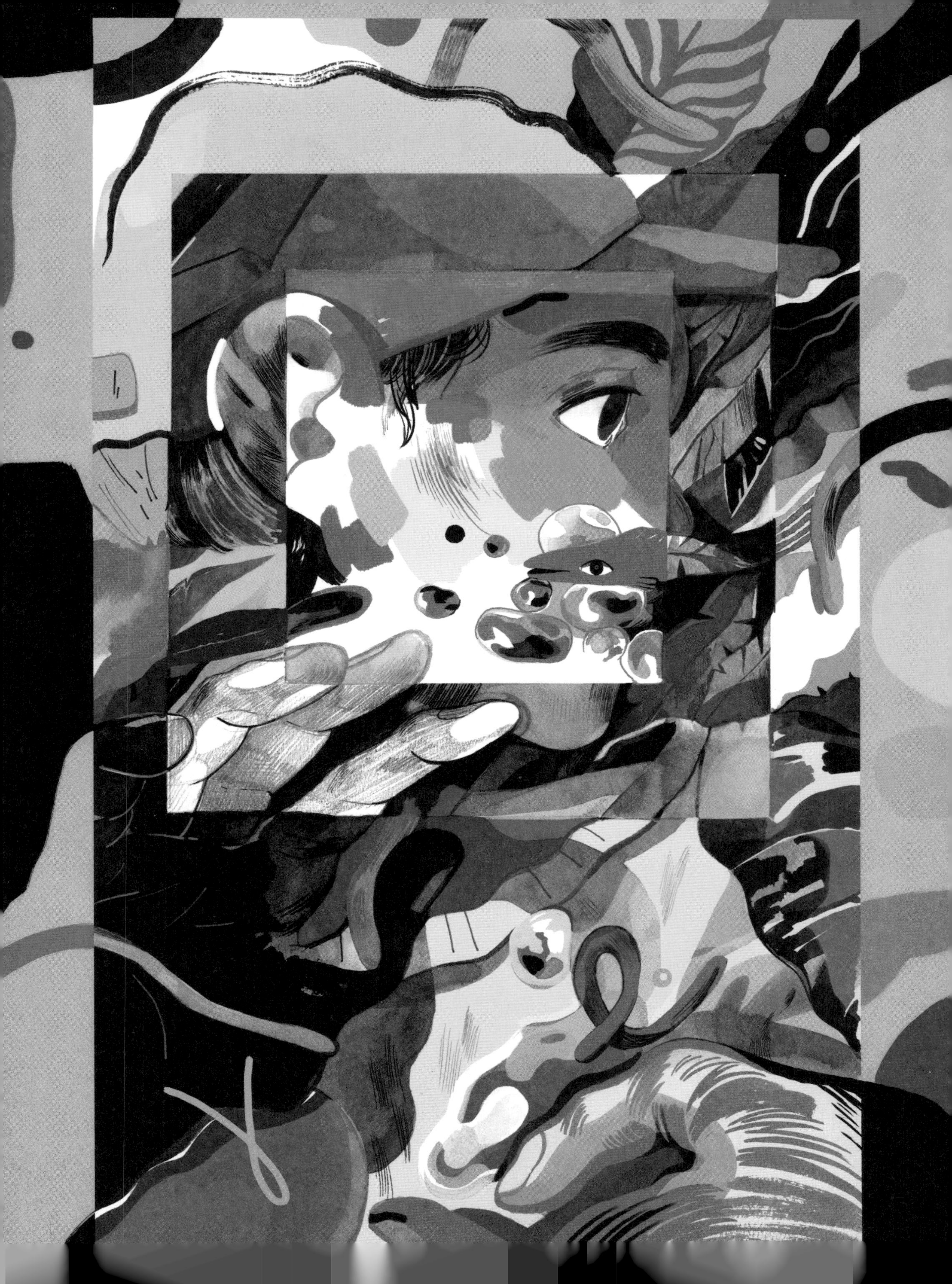

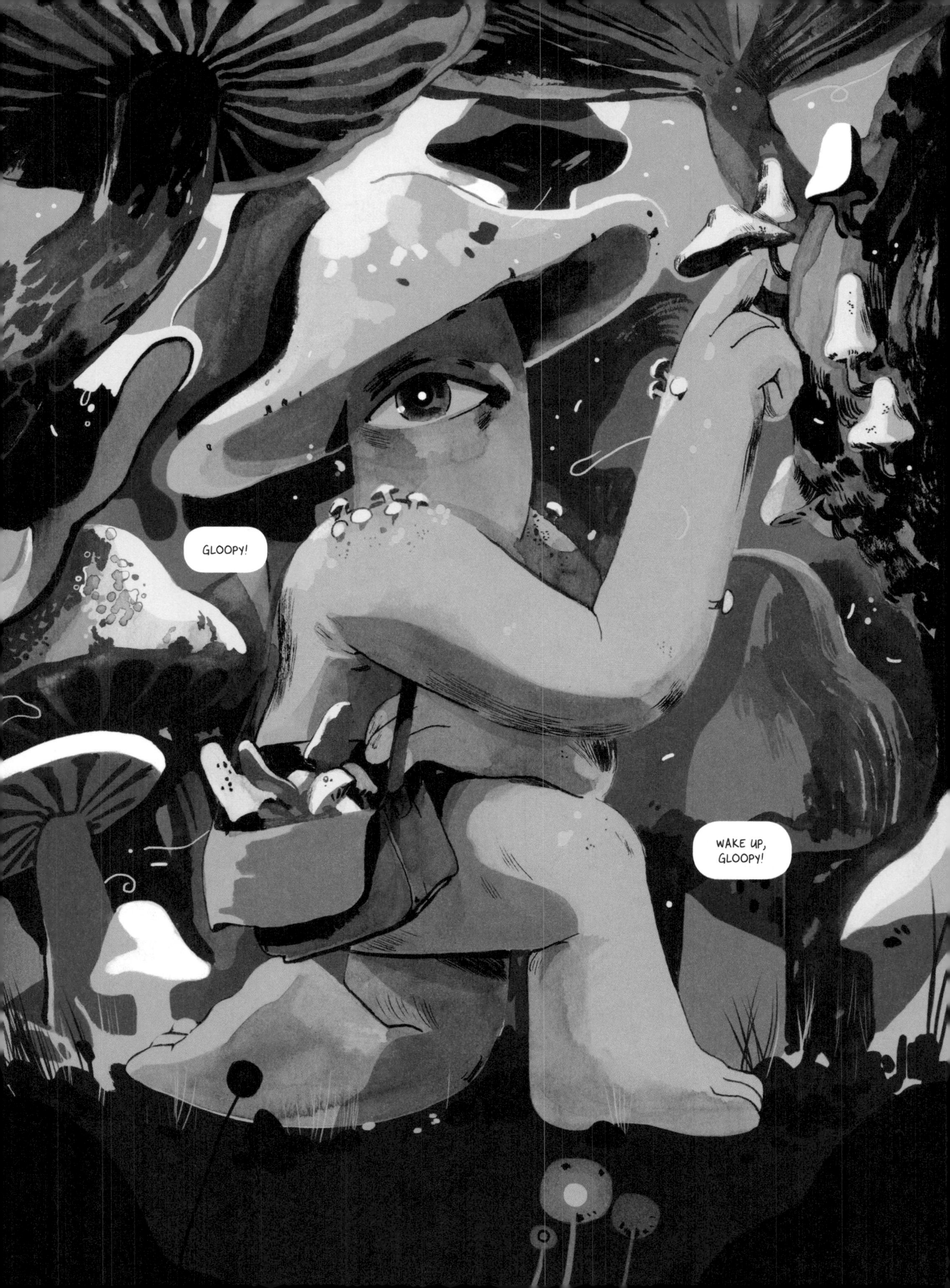
GLOOPY!
WAKE UP, GLOOPY!

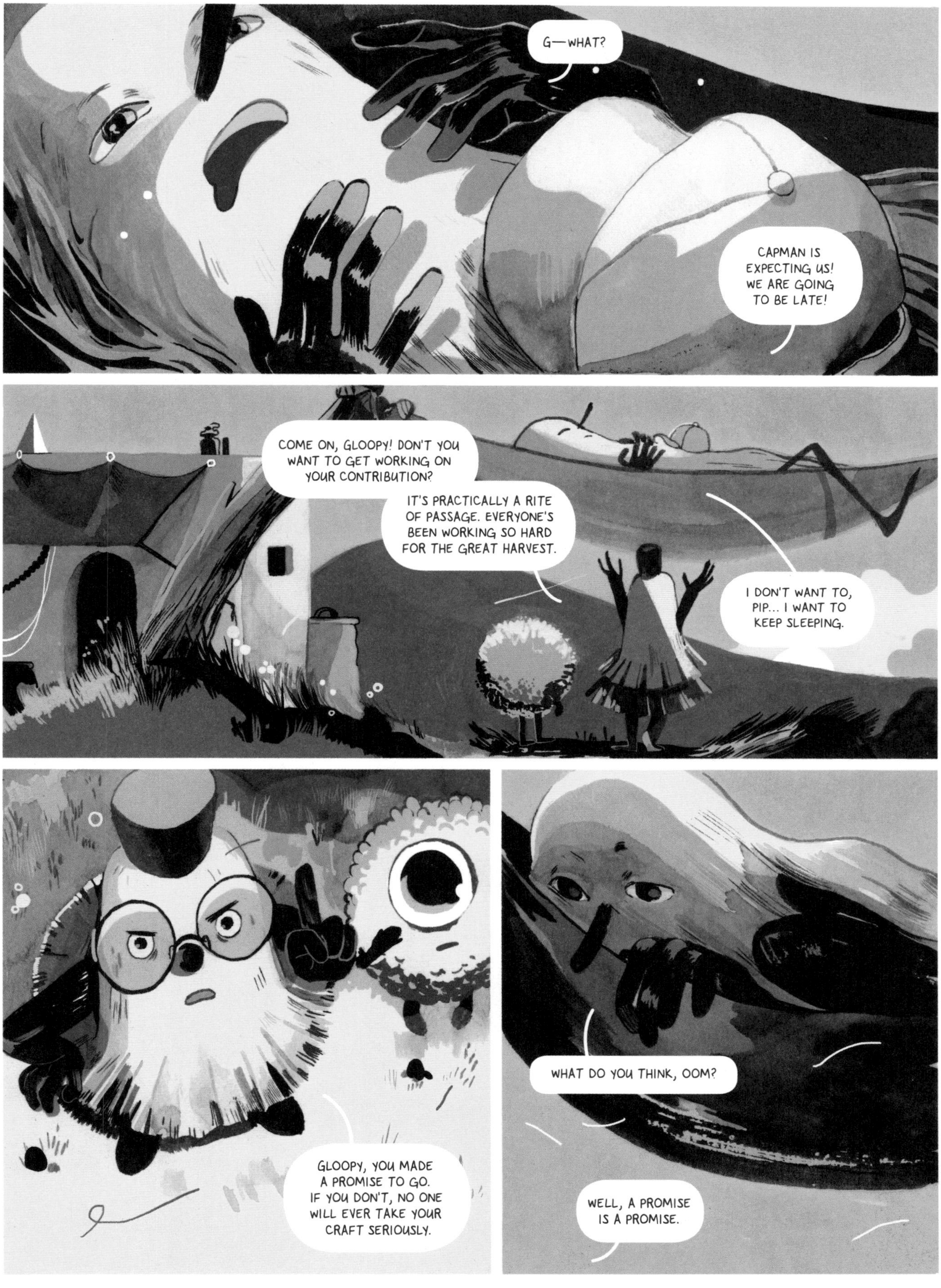
G—WHAT?
CAPMAN IS EXPECTING US! WE ARE GOING TO BE LATE!
COME ON, GLOOPY! DON'T YOU WANT TO GET WORKING ON YOUR CONTRIBUTION?
IT'S PRACTICALLY A RITE OF PASSAGE. EVERYONE'S BEEN WORKING SO HARD FOR THE GREAT HARVEST.
I DON'T WANT TO, PIP... I WANT TO KEEP SLEEPING.
GLOOPY, YOU MADE A PROMISE TO GO. IF YOU DON'T, NO ONE WILL EVER TAKE YOUR CRAFT SERIOUSLY.
WHAT DO YOU THINK, OOM?
WELL, A PROMISE IS A PROMISE.

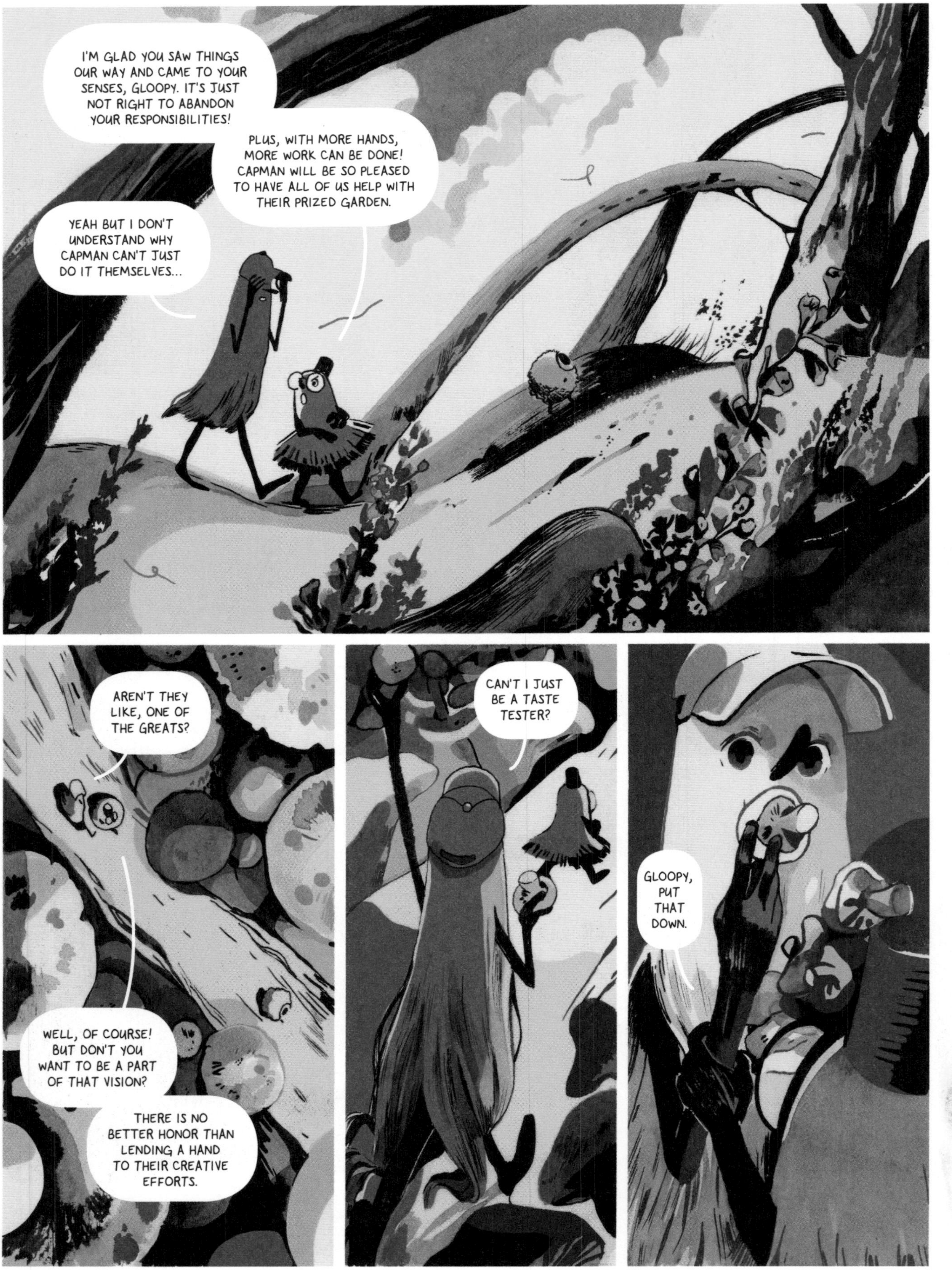
I'M GLAD YOU SAW THINGS OUR WAY AND CAME TO YOUR SENSES, GLOOPY. IT'S JUST NOT RIGHT TO ABANDON YOUR RESPONSIBILITIES!
PLUS, WITH MORE HANDS, MORE WORK CAN BE DONE! CAPMAN WILL BE SO PLEASED TO HAVE ALL OF US HELP WITH THEIR PRIZED GARDEN.
YEAH BUT I DON'T UNDERSTAND WHY CAPMAN CAN'T JUST DO IT THEMSELVES...
AREN'T THEY LIKE, ONE OF THE GREATS?
WELL, OF COURSE! BUT DON'T YOU WANT TO BE A PART OF THAT VISION?
THERE IS NO BETTER HONOR THAN LENDING A HAND TO THEIR CREATIVE EFFORTS.
CAN'T I JUST BE A TASTE TESTER?
GLOOPY, PUT THAT DOWN.

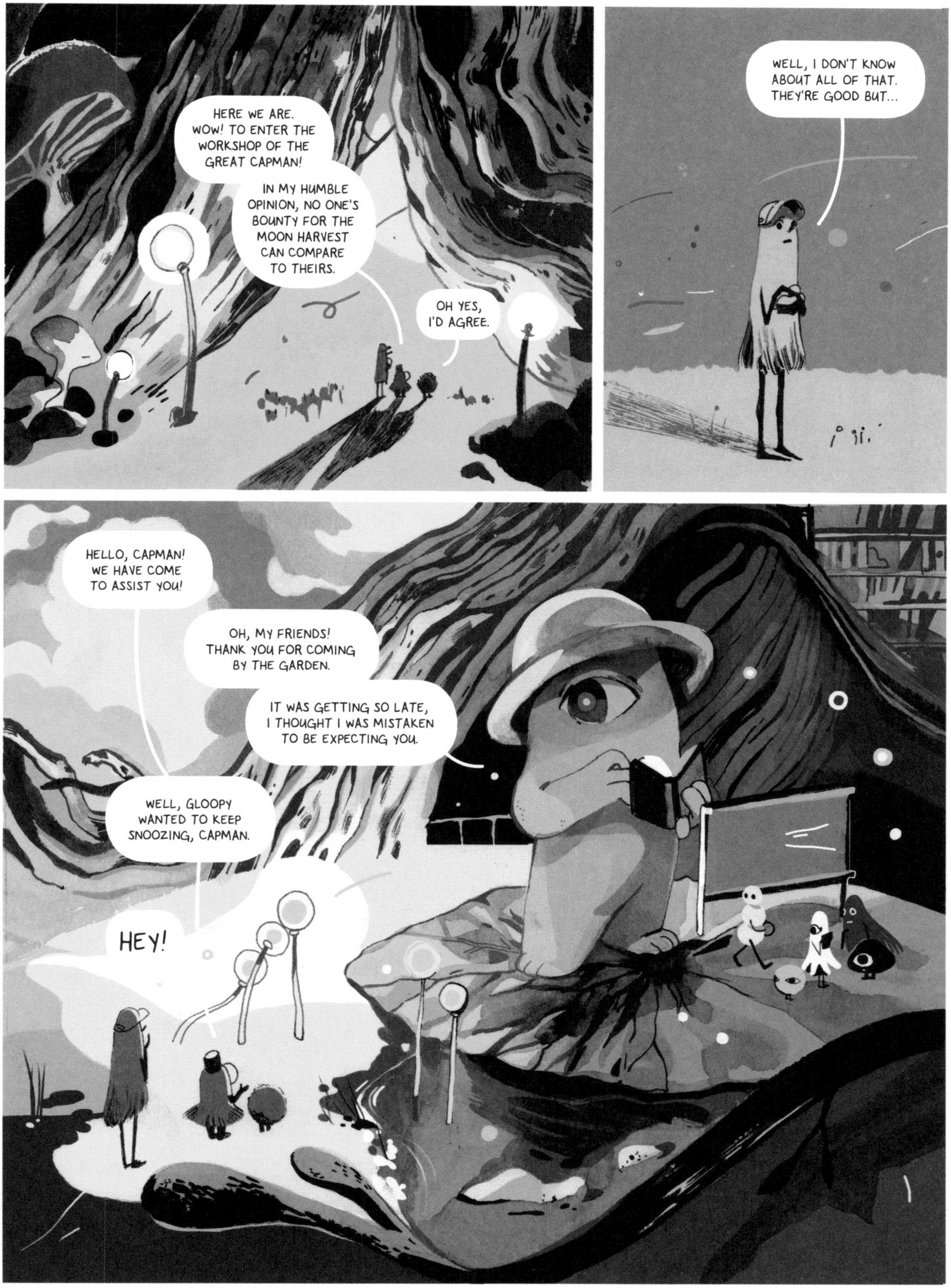
HERE WE ARE. WOW! TO ENTER THE WORKSHOP OF THE GREAT CAPMAN!
IN MY HUMBLE OPINION, NO ONE'S BOUNTY FOR THE MOON HARVEST CAN COMPARE TO THEIRS.
OH YES, I'D AGREE.
WELL, I DON'T KNOW ABOUT ALL OF THAT. THEY'RE GOOD BUT...
HELLO, CAPMAN! WE HAVE COME TO ASSIST YOU!
OH, MY FRIENDS! THANK YOU FOR COMING BY THE GARDEN.
IT WAS GETTING SO LATE, I THOUGHT I WAS MISTAKEN TO BE EXPECTING YOU.
WELL, GLOOPY WANTED TO KEEP SNOOZING, CAPMAN.
HEY!

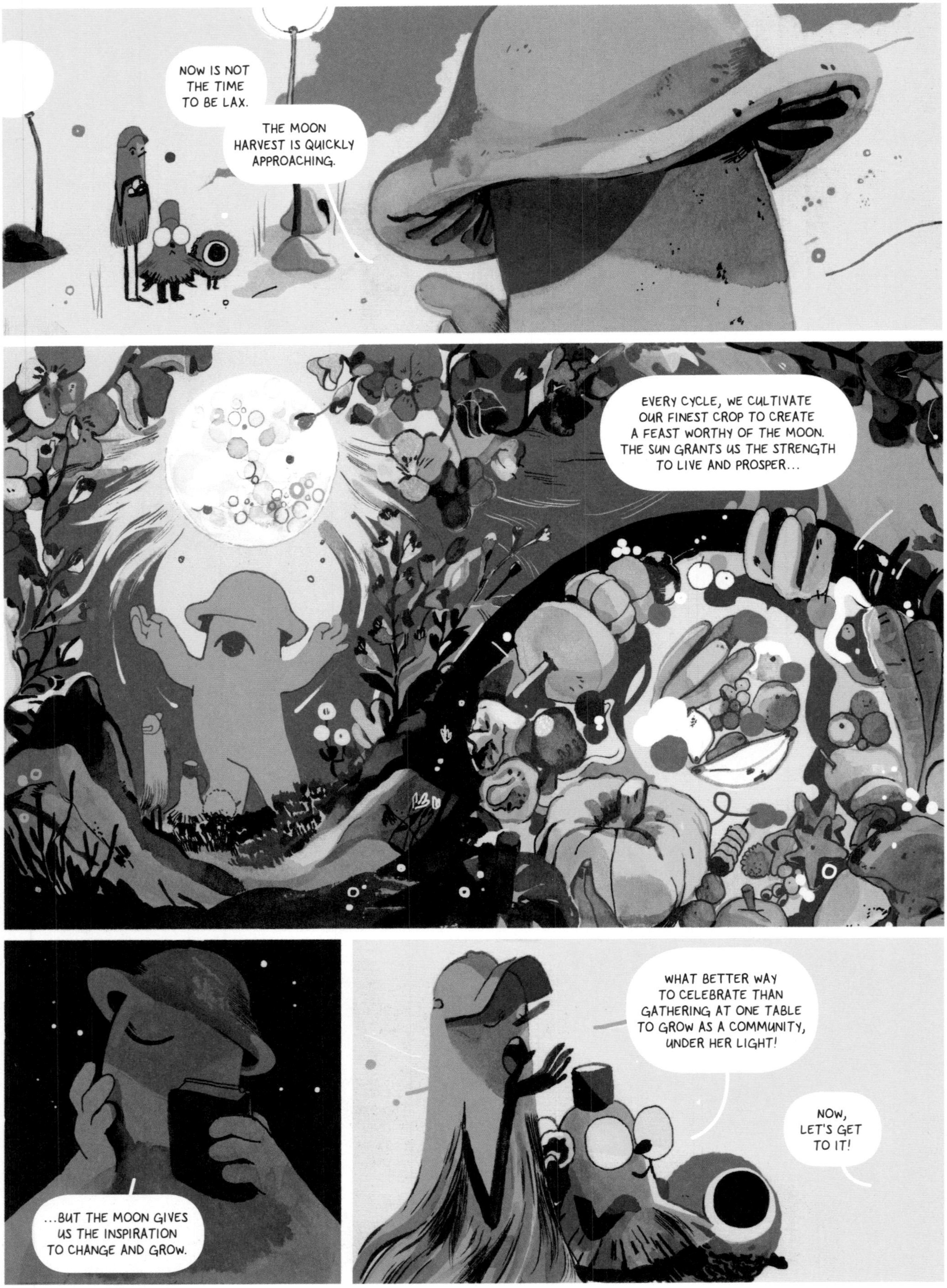
NOW IS NOT THE TIME TO BE LAX.
THE MOON HARVEST IS QUICKLY APPROACHING.
EVERY CYCLE, WE CULTIVATE OUR FINEST CROP TO CREATE A FEAST WORTHY OF THE MOON. THE SUN GRANTS US THE STRENGTH TO LIVE AND PROSPER...
...BUT THE MOON GIVES US THE INSPIRATION TO CHANGE AND GROW.
WHAT BETTER WAY TO CELEBRATE THAN GATHERING AT ONE TABLE TO GROW AS A COMMUNITY, UNDER HER LIGHT!
NOW, LET'S GET TO IT!

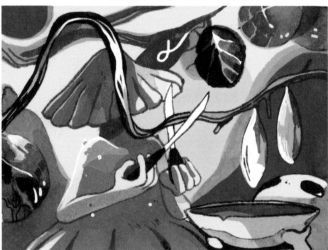

HEY, GLOOPY.
HELP ME WITH
THIS WATER?

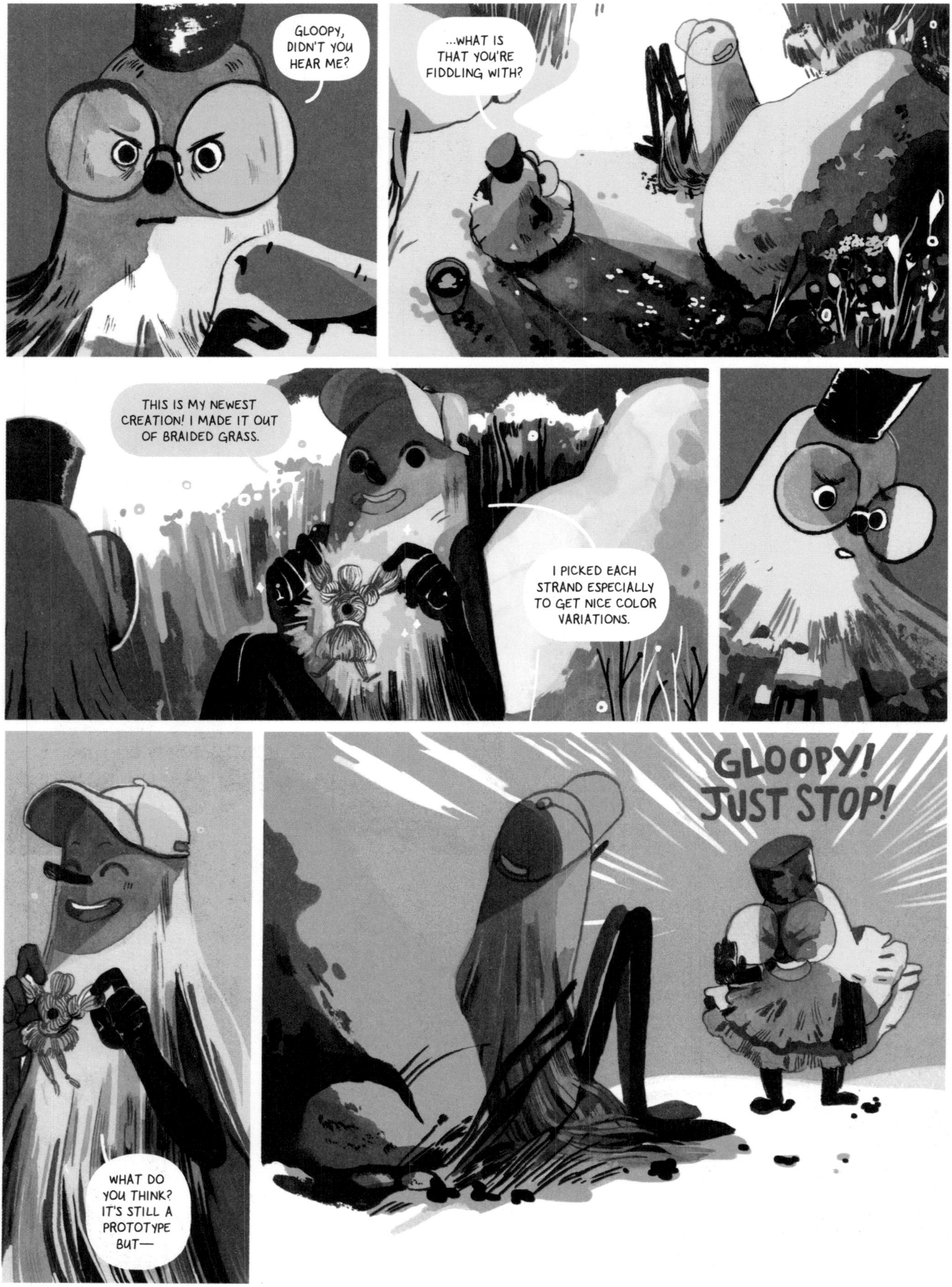
GLOOPY, DIDN'T YOU HEAR ME?
...WHAT IS THAT YOU'RE FIDDLING WITH?
THIS IS MY NEWEST CREATION! I MADE IT OUT OF BRAIDED GRASS.
I PICKED EACH STRAND ESPECIALLY TO GET NICE COLOR VARIATIONS.
WHAT DO YOU THINK? IT'S STILL A PROTOTYPE BUT—
GLOOPY! JUST STOP!

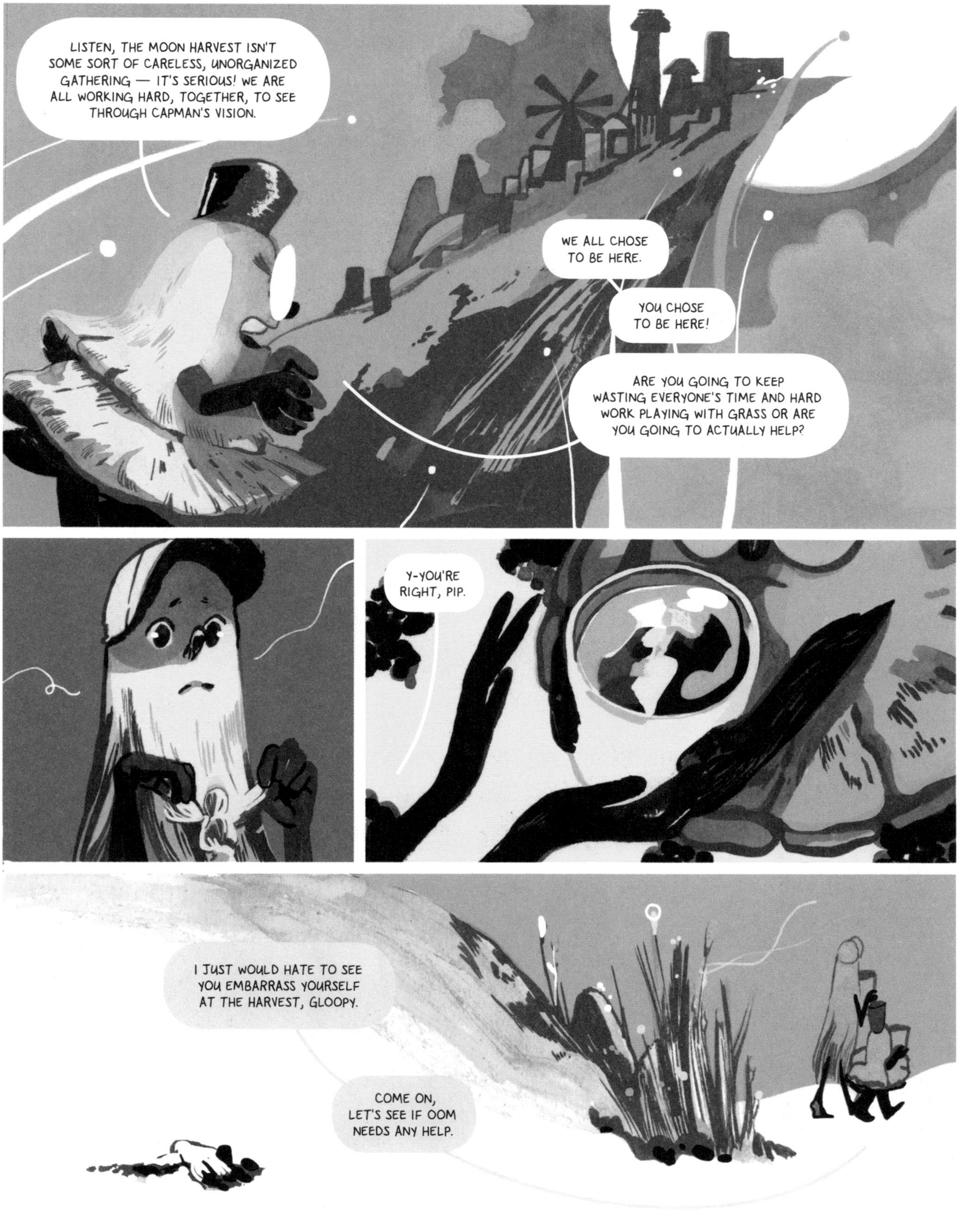
LISTEN, THE MOON HARVEST ISN'T SOME SORT OF CARELESS, UNORGANIZED GATHERING — IT'S SERIOUS! WE ARE ALL WORKING HARD, TOGETHER, TO SEE THROUGH CAPMAN'S VISION.
WE ALL CHOSE TO BE HERE.
YOU CHOSE TO BE HERE!
ARE YOU GOING TO KEEP WASTING EVERYONE'S TIME AND HARD WORK PLAYING WITH GRASS OR ARE YOU GOING TO ACTUALLY HELP?
Y-YOU'RE RIGHT, PIP.
I JUST WOULD HATE TO SEE YOU EMBARRASS YOURSELF AT THE HARVEST, GLOOPY.
COME ON, LET'S SEE IF OOM NEEDS ANY HELP.

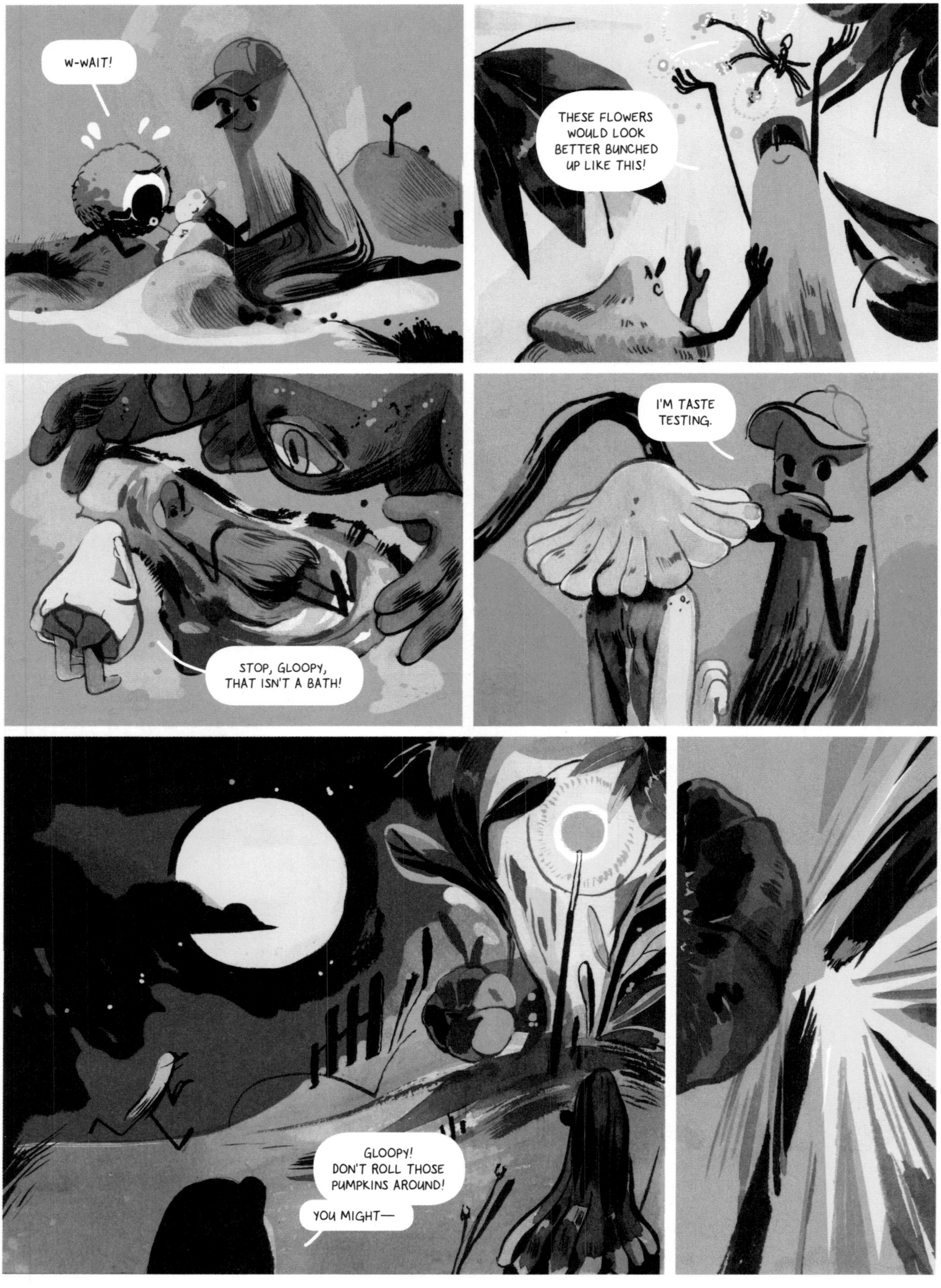
W-WAIT!
THESE FLOWERS WOULD LOOK BETTER BUNCHED UP LIKE THIS!
STOP, GLOOPY, THAT ISN'T A BATH!
I'M TASTE TESTING.
GLOOPY! DON'T ROLL THOSE PUMPKINS AROUND!
YOU MIGHT—

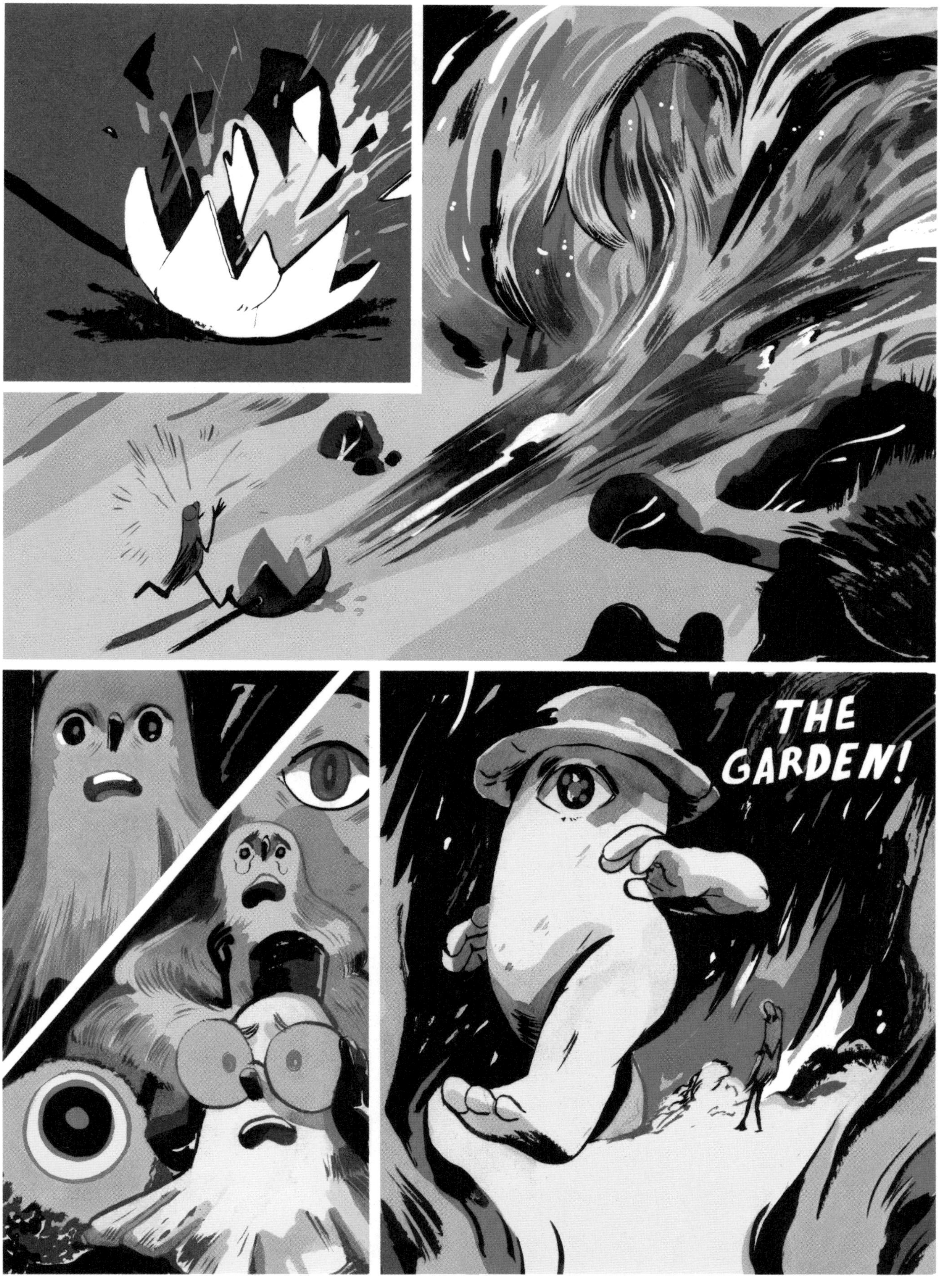
THE GARDEN!

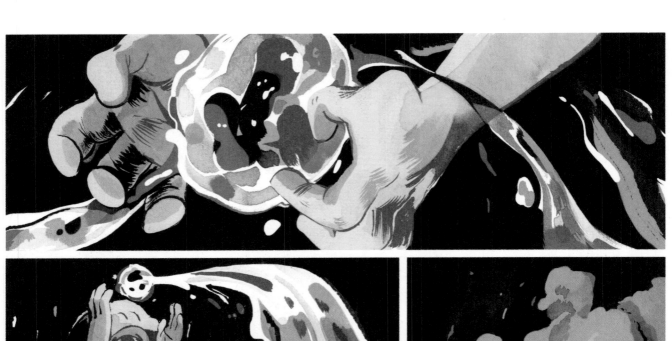

IT'S GONE...

OH, GLOOPY.

YOU'VE HELPED ENOUGH.
I-I THINK YOU SHOULD LEAVE.

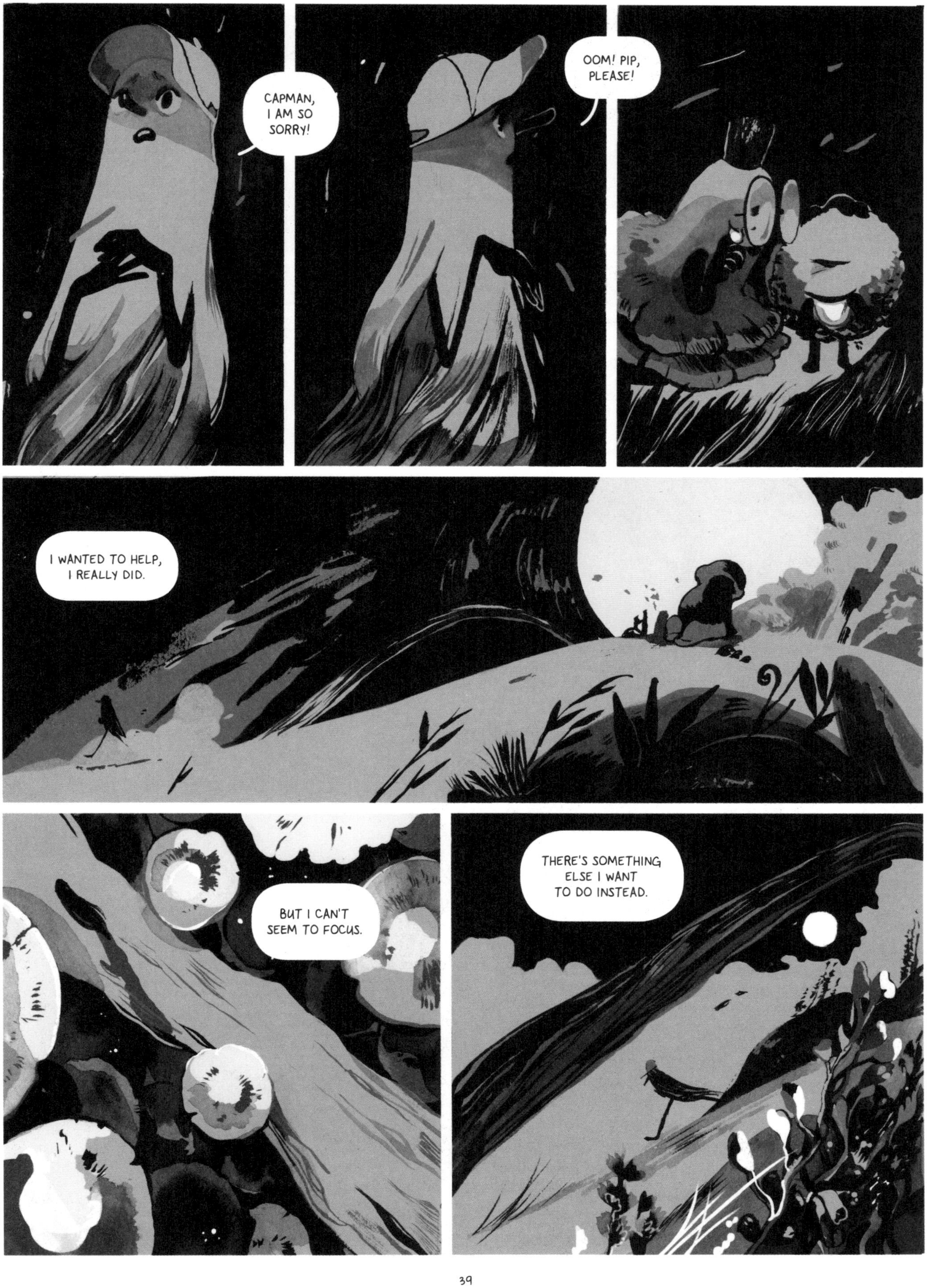
CAPMAN, I AM SO SORRY!
OOM! PIP, PLEASE!
I WANTED TO HELP, I REALLY DID.
BUT I CAN'T SEEM TO FOCUS.
THERE'S SOMETHING ELSE I WANT TO DO INSTEAD.

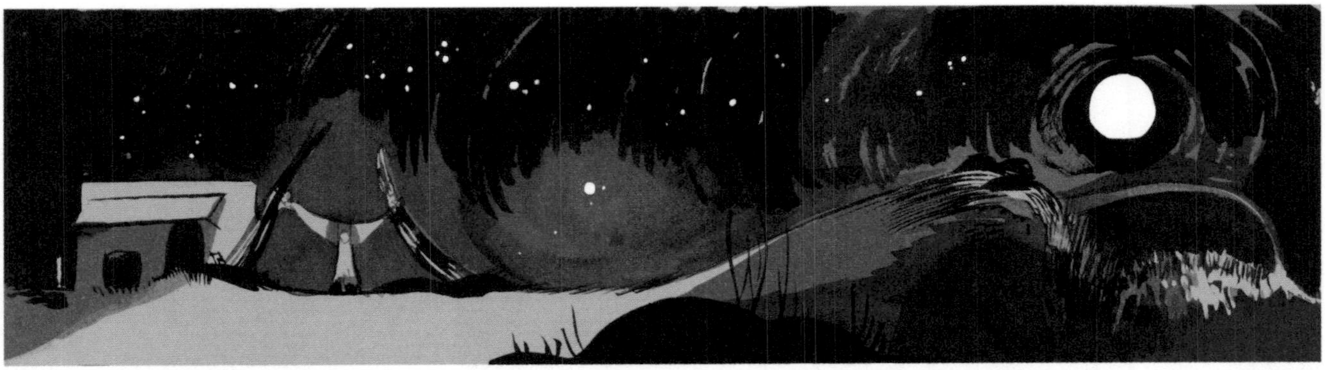

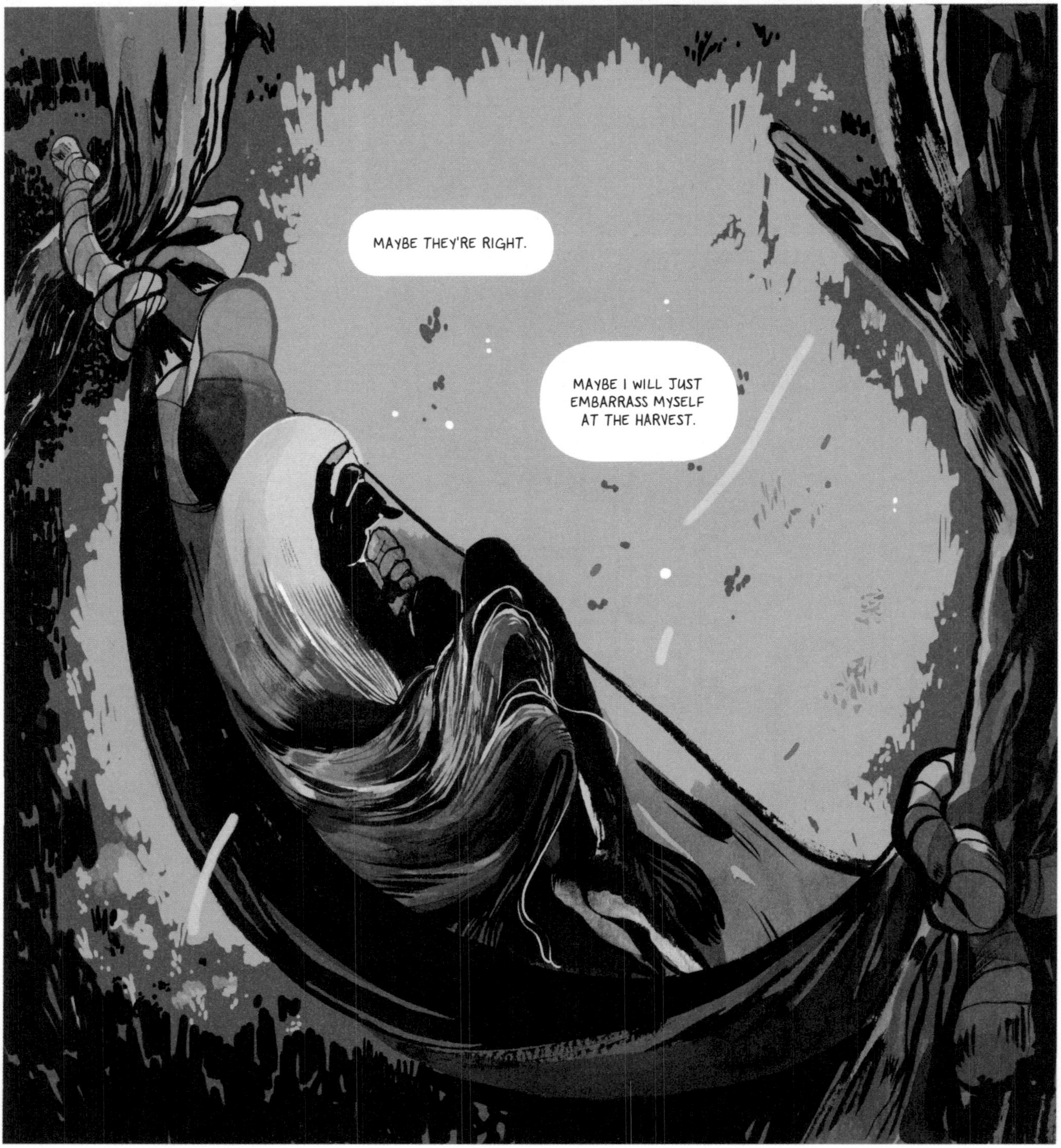
MAYBE THEY'RE RIGHT.
MAYBE I WILL JUST EMBARRASS MYSELF AT THE HARVEST.

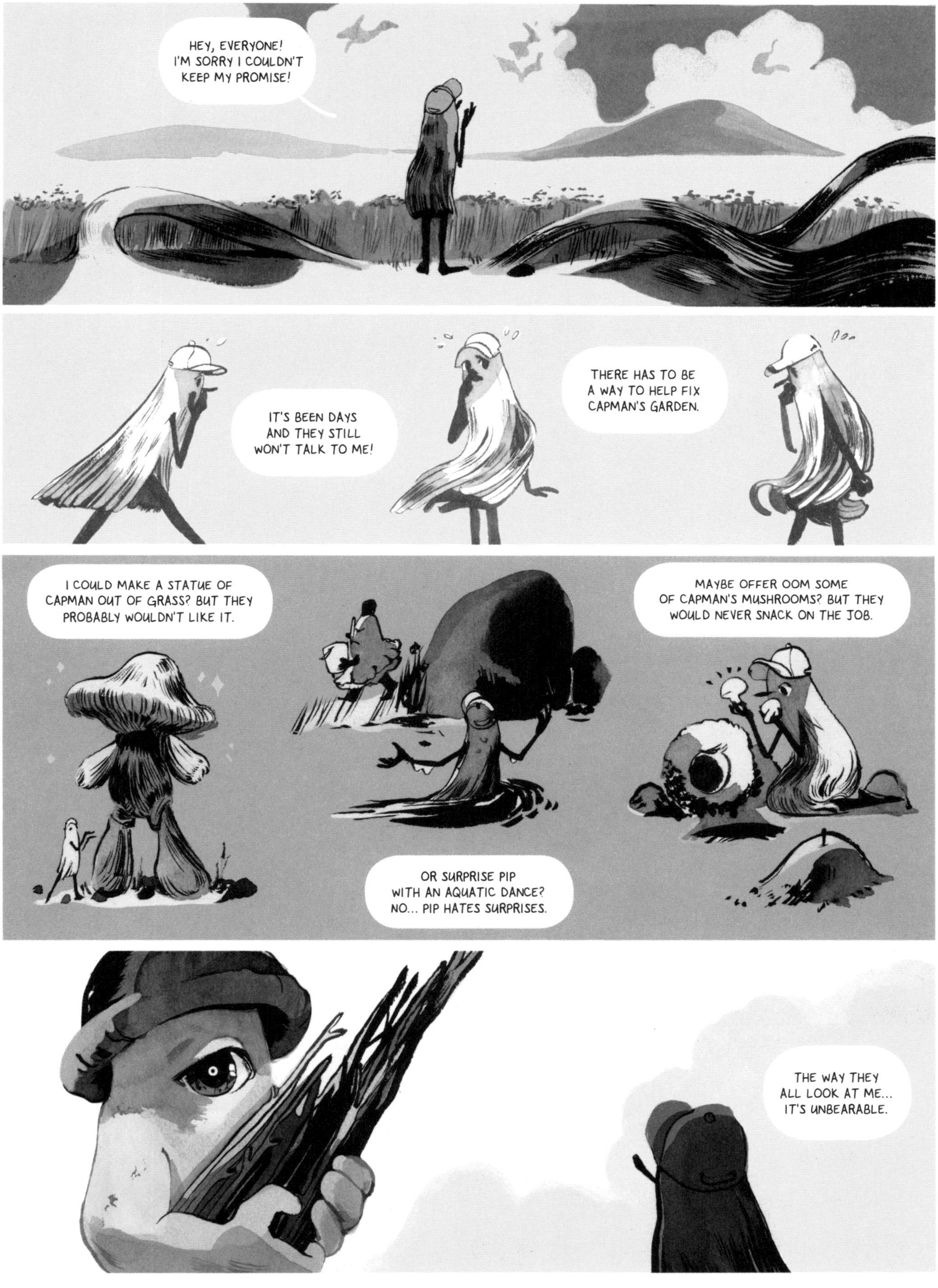
HEY, EVERYONE! I'M SORRY I COULDN'T KEEP MY PROMISE!
IT'S BEEN DAYS AND THEY STILL WON'T TALK TO ME!
THERE HAS TO BE A WAY TO HELP FIX CAPMAN'S GARDEN.
I COULD MAKE A STATUE OF CAPMAN OUT OF GRASS? BUT THEY PROBABLY WOULDN'T LIKE IT.
MAYBE OFFER OOM SOME OF CAPMAN'S MUSHROOMS? BUT THEY WOULD NEVER SNACK ON THE JOB.
OR SURPRISE PIP WITH AN AQUATIC DANCE? NO... PIP HATES SURPRISES.
THE WAY THEY ALL LOOK AT ME... IT'S UNBEARABLE.

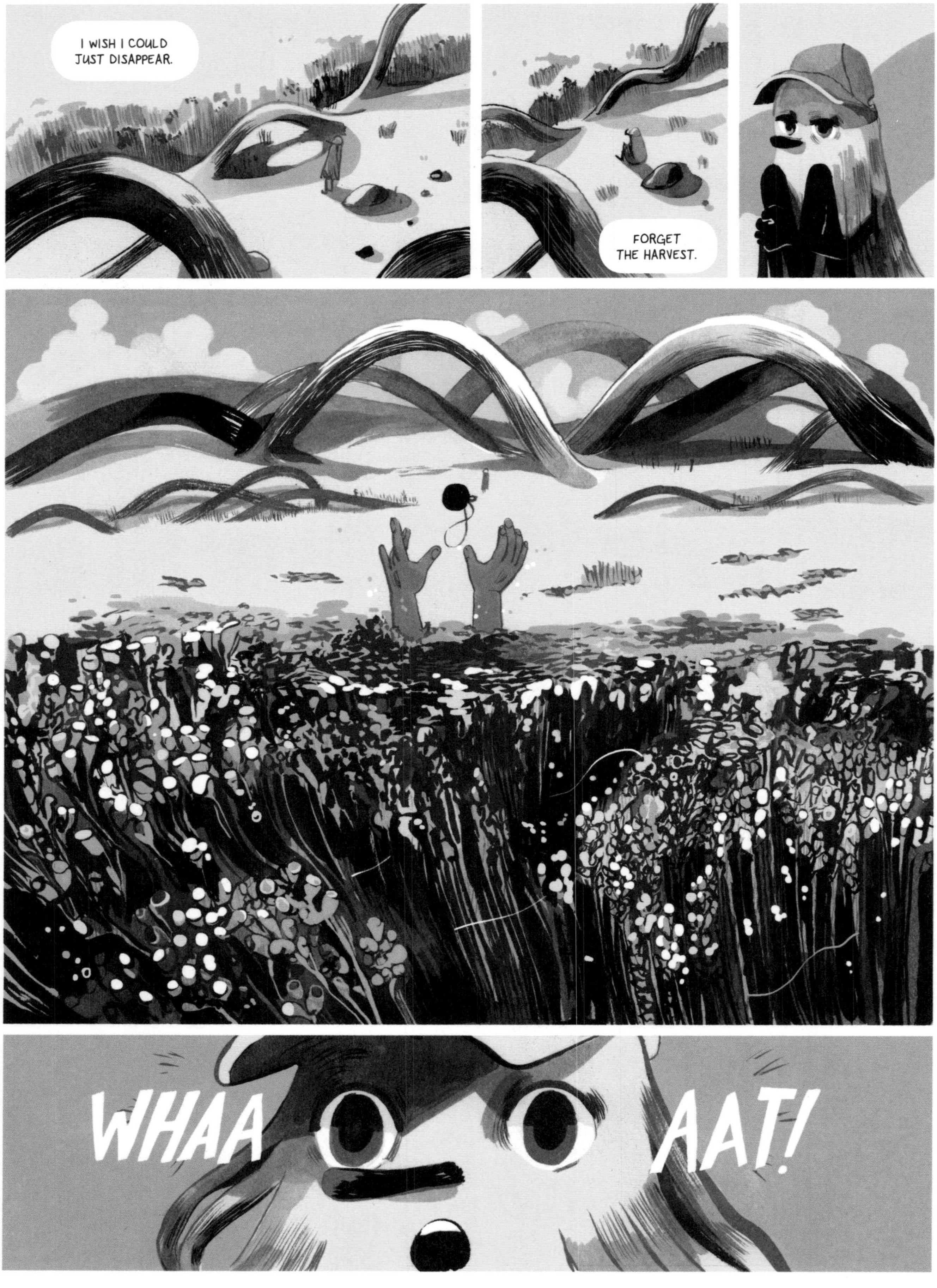
I WISH I COULD JUST DISAPPEAR.
FORGET THE HARVEST.
WHAA AAT!

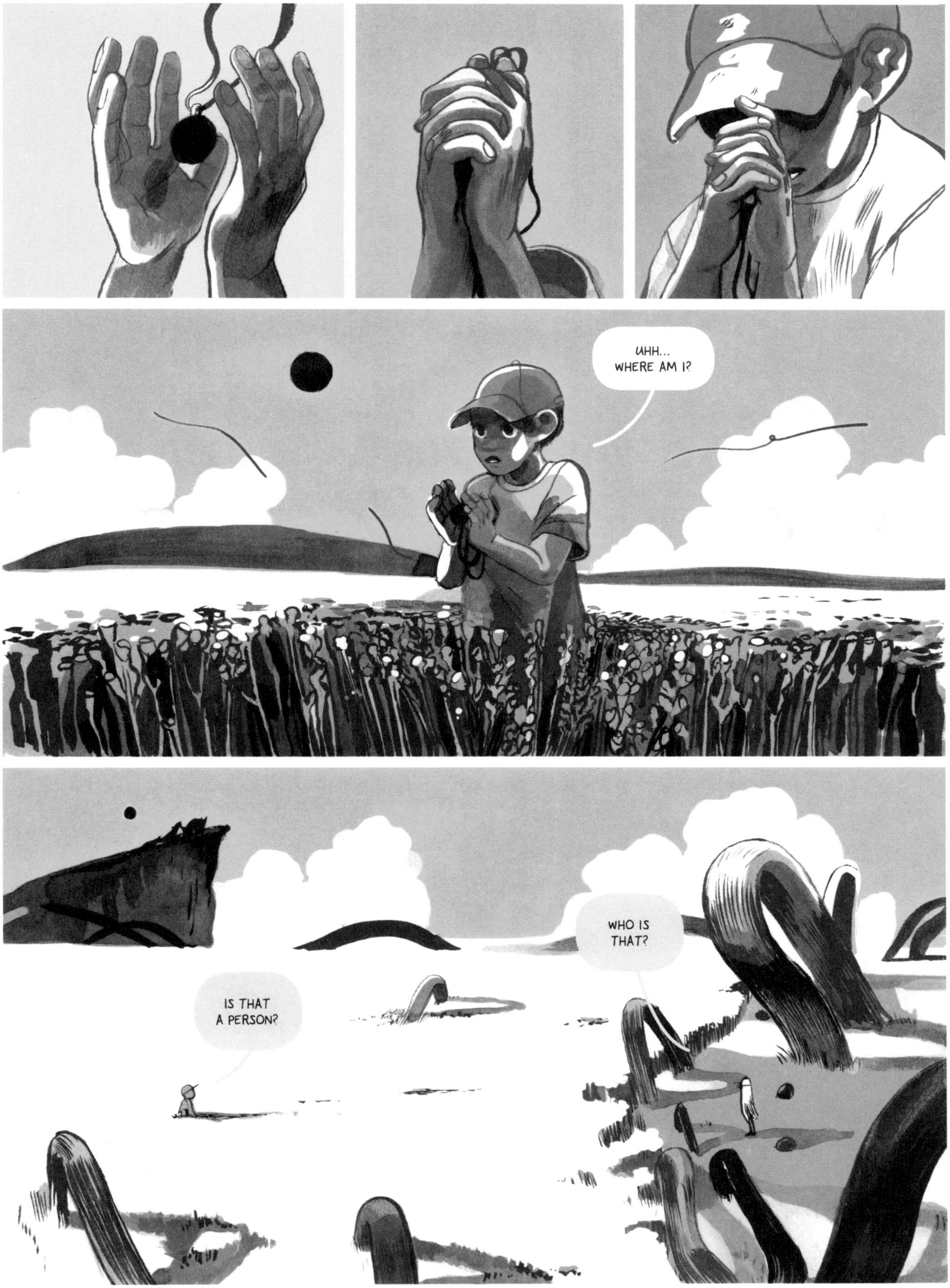
UHH...
WHERE AM I?
WHO IS THAT?
IS THAT A PERSON?

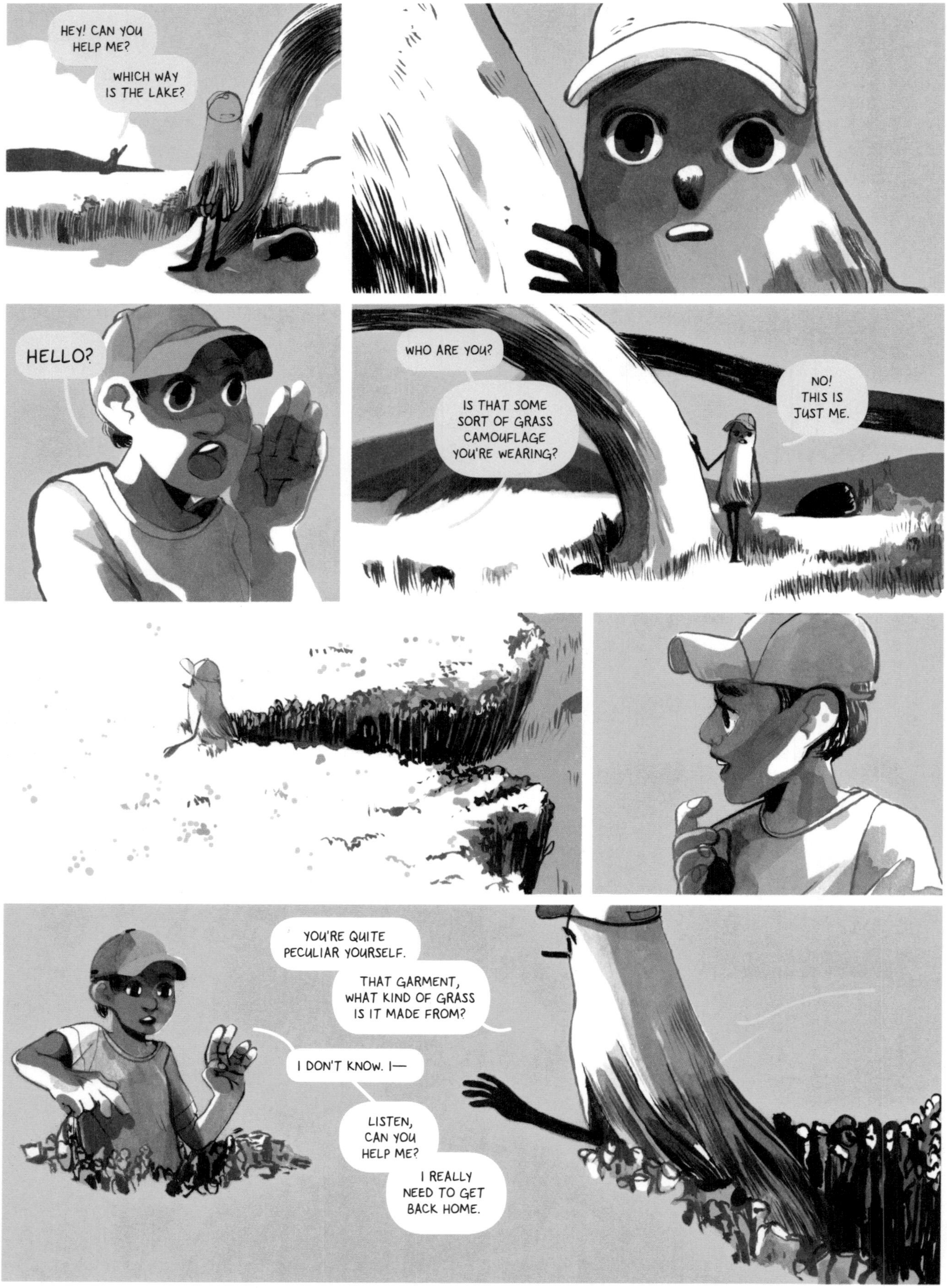
HEY! CAN YOU HELP ME?
WHICH WAY IS THE LAKE?
HELLO?
WHO ARE YOU?
IS THAT SOME SORT OF GRASS CAMOUFLAGE YOU'RE WEARING?
NO! THIS IS JUST ME.
YOU'RE QUITE PECULIAR YOURSELF.
THAT GARMENT, WHAT KIND OF GRASS IS IT MADE FROM?
I DON'T KNOW. I—
LISTEN, CAN YOU HELP ME?
I REALLY NEED TO GET BACK HOME.

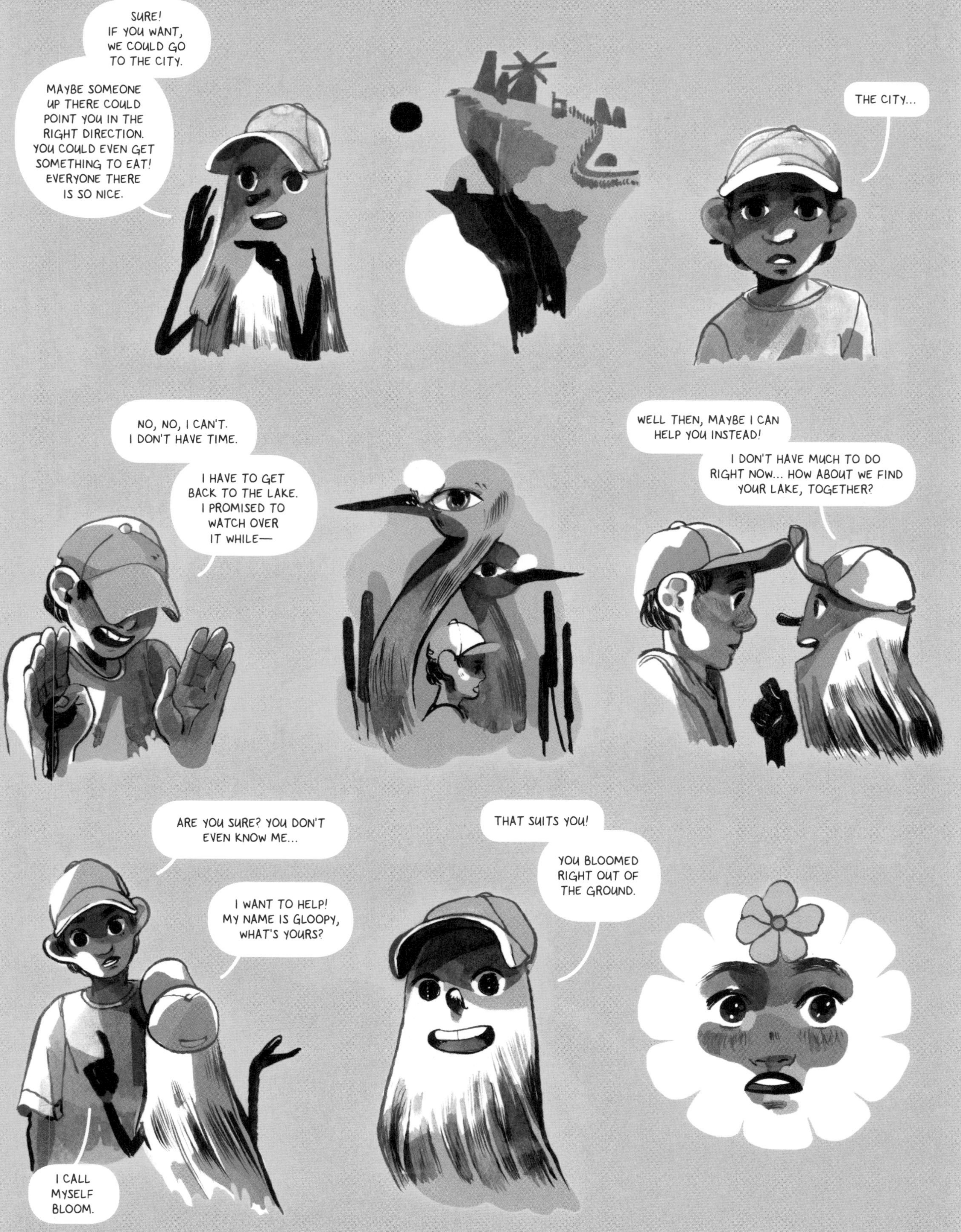
SURE! IF YOU WANT, WE COULD GO TO THE CITY.
MAYBE SOMEONE UP THERE COULD POINT YOU IN THE RIGHT DIRECTION. YOU COULD EVEN GET SOMETHING TO EAT! EVERYONE THERE IS SO NICE.
THE CITY...
NO, NO, I CAN'T. I DON'T HAVE TIME.
I HAVE TO GET BACK TO THE LAKE. I PROMISED TO WATCH OVER IT WHILE—
WELL THEN, MAYBE I CAN HELP YOU INSTEAD!
I DON'T HAVE MUCH TO DO RIGHT NOW... HOW ABOUT WE FIND YOUR LAKE, TOGETHER?
ARE YOU SURE? YOU DON'T EVEN KNOW ME...
I WANT TO HELP! MY NAME IS GLOOPY, WHAT'S YOURS?
I CALL MYSELF BLOOM.
THAT SUITS YOU!
YOU BLOOMED RIGHT OUT OF THE GROUND.

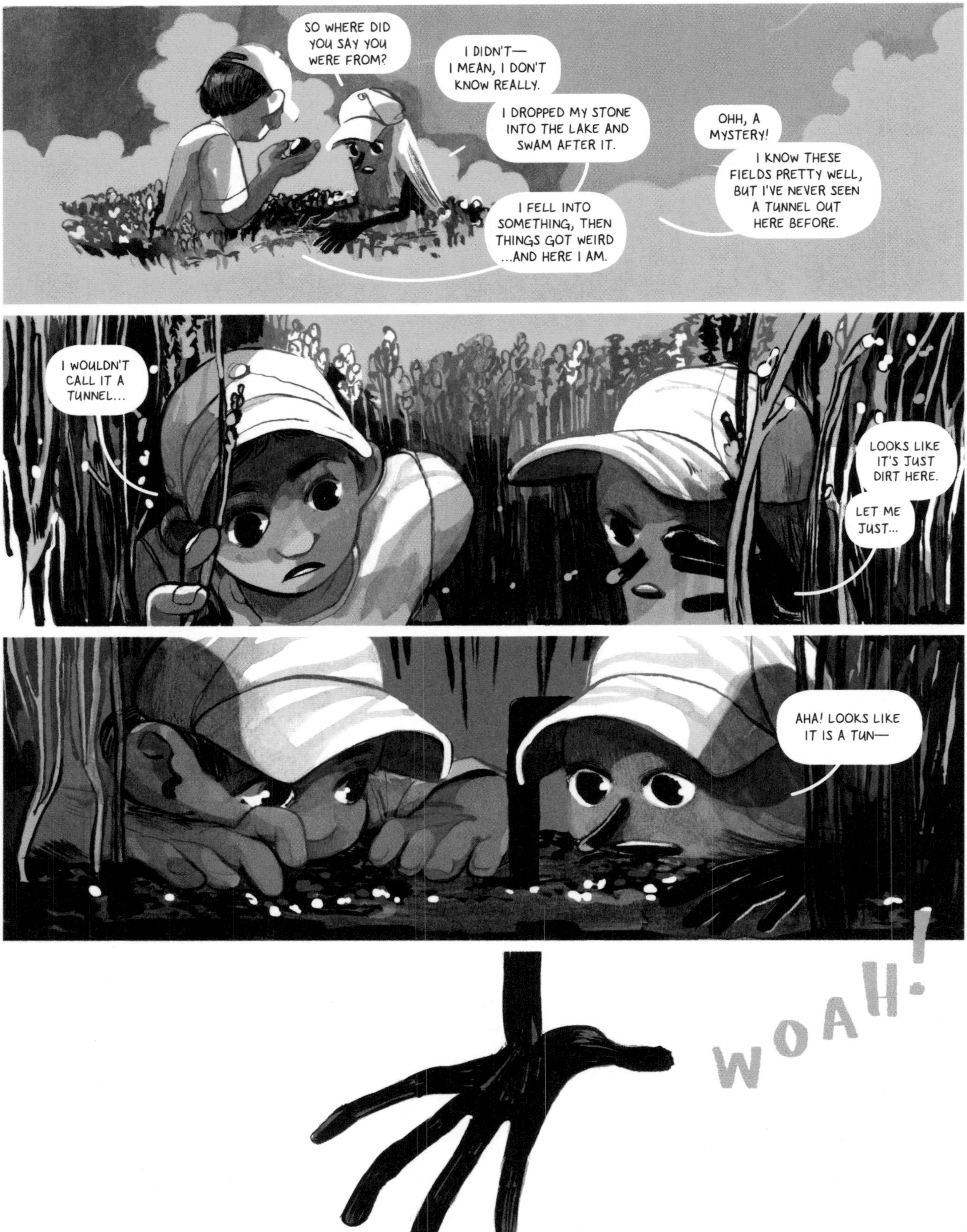
SO WHERE DID YOU SAY YOU WERE FROM?
I DIDN'T— I MEAN, I DON'T KNOW REALLY.
I DROPPED MY STONE INTO THE LAKE AND SWAM AFTER IT.
I FELL INTO SOMETHING, THEN THINGS GOT WEIRD ...AND HERE I AM.
OHH, A MYSTERY!
I KNOW THESE FIELDS PRETTY WELL, BUT I'VE NEVER SEEN A TUNNEL OUT HERE BEFORE.
I WOULDN'T CALL IT A TUNNEL...
LOOKS LIKE IT'S JUST DIRT HERE.
LET ME JUST...
AHA! LOOKS LIKE IT IS A TUN—
WOAH!

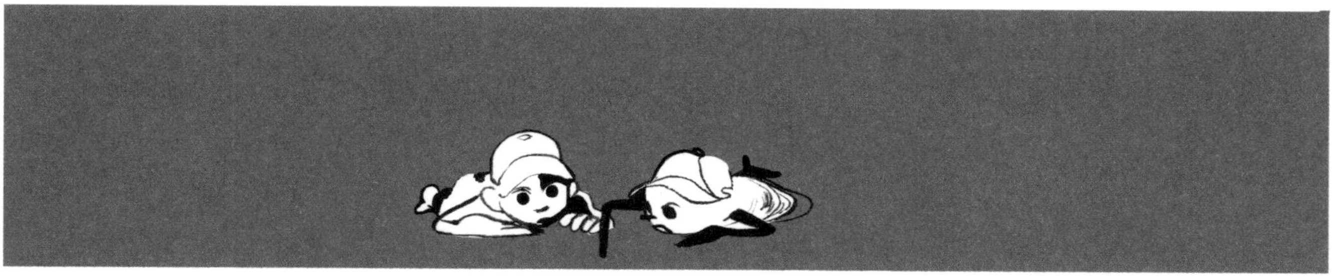
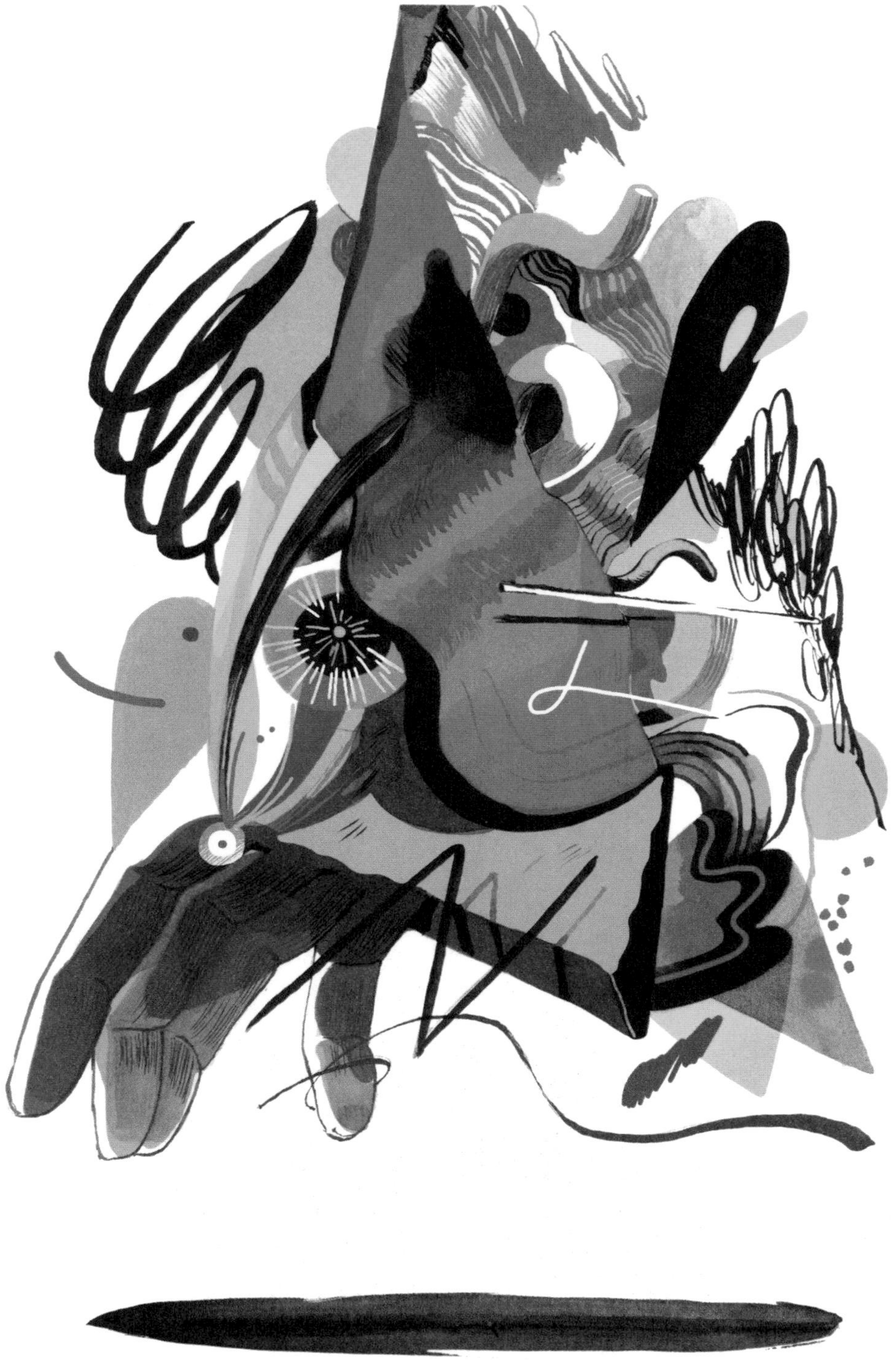

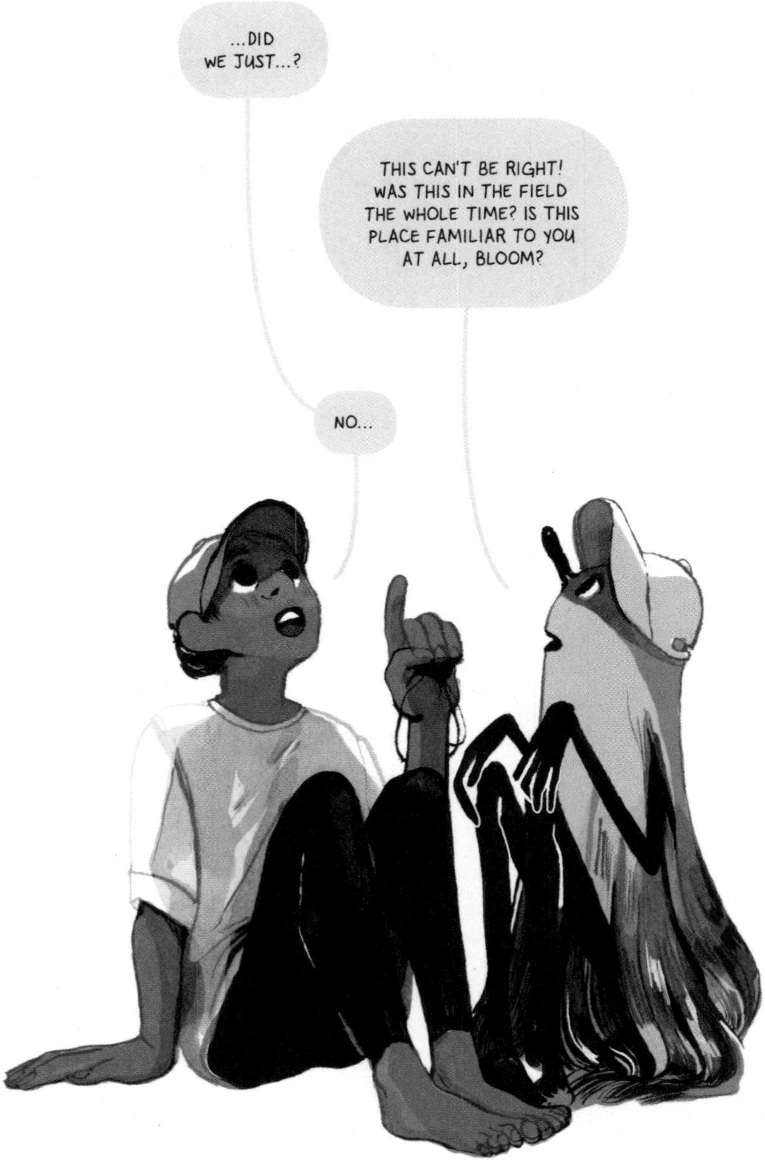
...DID WE JUST...?
THIS CAN'T BE RIGHT! WAS THIS IN THE FIELD THE WHOLE TIME? IS THIS PLACE FAMILIAR TO YOU AT ALL, BLOOM?
NO...

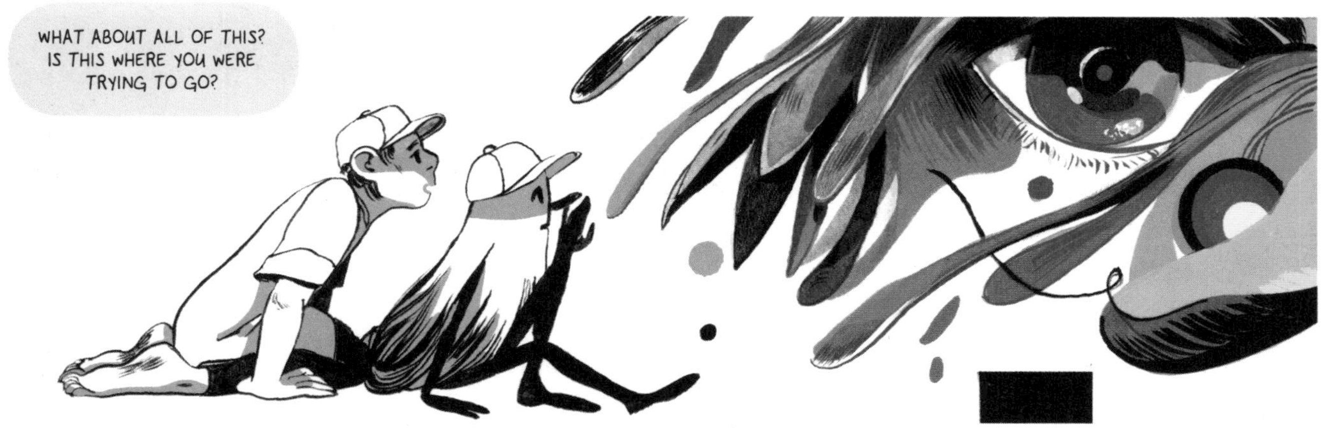
WHAT ABOUT ALL OF THIS? IS THIS WHERE YOU WERE TRYING TO GO?

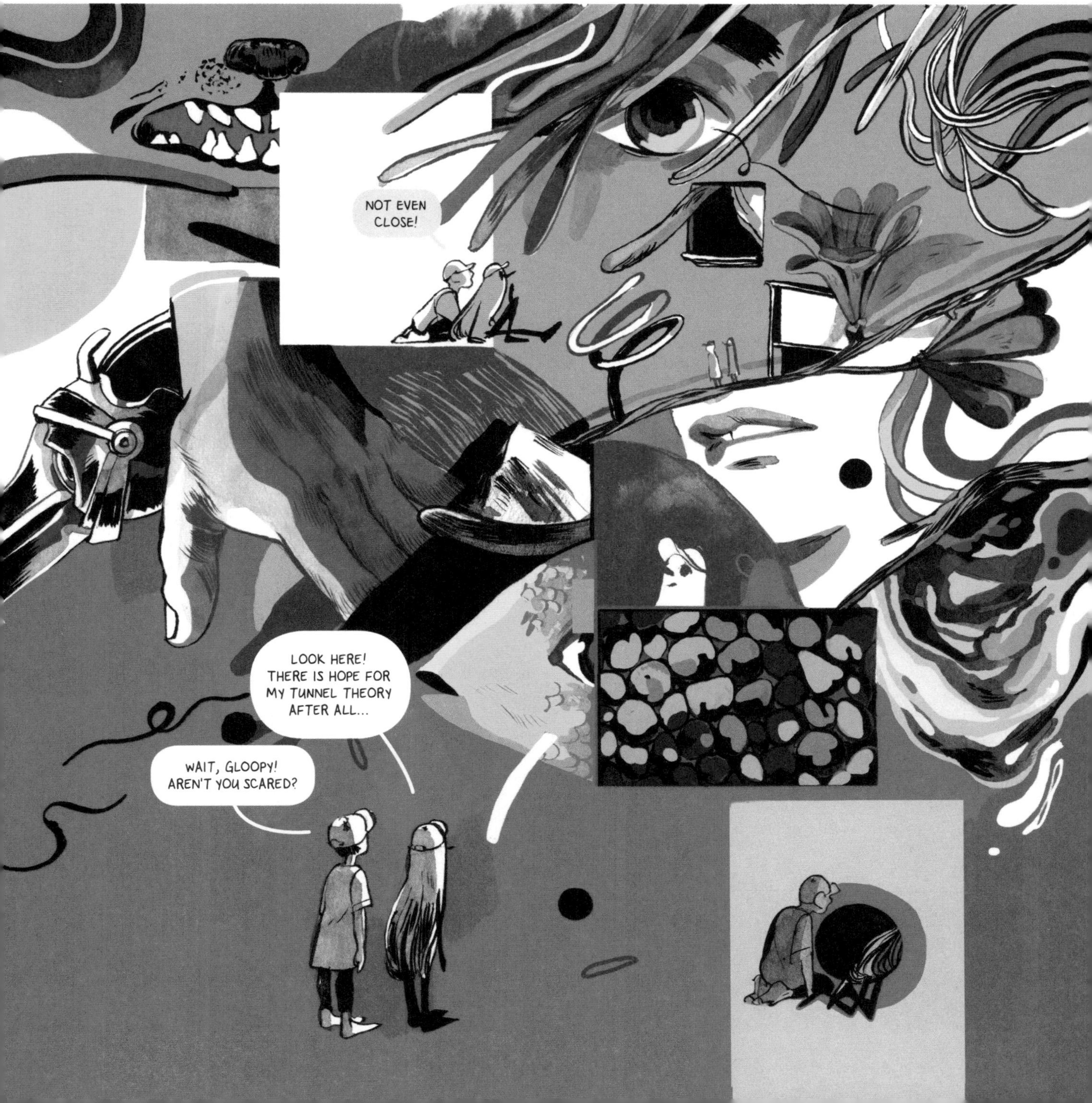
NOT EVEN CLOSE!
LOOK HERE! THERE IS HOPE FOR MY TUNNEL THEORY AFTER ALL...
WAIT, GLOOPY! AREN'T YOU SCARED?

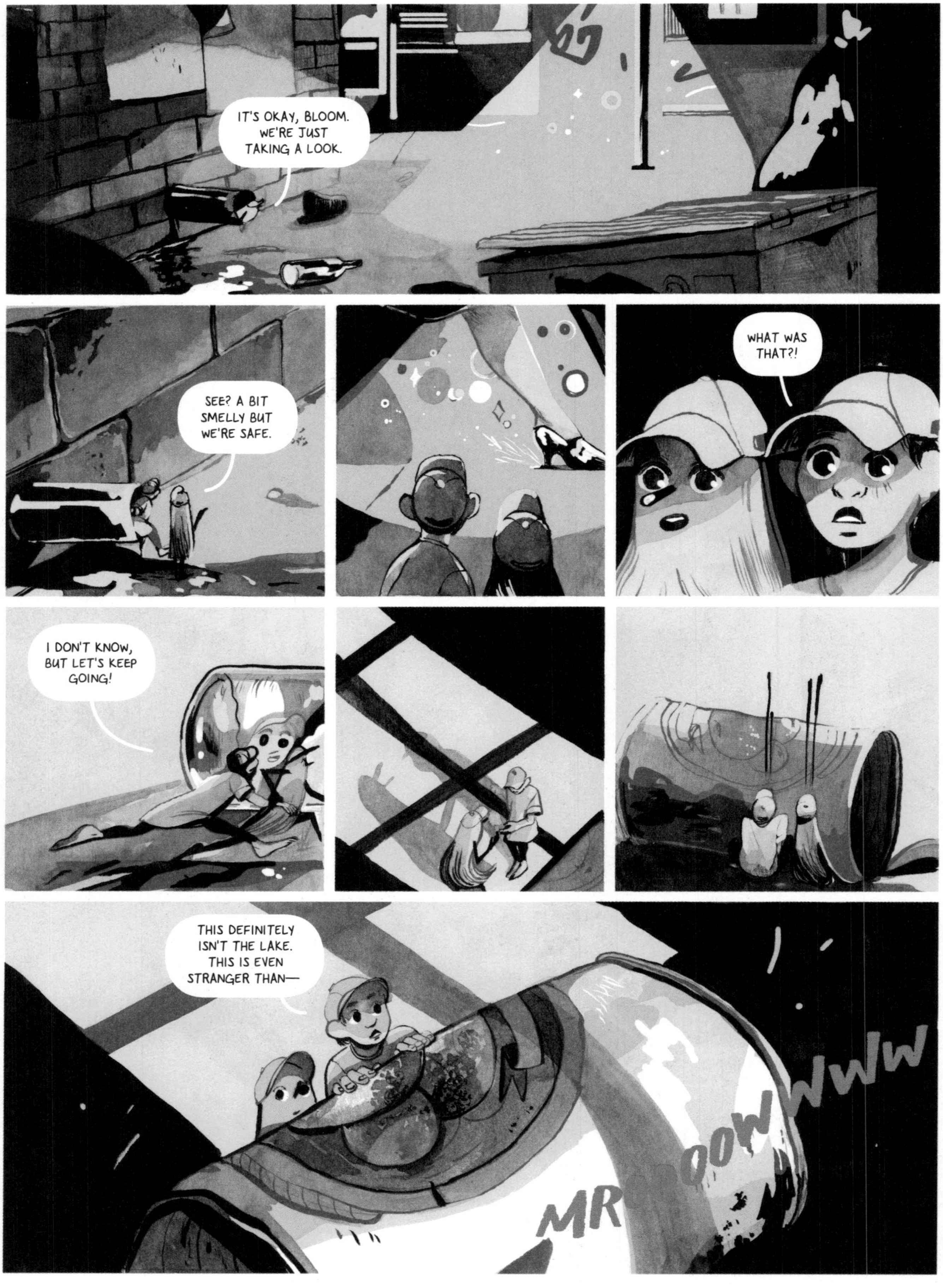
IT'S OKAY, BLOOM. WE'RE JUST TAKING A LOOK.
SEE? A BIT SMELLY BUT WE'RE SAFE.
WHAT WAS THAT?!
I DON'T KNOW, BUT LET'S KEEP GOING!
THIS DEFINITELY ISN'T THE LAKE. THIS IS EVEN STRANGER THAN—
MROOOOWWWW

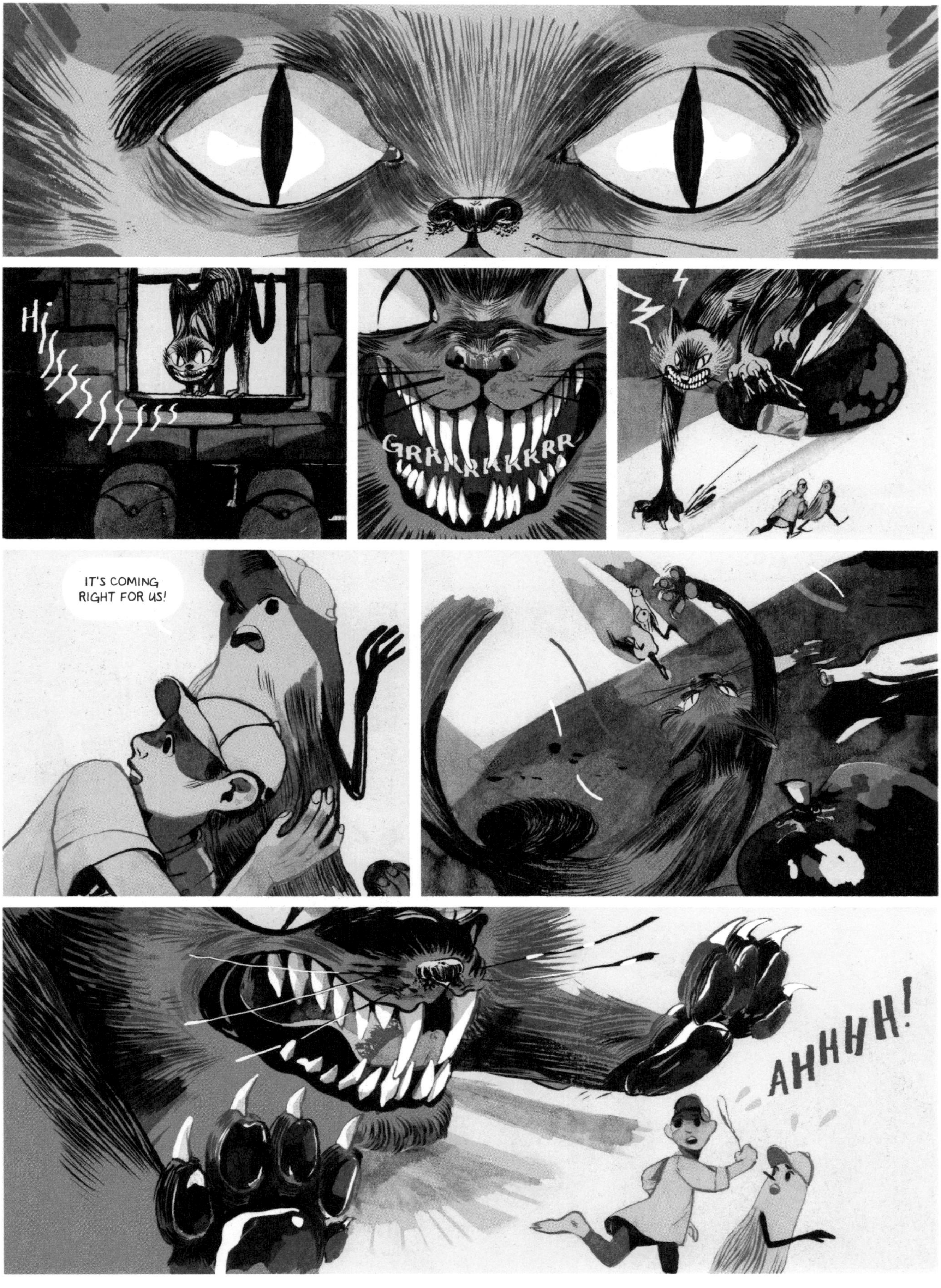
HISSSSSSSSSS
GRRRRRRRRRR
IT'S COMING RIGHT FOR US!
AHHHH!

LOOK!
ANOTHER TUNNEL,
QUICK!

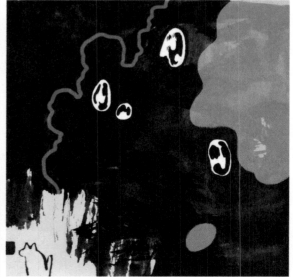

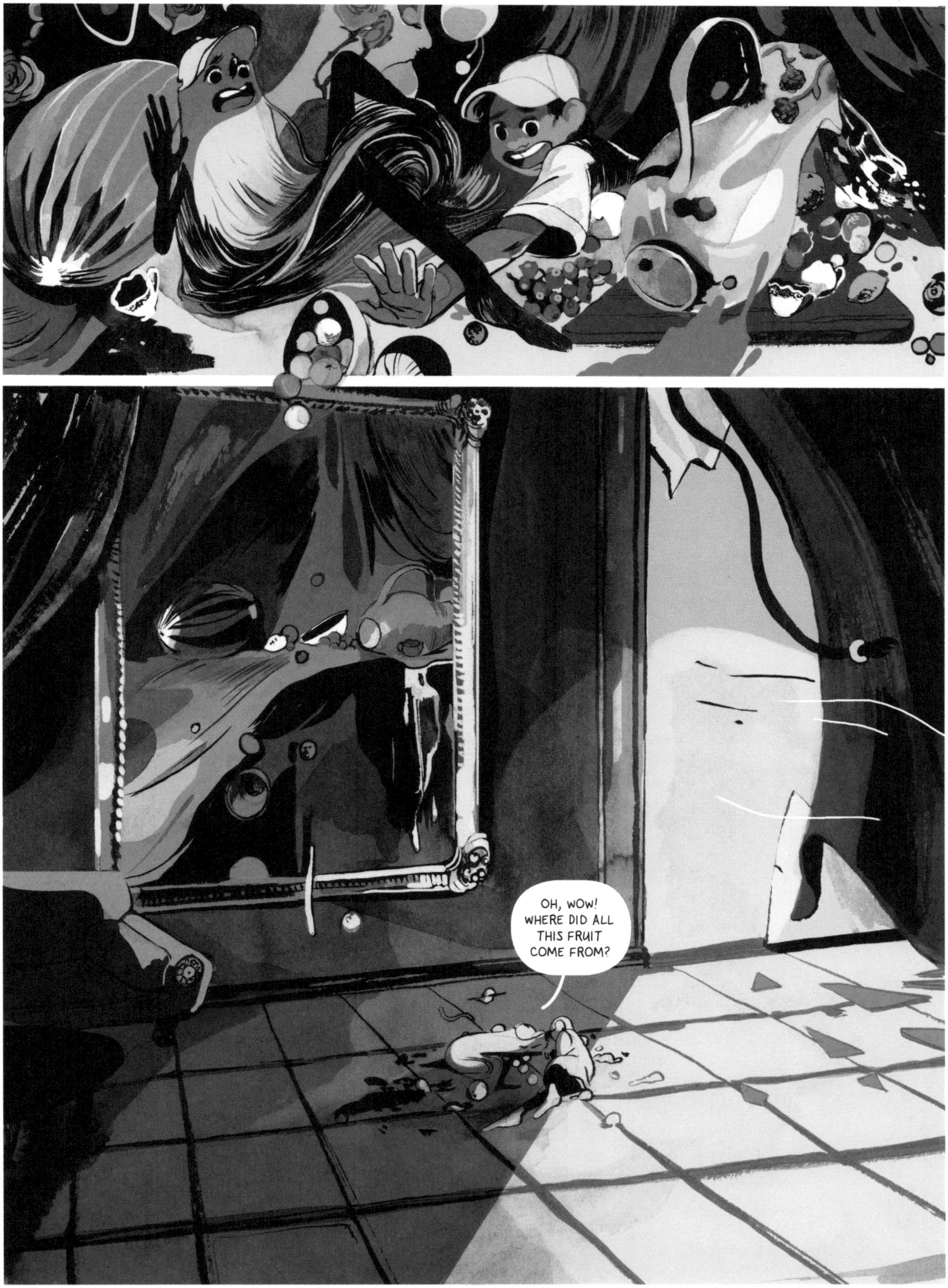
OH, WOW! WHERE DID ALL THIS FRUIT COME FROM?

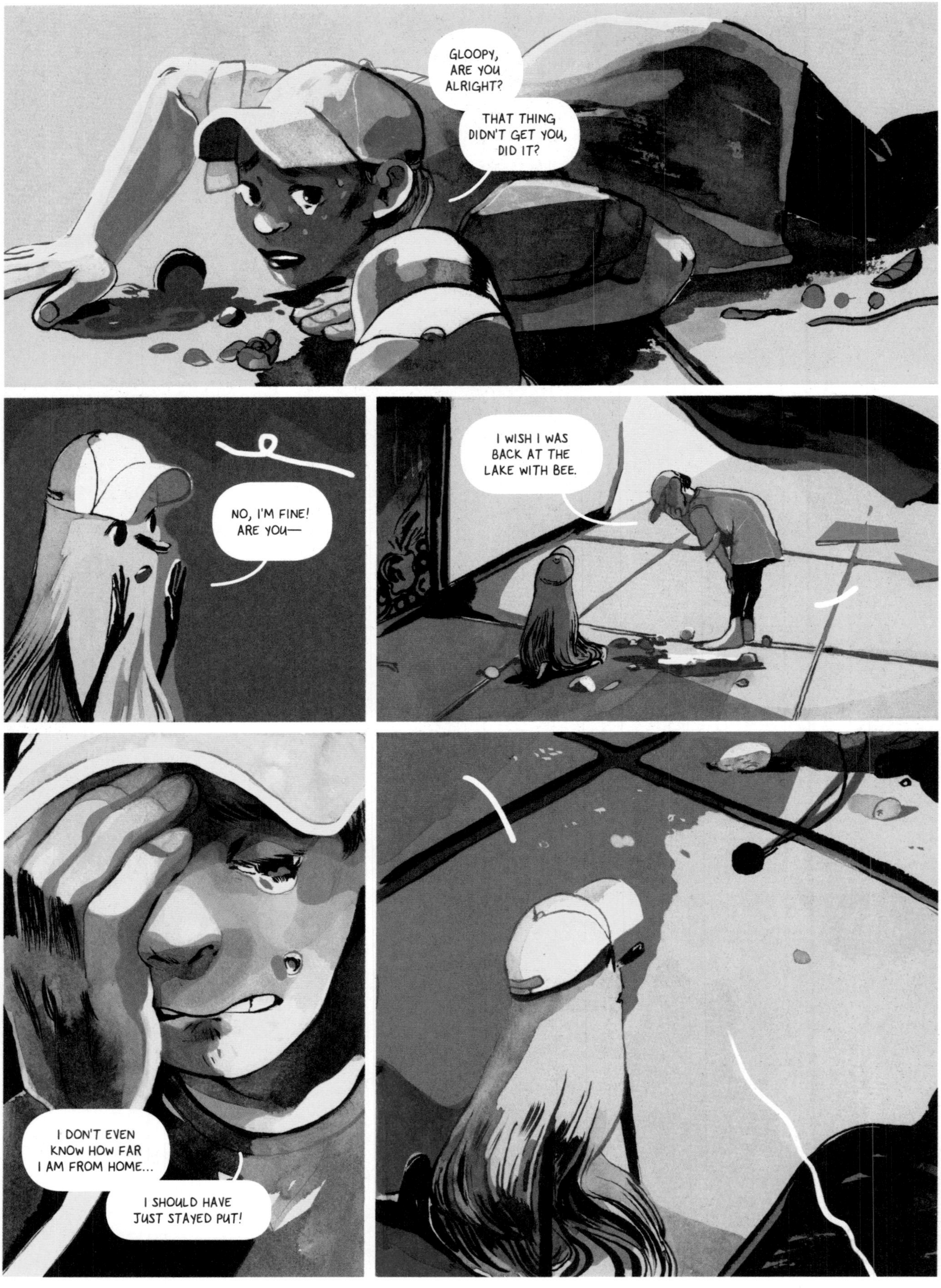
GLOOPY, ARE YOU ALRIGHT?
THAT THING DIDN'T GET YOU, DID IT?
NO, I'M FINE! ARE YOU—
I WISH I WAS BACK AT THE LAKE WITH BEE.
I DON'T EVEN KNOW HOW FAR I AM FROM HOME...
I SHOULD HAVE JUST STAYED PUT!

IT'S OKAY, BLOOM. HERE, LOOK, YOU DROPPED THIS.

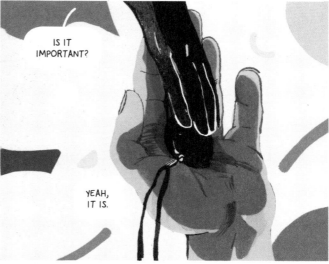

IS IT IMPORTANT?

YEAH, IT IS.

DON'T WORRY ABOUT ALL THIS, WE'LL FIGURE IT OUT!

JUST LOOK AT THIS PLACE! I'VE NEVER SEEN ANYTHING LIKE IT!

THIS ONE LOOKS LIKE BACK HOME...

...OH, AND THIS ONE HAS SOME MORE FRUIT. I BET PIP WOULD LIKE IT.

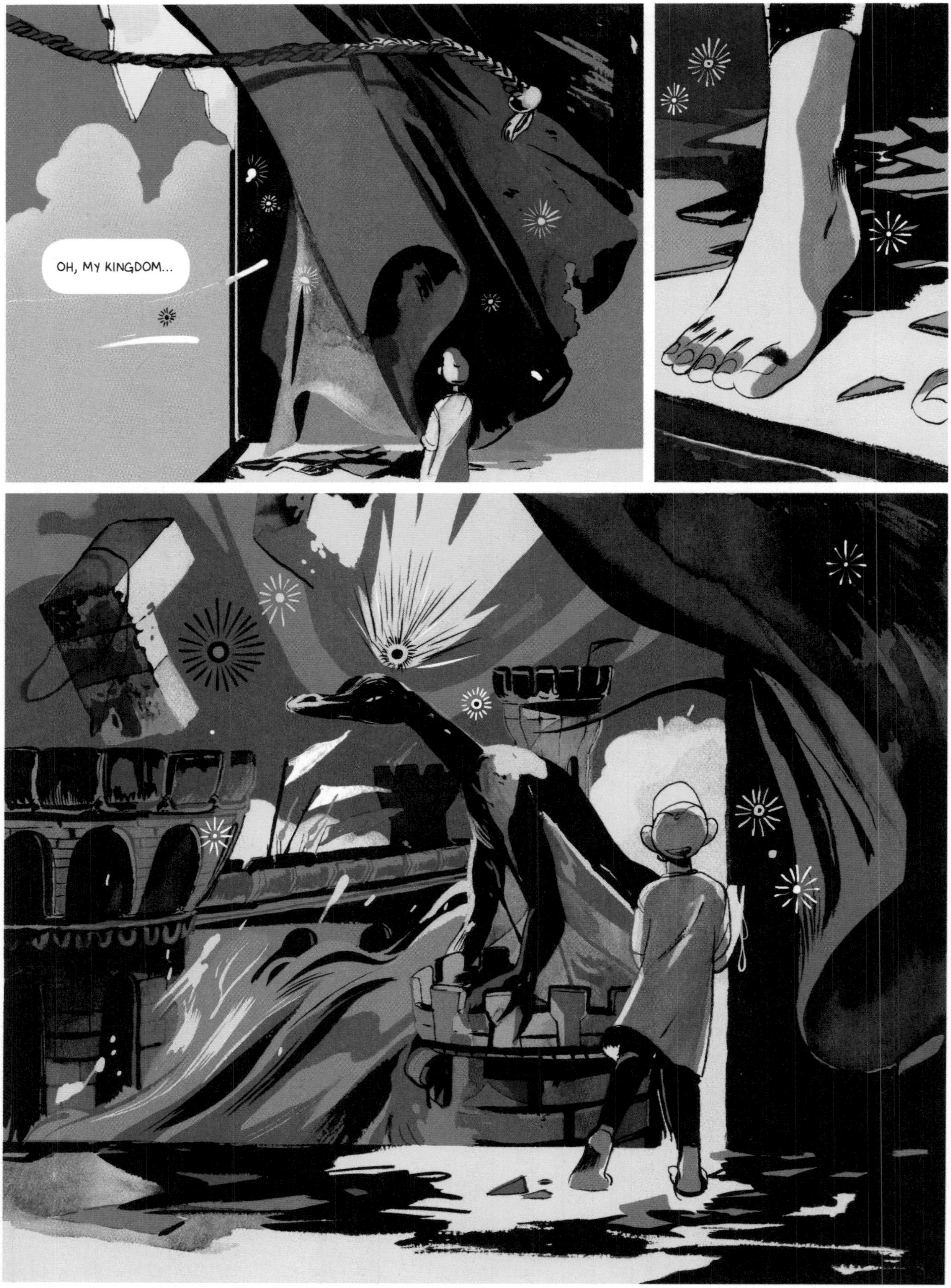
OH, MY KINGDOM...

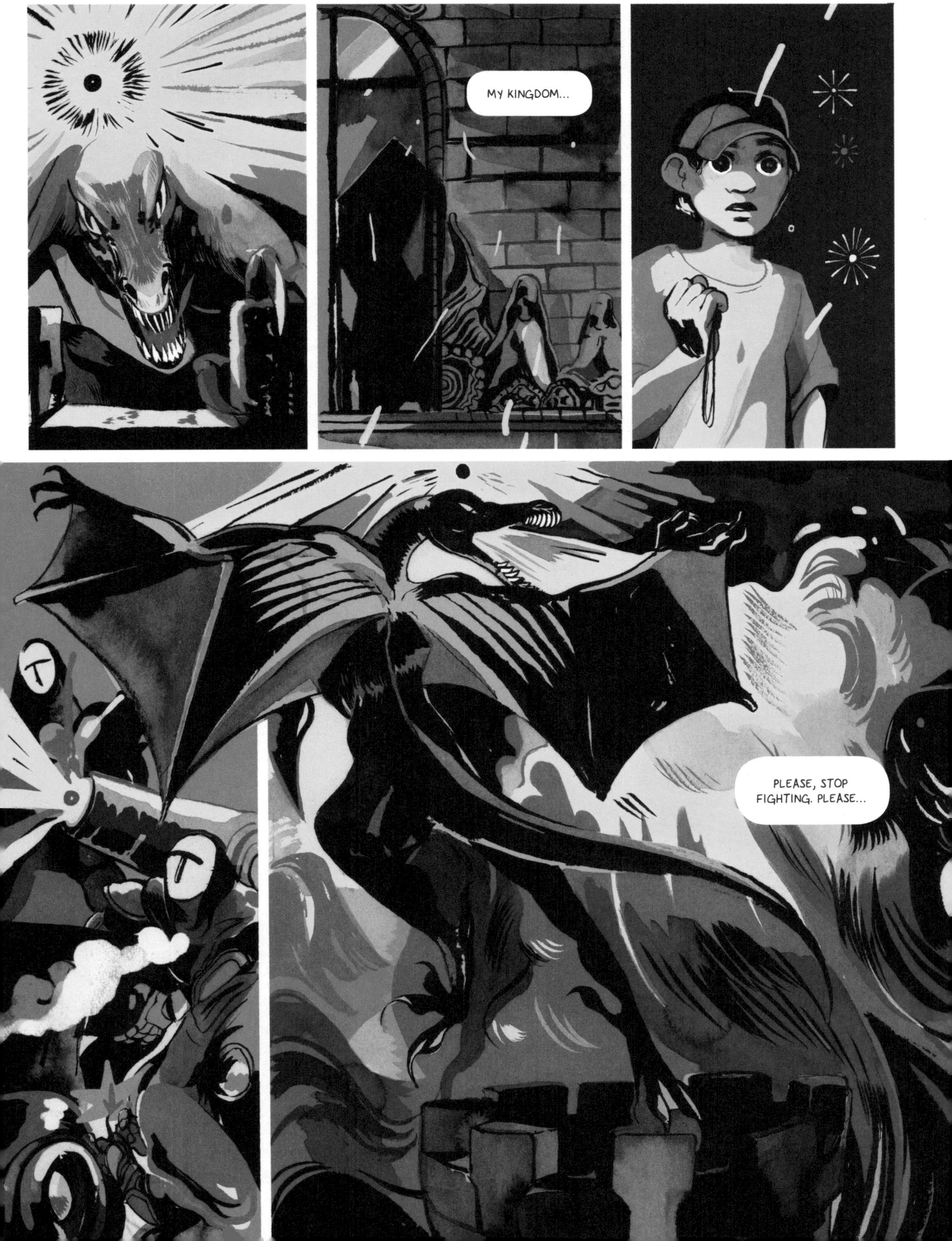
MY KINGDOM...
PLEASE, STOP FIGHTING. PLEASE...

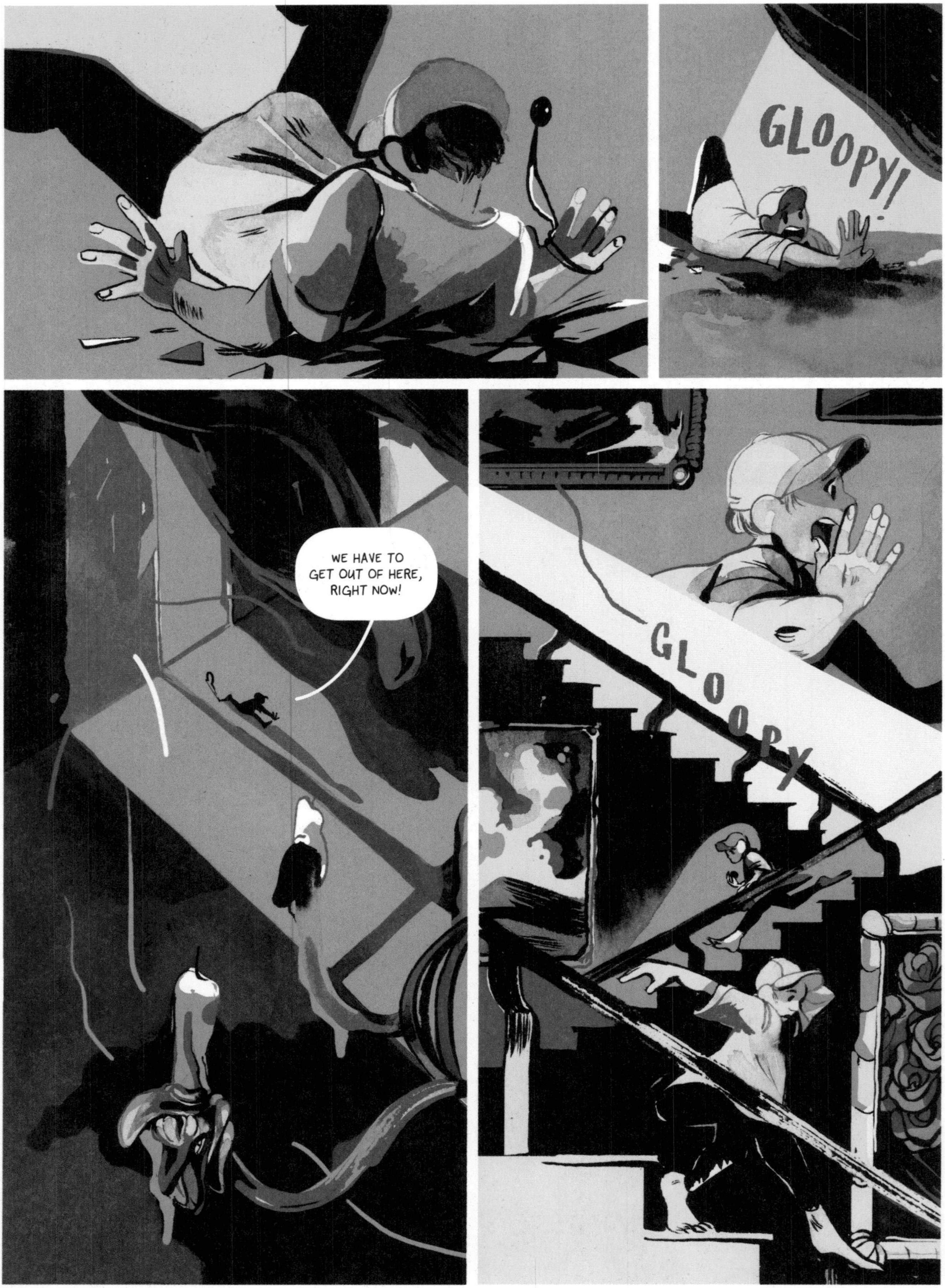
GLOOPY!
WE HAVE TO GET OUT OF HERE, RIGHT NOW!
GLOOPY

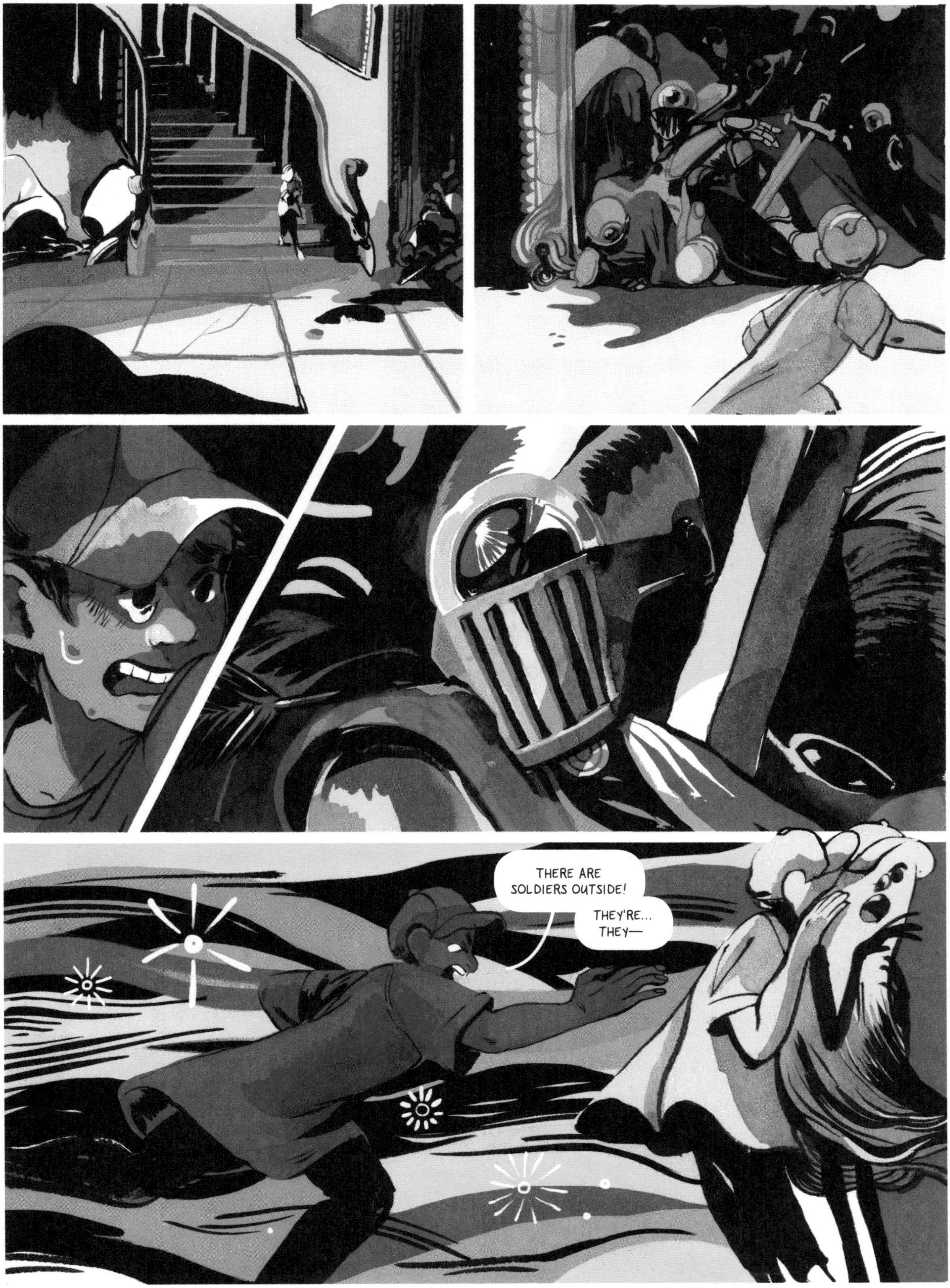
THERE ARE SOLDIERS OUTSIDE!
THEY'RE... THEY—

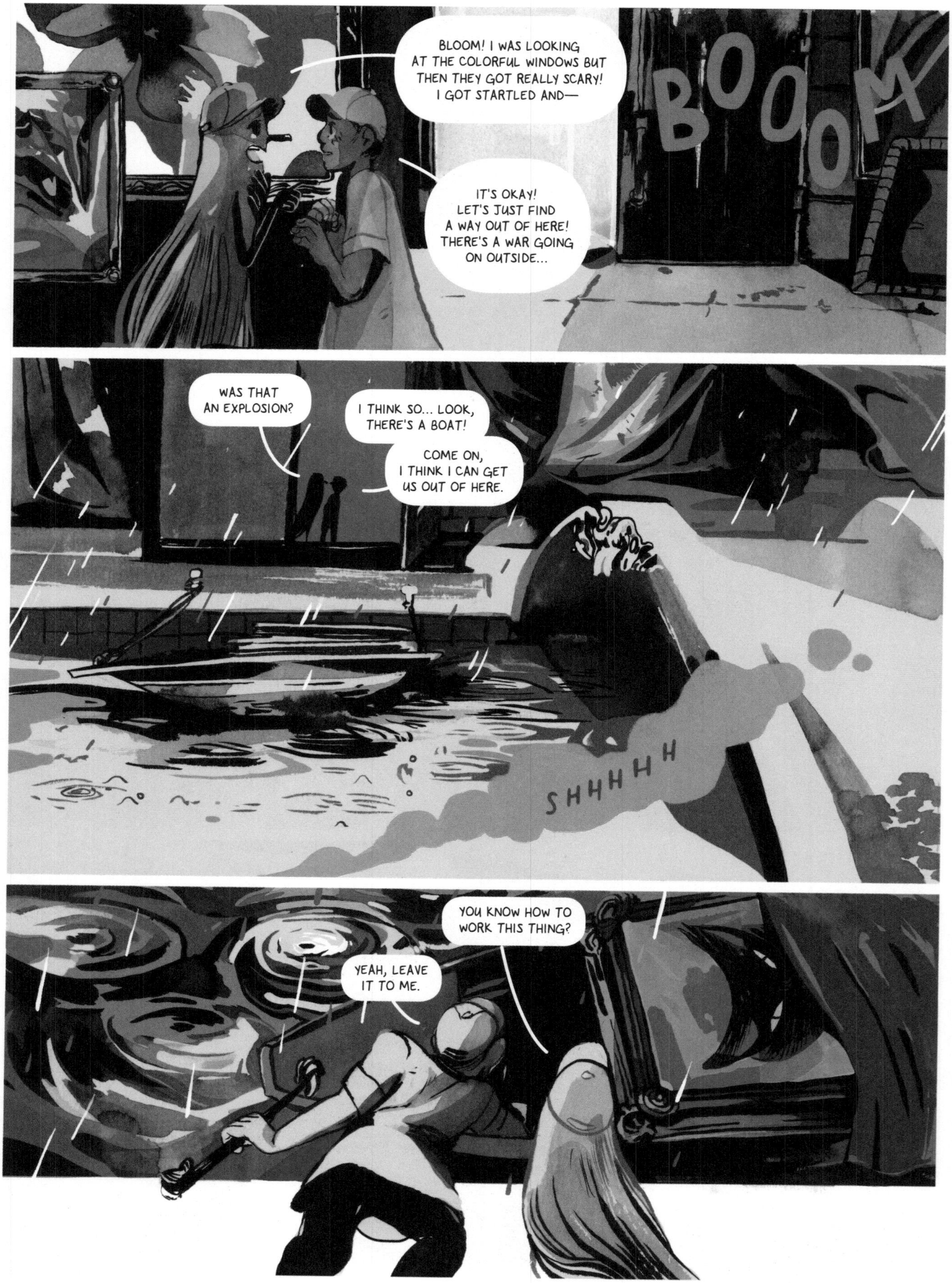
BLOOM! I WAS LOOKING AT THE COLORFUL WINDOWS BUT THEN THEY GOT REALLY SCARY! I GOT STARTLED AND—
BOOOM
IT'S OKAY! LET'S JUST FIND A WAY OUT OF HERE! THERE'S A WAR GOING ON OUTSIDE...
WAS THAT AN EXPLOSION?
I THINK SO... LOOK, THERE'S A BOAT!
COME ON, I THINK I CAN GET US OUT OF HERE.
SHHHHH
YOU KNOW HOW TO WORK THIS THING?
YEAH, LEAVE IT TO ME.

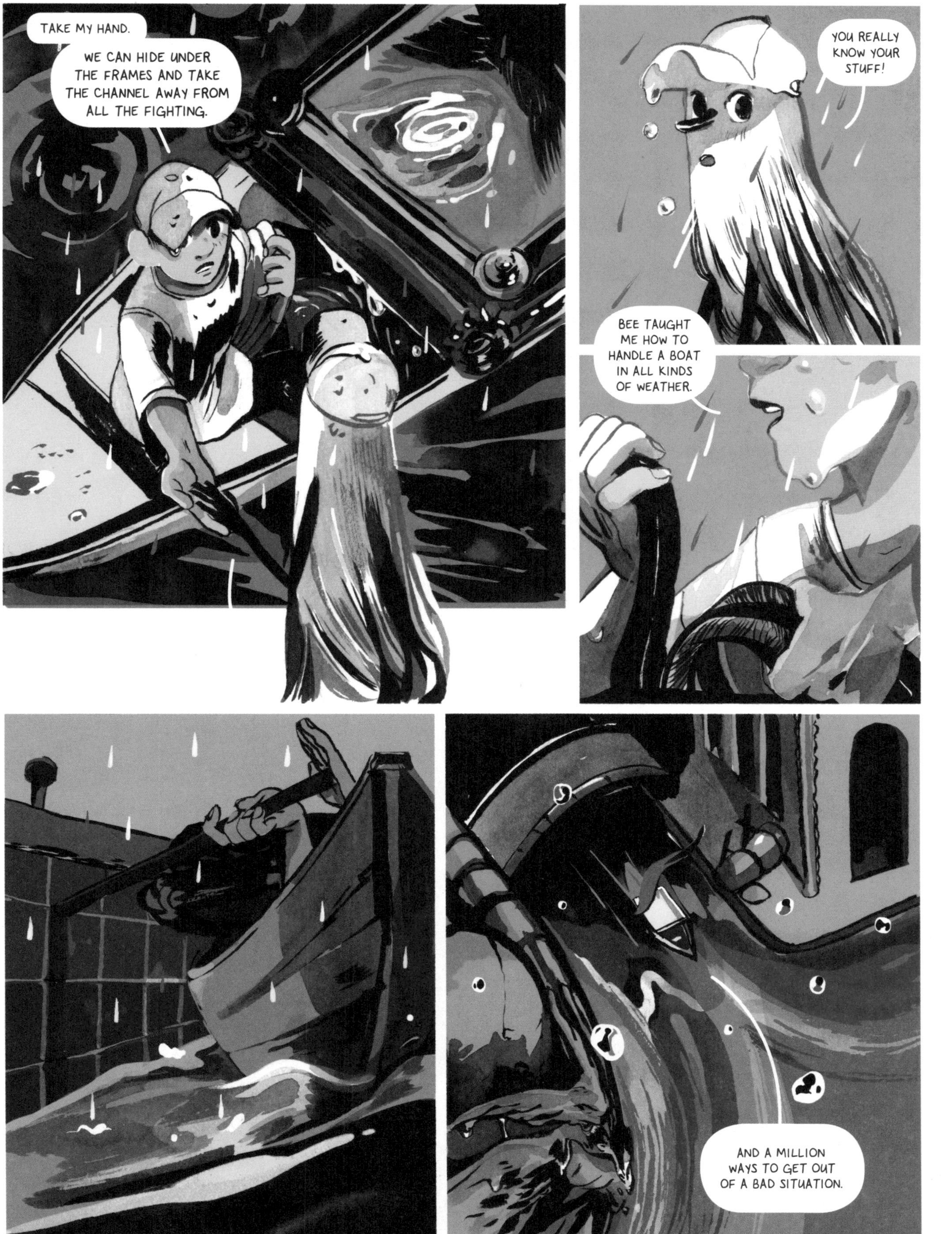
TAKE MY HAND.
WE CAN HIDE UNDER THE FRAMES AND TAKE THE CHANNEL AWAY FROM ALL THE FIGHTING.
YOU REALLY KNOW YOUR STUFF!
BEE TAUGHT ME HOW TO HANDLE A BOAT IN ALL KINDS OF WEATHER.
AND A MILLION WAYS TO GET OUT OF A BAD SITUATION.

WHO IS BEE? YOUR PARENT?

THEY— THEY'RE VERY IMPORTANT TO ME.

AND THIS PLACE, IT REMINDS ME OF SOMETHING THEY SAID.

ABOUT HOW THERE WAS A BIG TEAR IN THE WORLD THAT DIVIDED EVERYONE...

...AND THE MACHINES THEY CREATED TO MAKE THE WORLD BETTER WERE USED TO HURT EACH OTHER INSTEAD...

UNTIL ONLY THE MACHINES WERE LEFT.

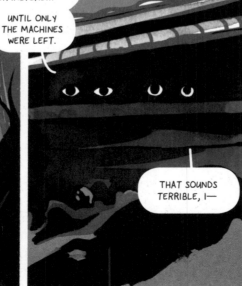

THAT SOUNDS TERRIBLE, I—

OH NO

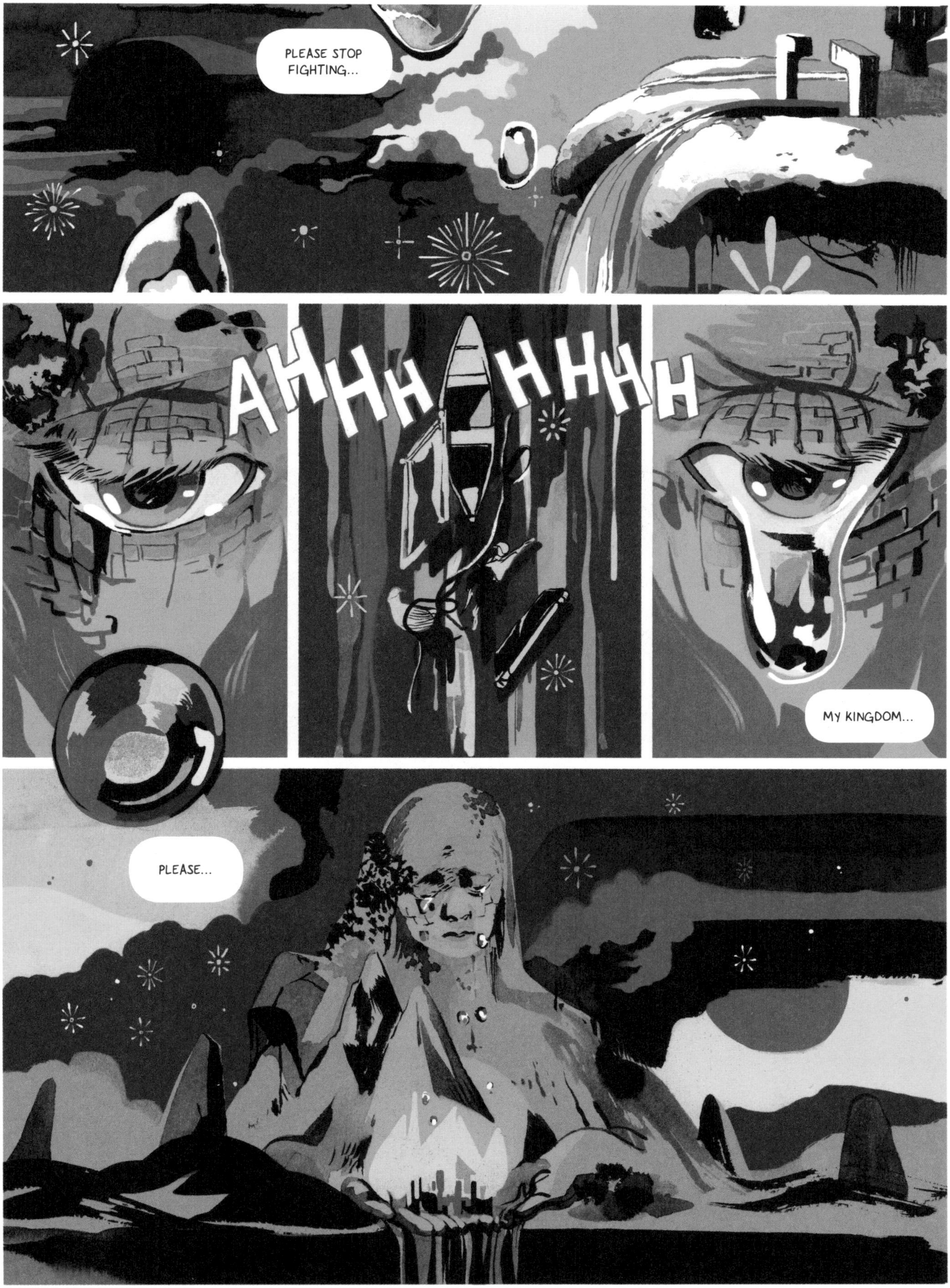
PLEASE STOP FIGHTING...
AHHHHHHHH
MY KINGDOM...
PLEASE...

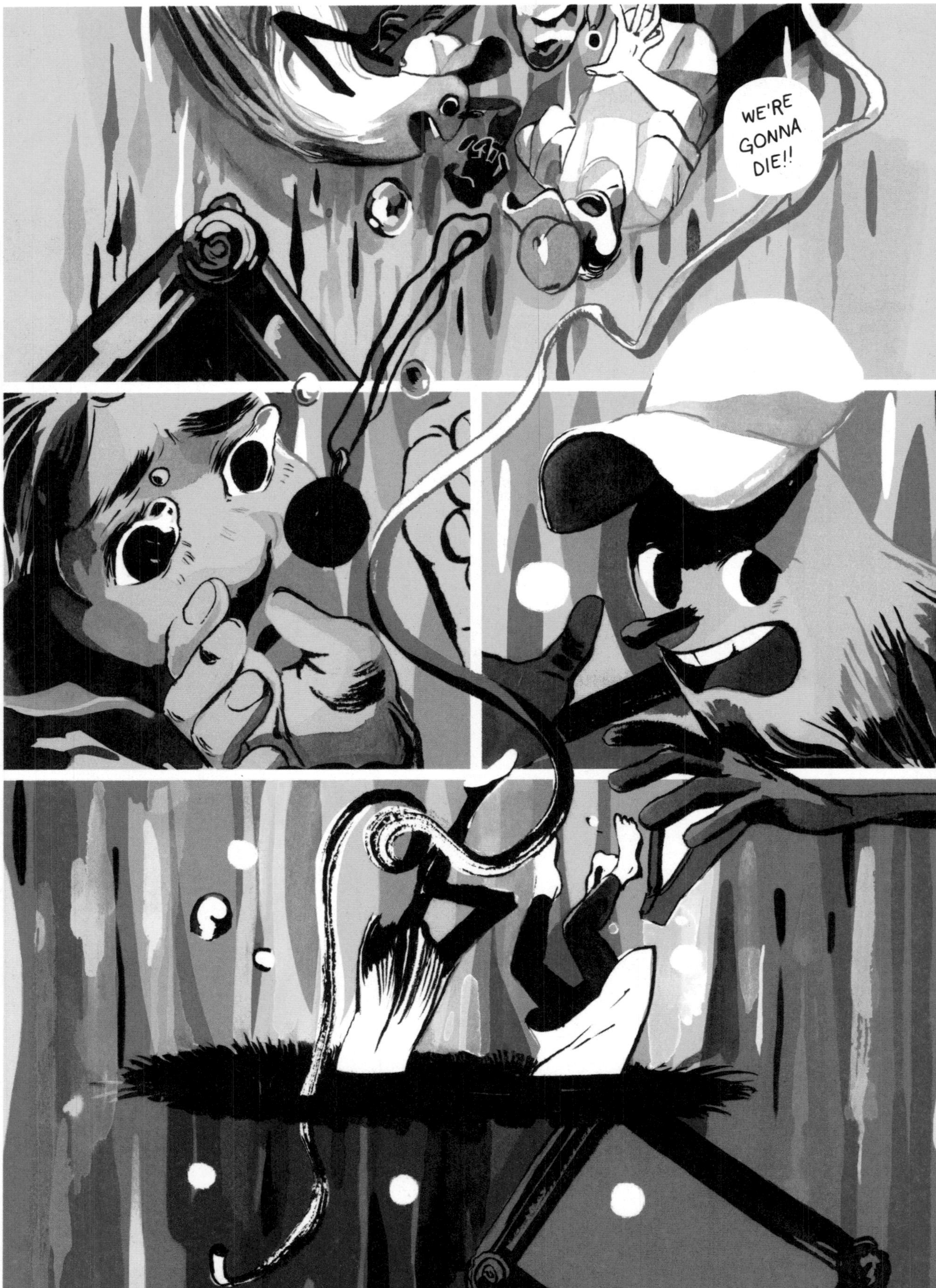
WE'RE GONNA DIE!!

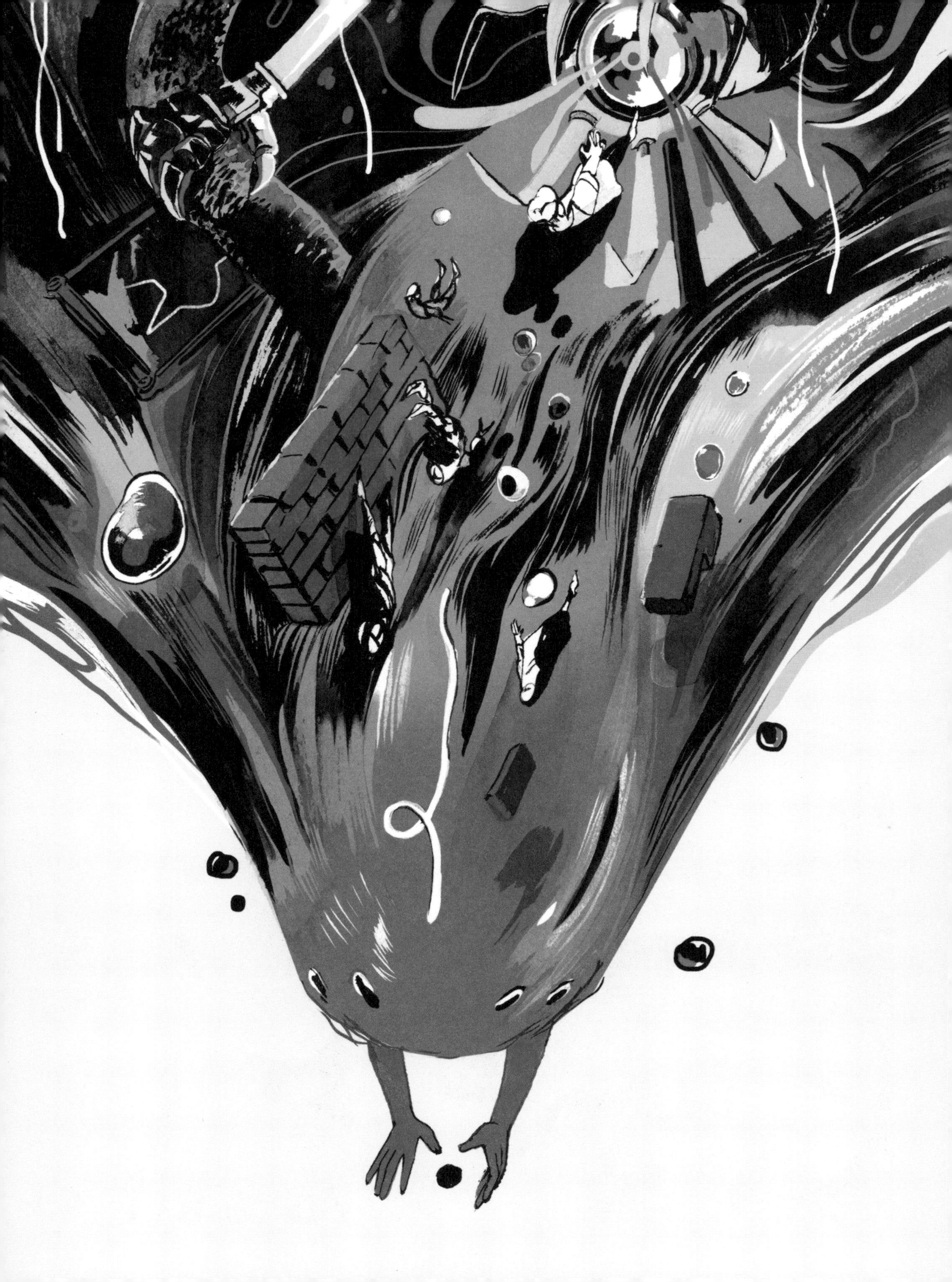

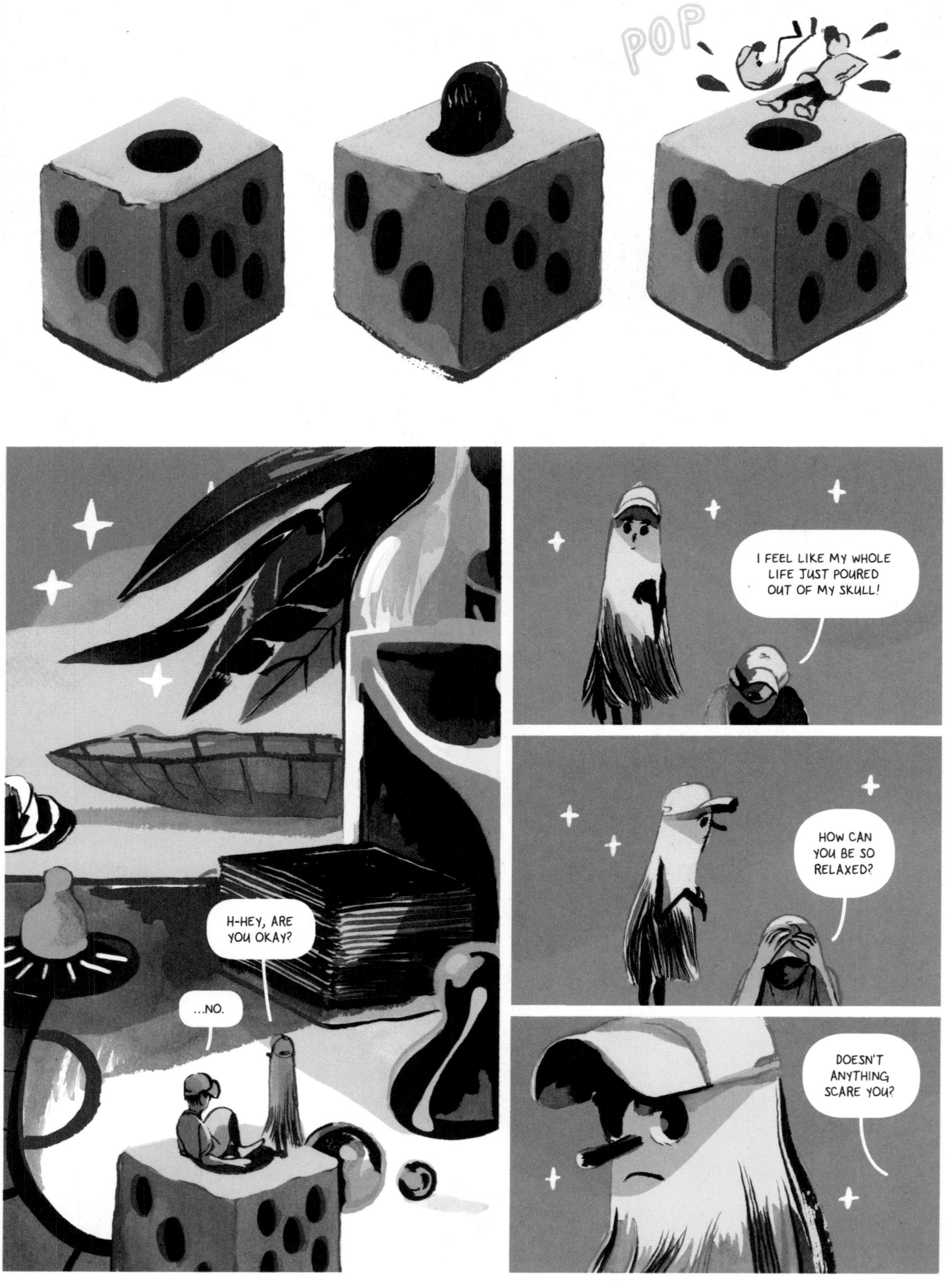
POP
H-HEY, ARE YOU OKAY?
...NO.
I FEEL LIKE MY WHOLE LIFE JUST POURED OUT OF MY SKULL!
HOW CAN YOU BE SO RELAXED?
DOESN'T ANYTHING SCARE YOU?

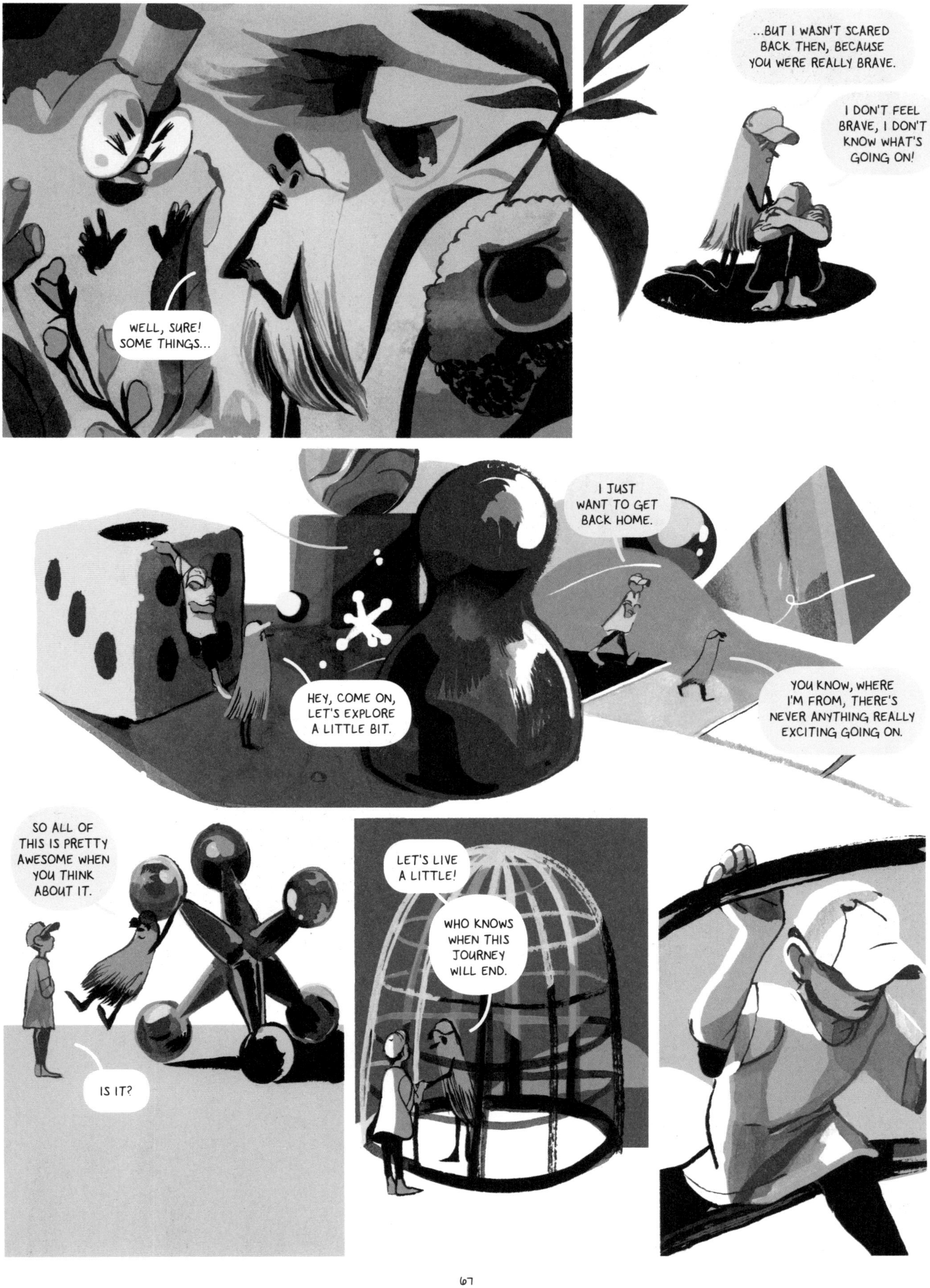
WELL, SURE! SOME THINGS...
...BUT I WASN'T SCARED BACK THEN, BECAUSE YOU WERE REALLY BRAVE.
I DON'T FEEL BRAVE, I DON'T KNOW WHAT'S GOING ON!
HEY, COME ON, LET'S EXPLORE A LITTLE BIT.
I JUST WANT TO GET BACK HOME.
YOU KNOW, WHERE I'M FROM, THERE'S NEVER ANYTHING REALLY EXCITING GOING ON.
SO ALL OF THIS IS PRETTY AWESOME WHEN YOU THINK ABOUT IT.
IS IT?
LET'S LIVE A LITTLE!
WHO KNOWS WHEN THIS JOURNEY WILL END.

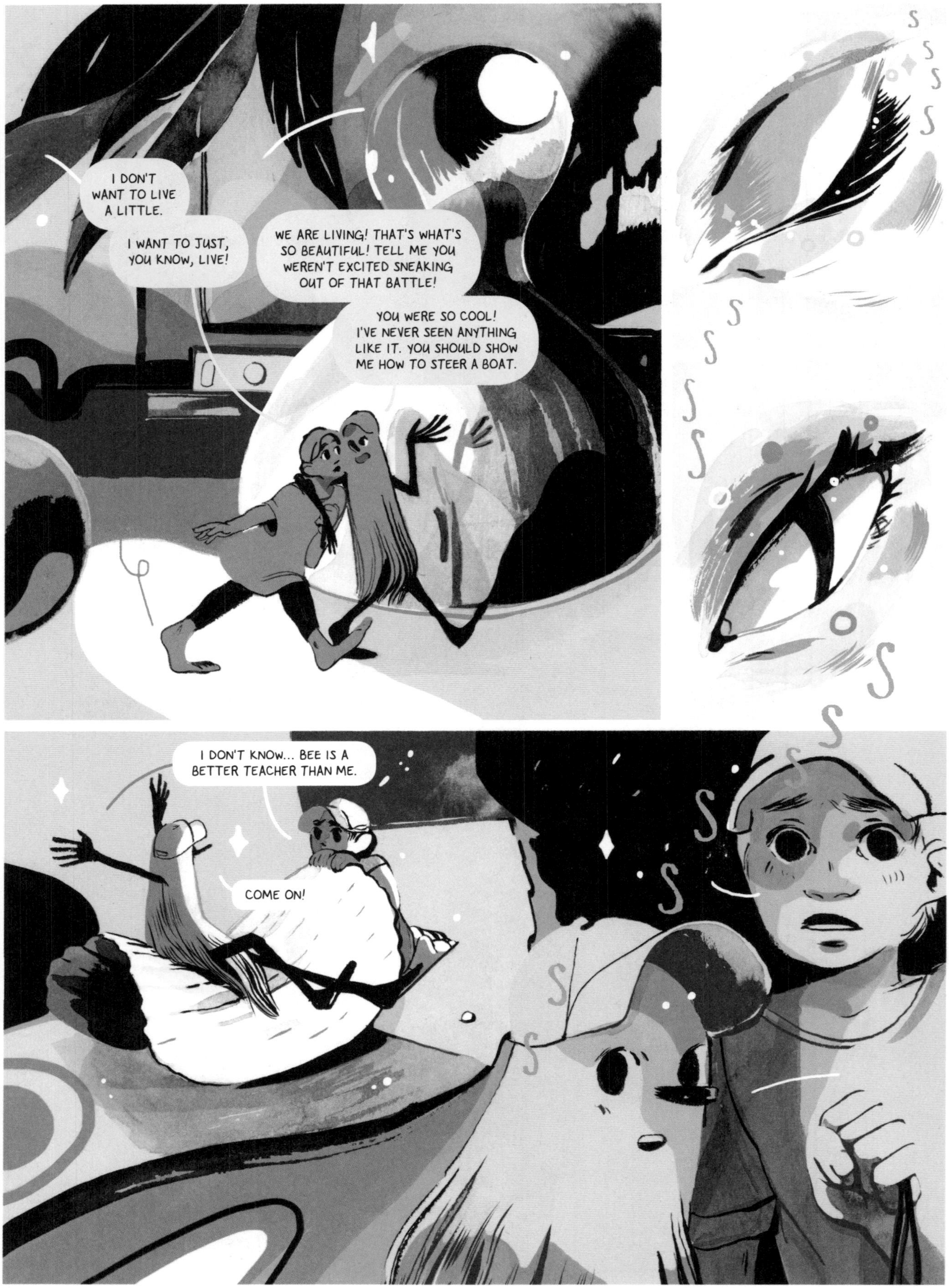
I DON'T WANT TO LIVE A LITTLE.
I WANT TO JUST, YOU KNOW, LIVE!
WE ARE LIVING! THAT'S WHAT'S SO BEAUTIFUL! TELL ME YOU WEREN'T EXCITED SNEAKING OUT OF THAT BATTLE!
YOU WERE SO COOL! I'VE NEVER SEEN ANYTHING LIKE IT. YOU SHOULD SHOW ME HOW TO STEER A BOAT.
I DON'T KNOW... BEE IS A BETTER TEACHER THAN ME.
COME ON!

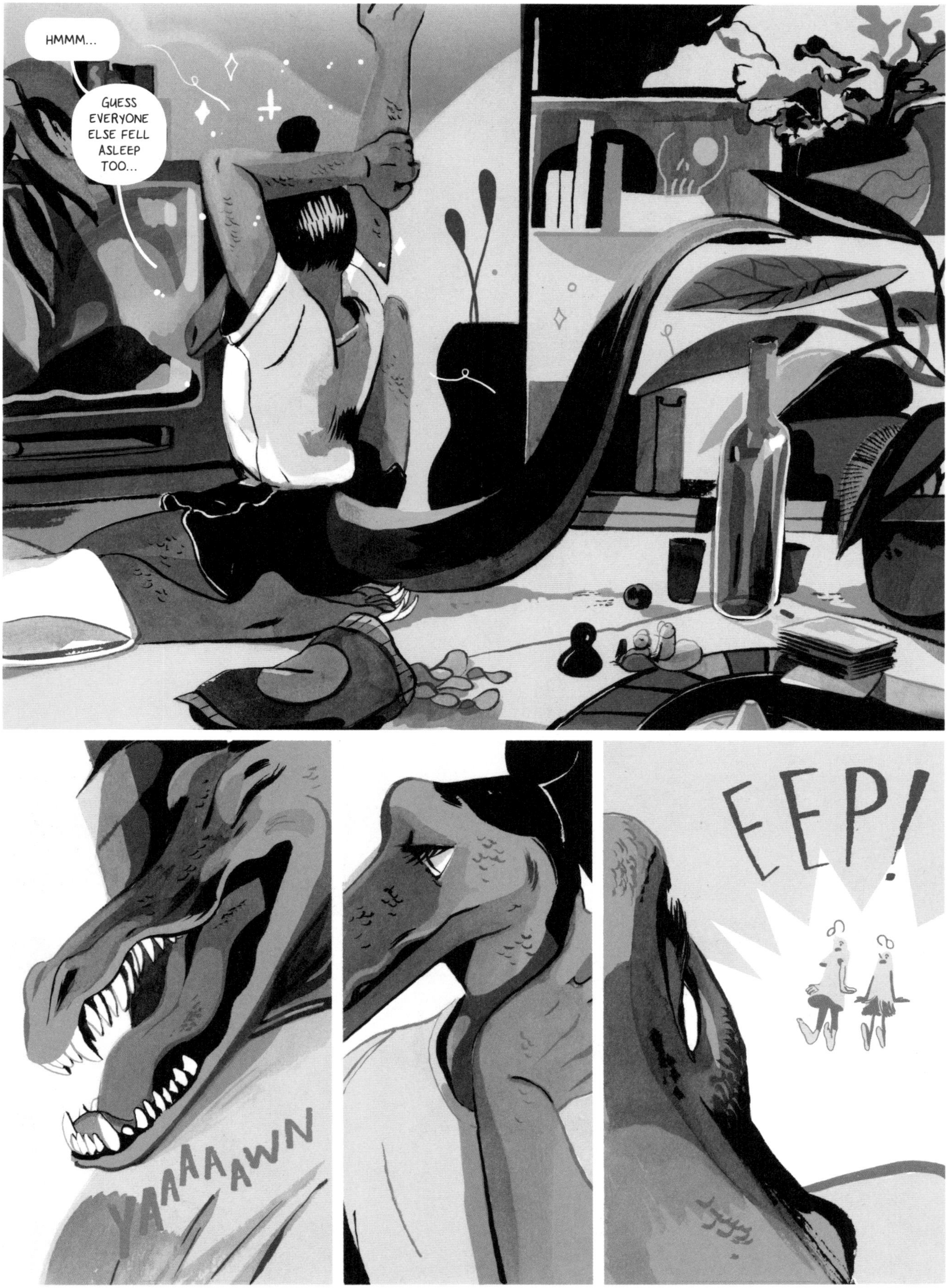
HMMM...
GUESS EVERYONE ELSE FELL ASLEEP TOO...
YAAAAAWN
EEP!

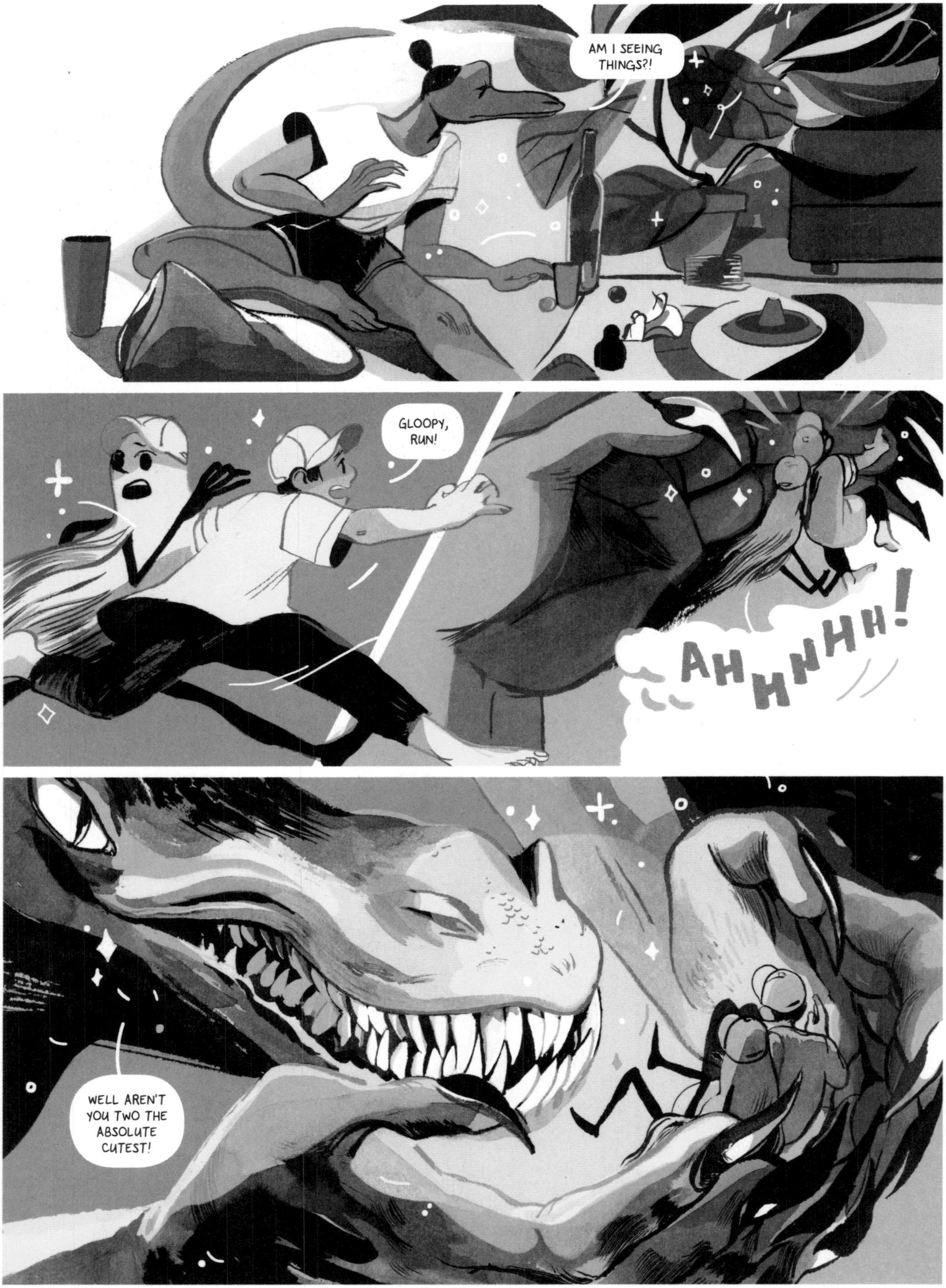
AM I SEEING THINGS?!
GLOOPY, RUN!
AHHHHH!
WELL AREN'T YOU TWO THE ABSOLUTE CUTEST!

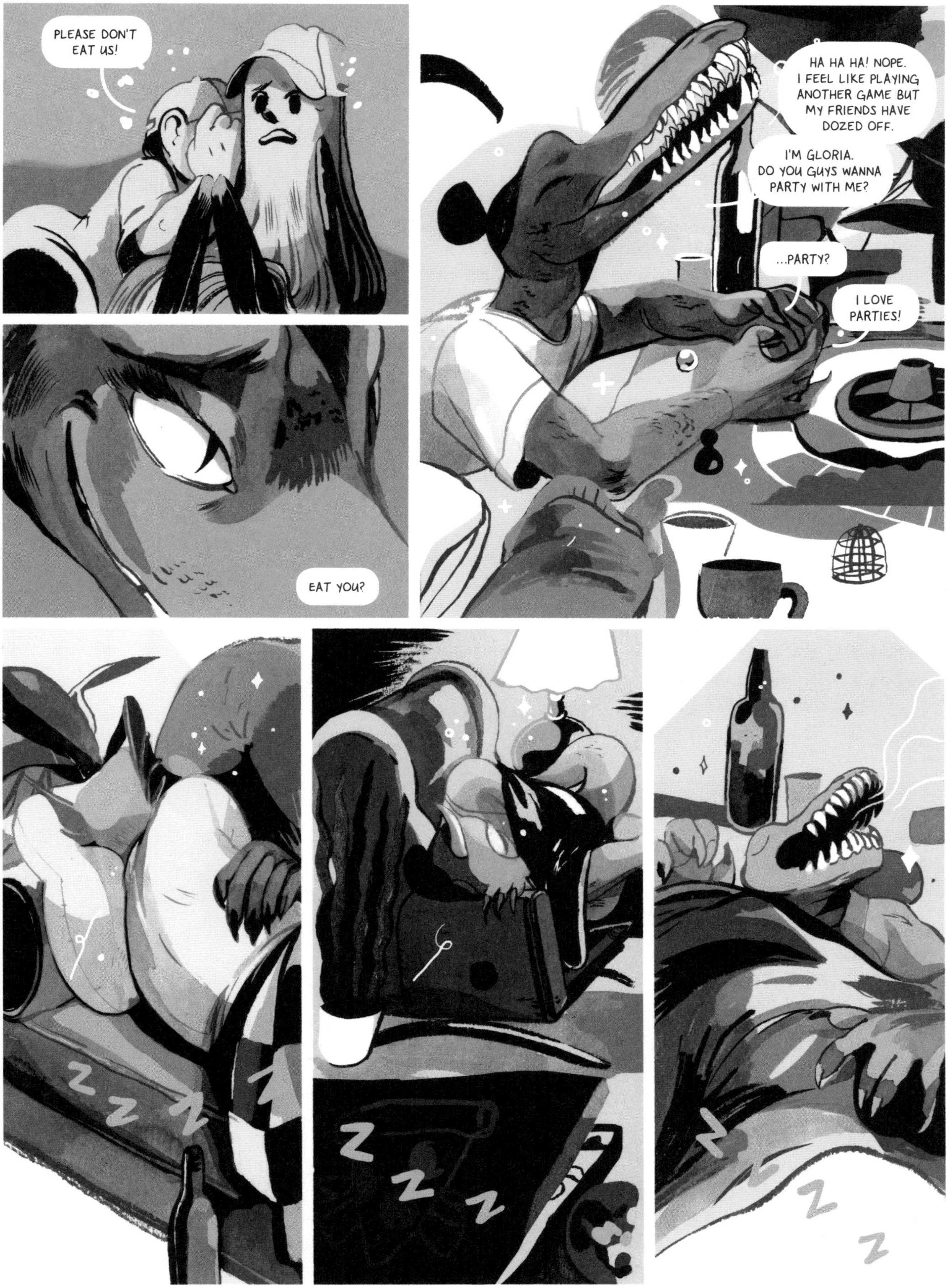
PLEASE DON'T EAT US!
EAT YOU?
HA HA HA! NOPE. I FEEL LIKE PLAYING ANOTHER GAME BUT MY FRIENDS HAVE DOZED OFF.
I'M GLORIA. DO YOU GUYS WANNA PARTY WITH ME?
...PARTY?
I LOVE PARTIES!
Z Z Z
Z Z Z
Z Z Z

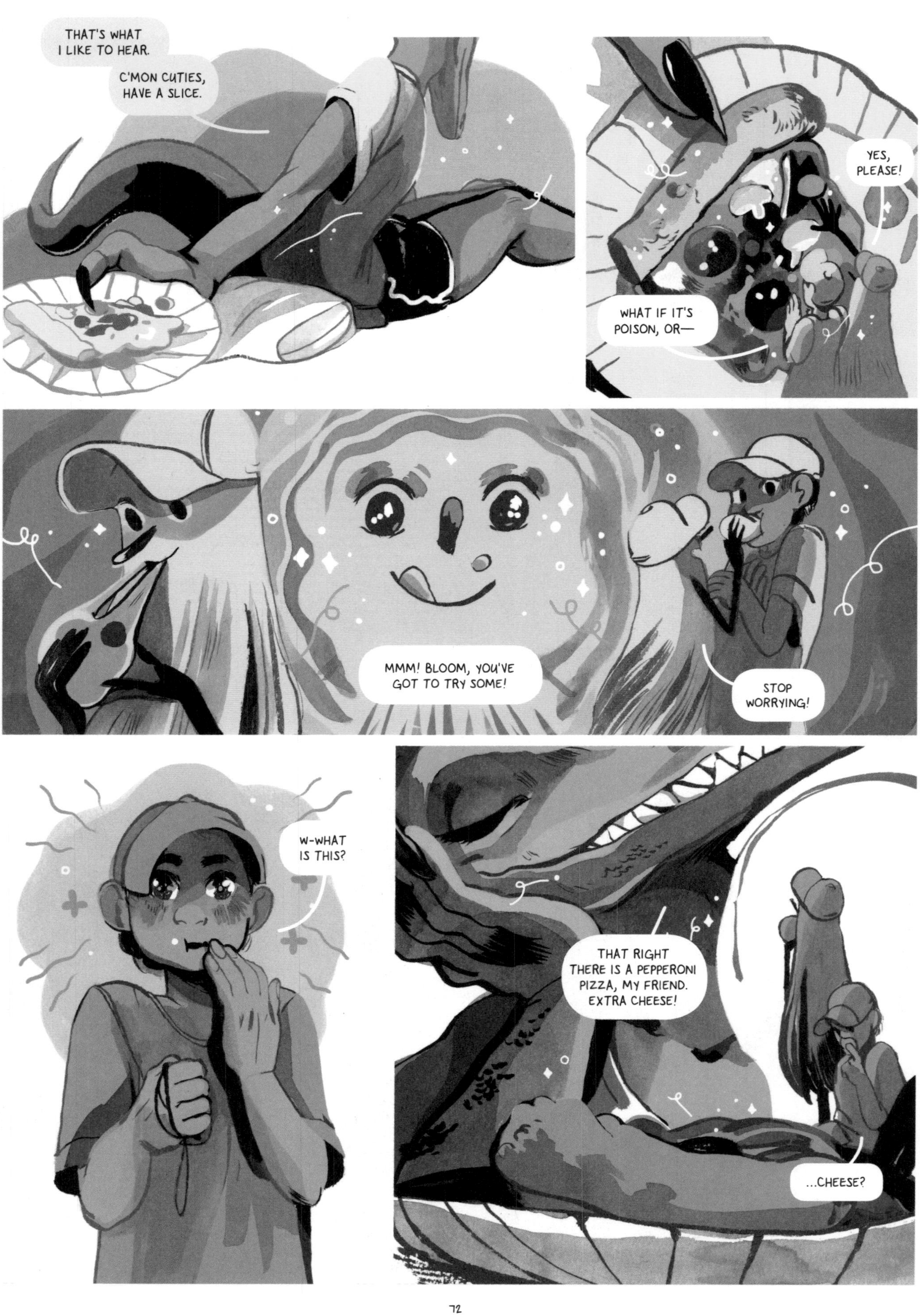
THAT'S WHAT I LIKE TO HEAR.
C'MON CUTIES, HAVE A SLICE.
YES, PLEASE!
WHAT IF IT'S POISON, OR—
MMM! BLOOM, YOU'VE GOT TO TRY SOME!
STOP WORRYING!
W-WHAT IS THIS?
THAT RIGHT THERE IS A PEPPERONI PIZZA, MY FRIEND. EXTRA CHEESE!
...CHEESE?

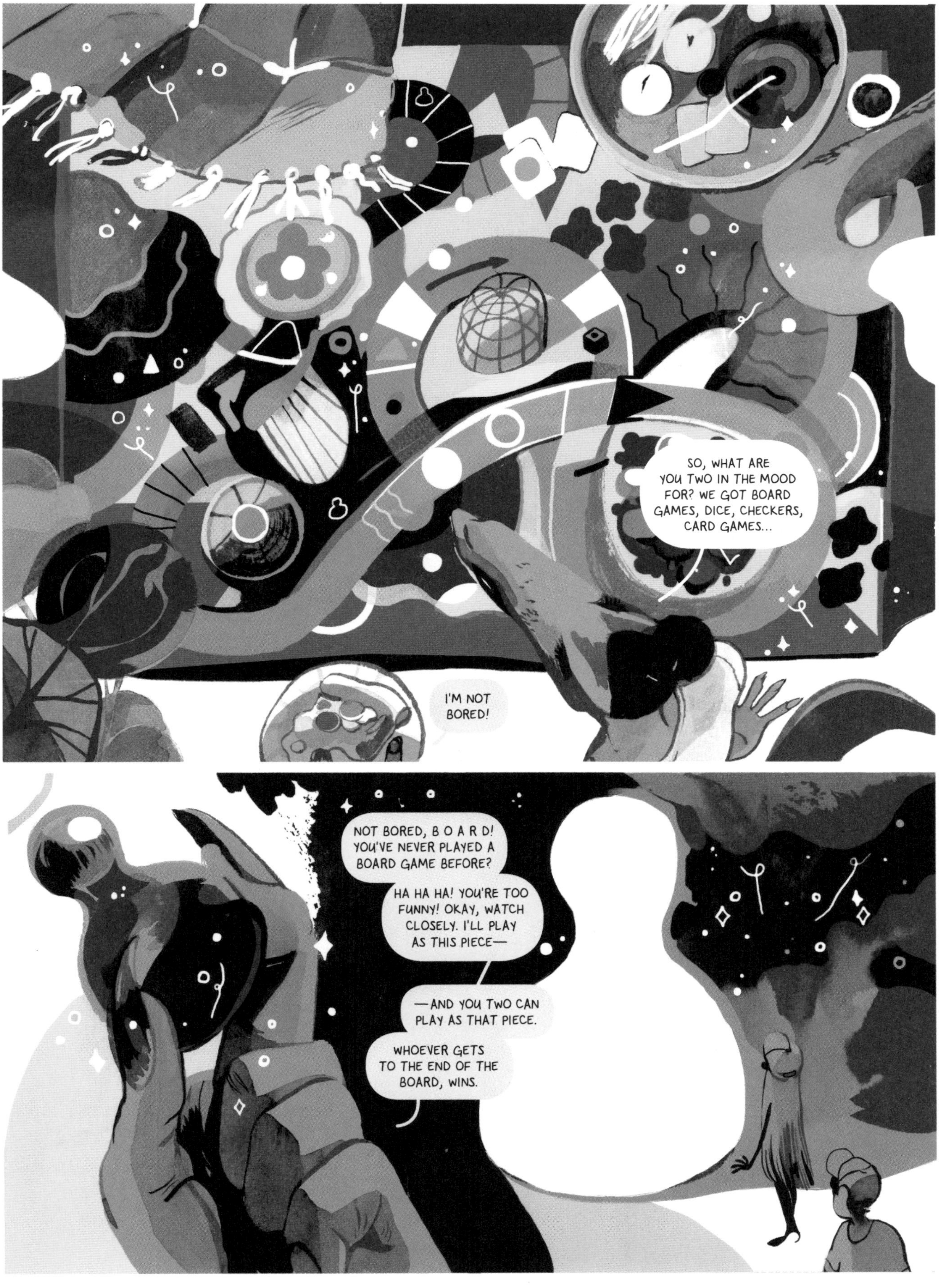
SO, WHAT ARE YOU TWO IN THE MOOD FOR? WE GOT BOARD GAMES, DICE, CHECKERS, CARD GAMES...
I'M NOT BORED!
NOT BORED, B O A R D! YOU'VE NEVER PLAYED A BOARD GAME BEFORE?
HA HA HA! YOU'RE TOO FUNNY! OKAY, WATCH CLOSELY. I'LL PLAY AS THIS PIECE—
—AND YOU TWO CAN PLAY AS THAT PIECE.
WHOEVER GETS TO THE END OF THE BOARD, WINS.

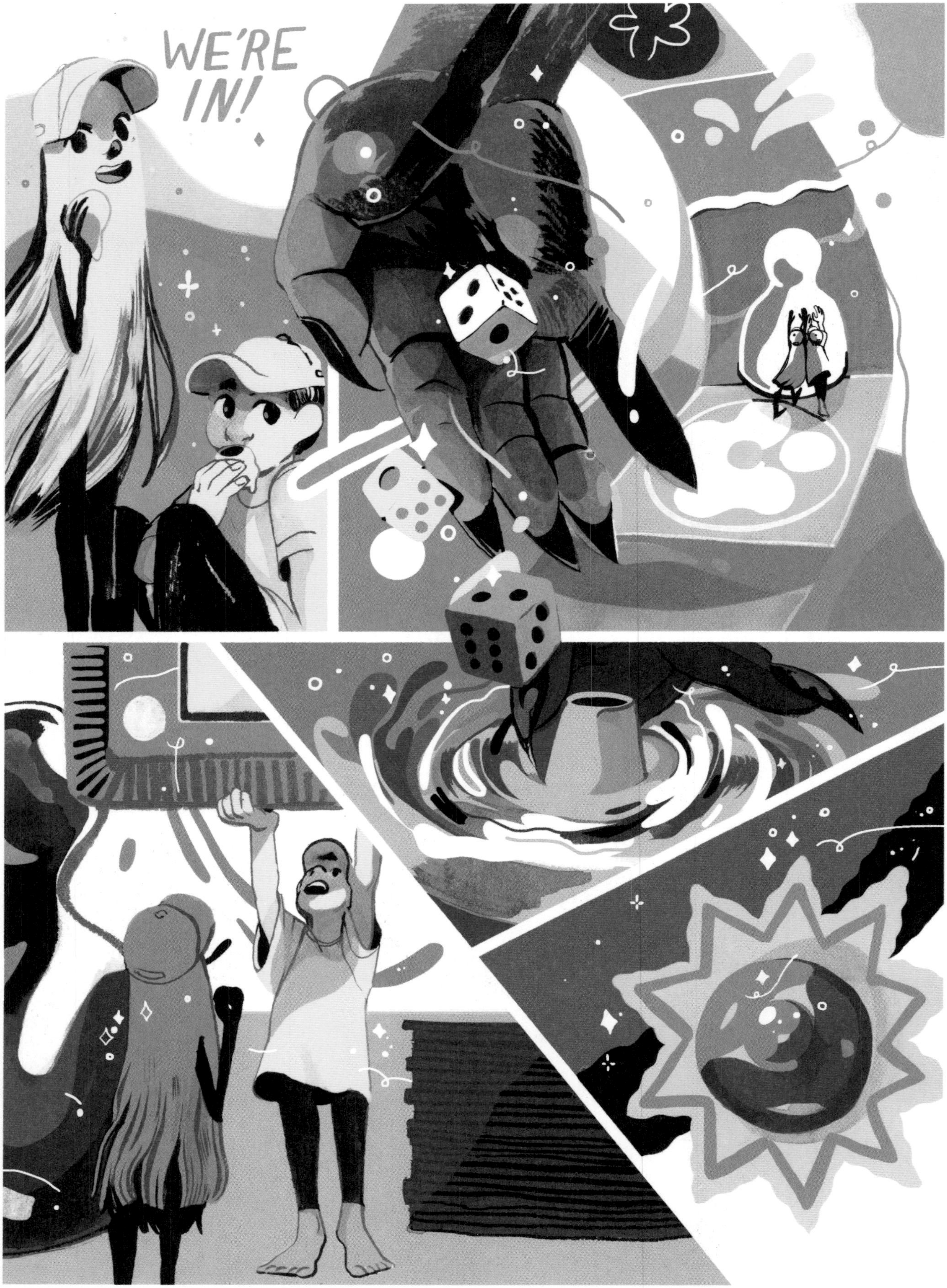
WE'RE IN!

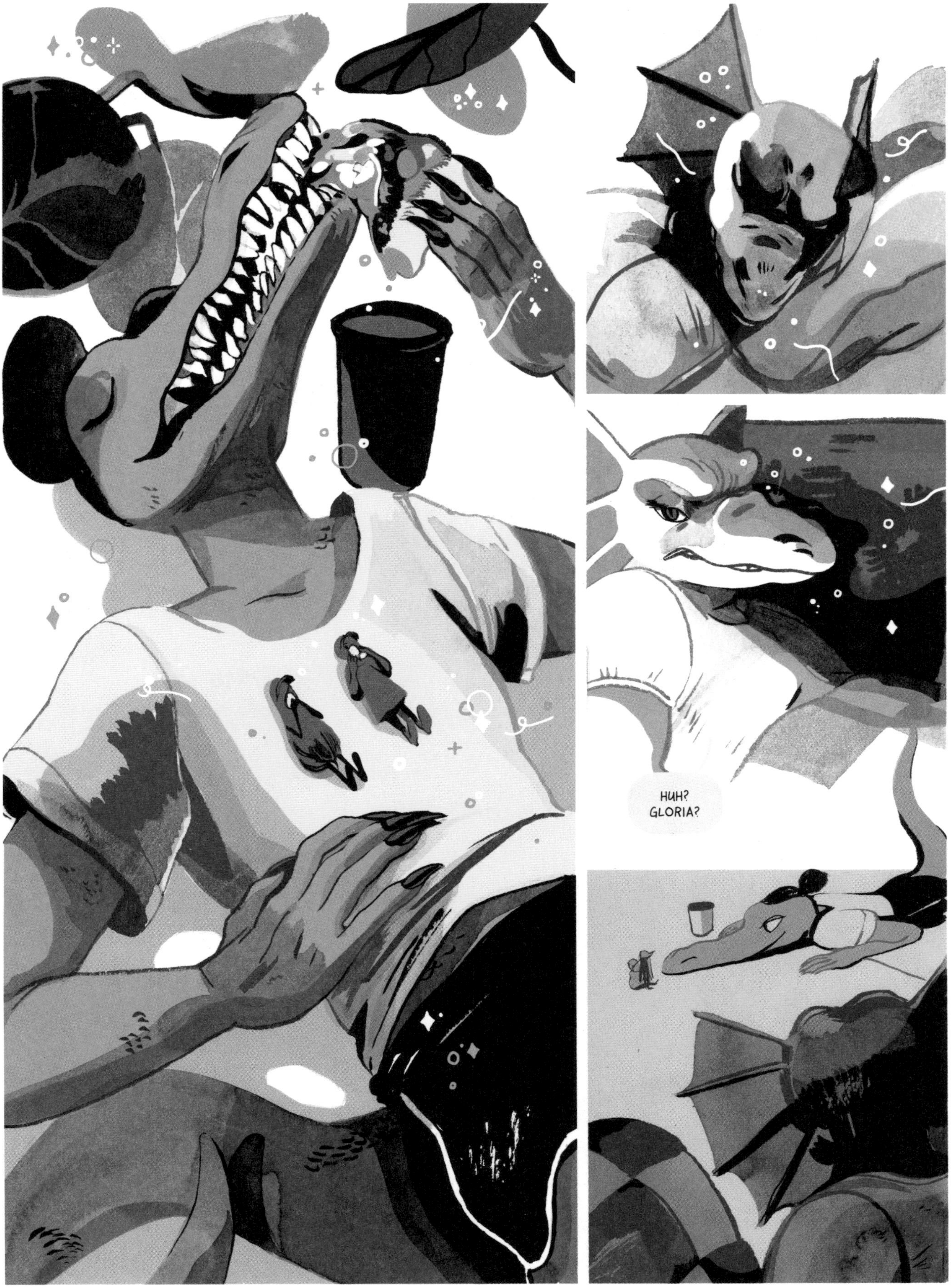
HUH?
GLORIA?

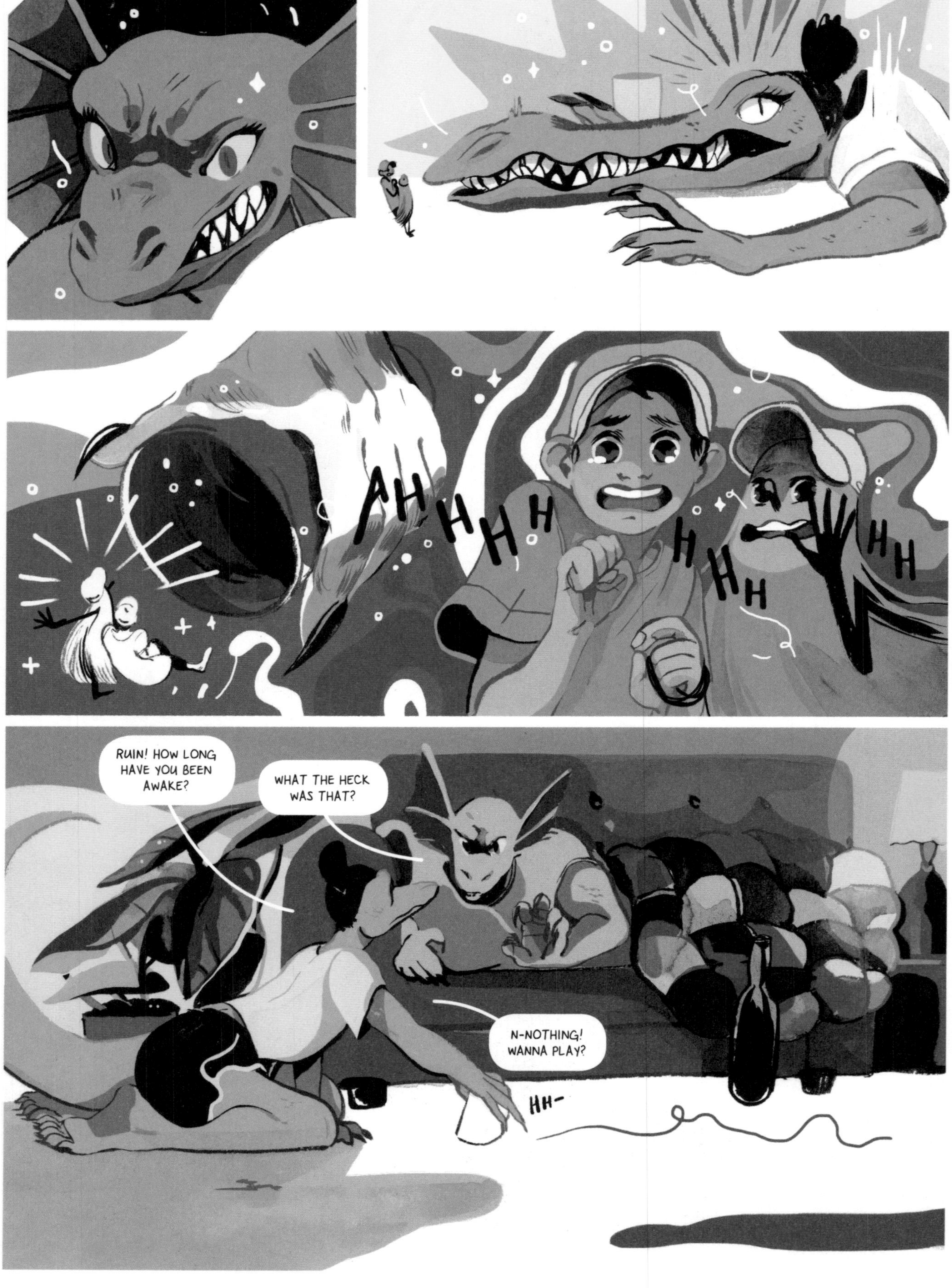
AHHHHH
HHHHH
RUIN! HOW LONG HAVE YOU BEEN AWAKE?
WHAT THE HECK WAS THAT?
N-NOTHING! WANNA PLAY?
HH-

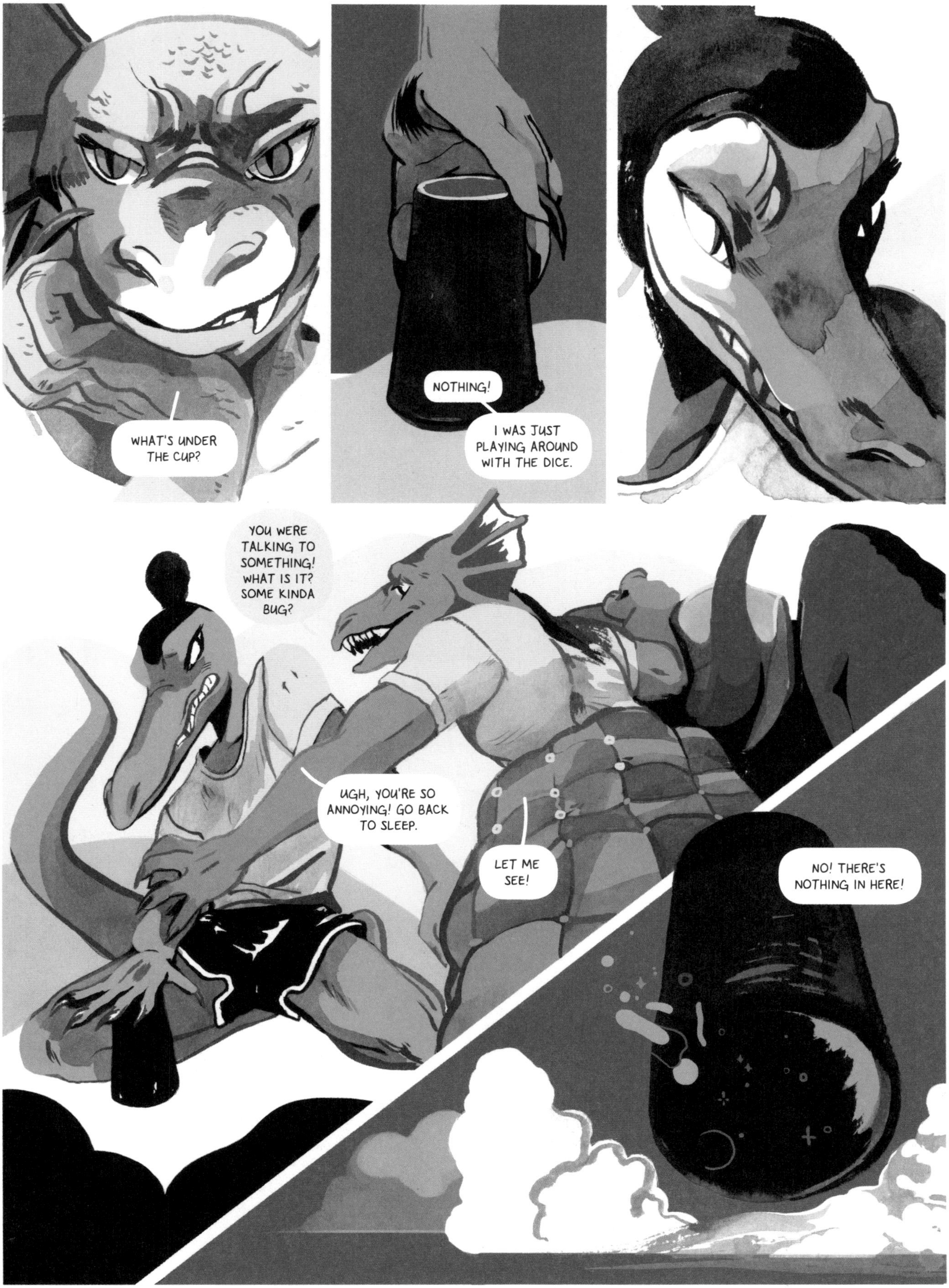
WHAT'S UNDER THE CUP?
NOTHING!
I WAS JUST PLAYING AROUND WITH THE DICE.
YOU WERE TALKING TO SOMETHING! WHAT IS IT? SOME KINDA BUG?
UGH, YOU'RE SO ANNOYING! GO BACK TO SLEEP.
LET ME SEE!
NO! THERE'S NOTHING IN HERE!

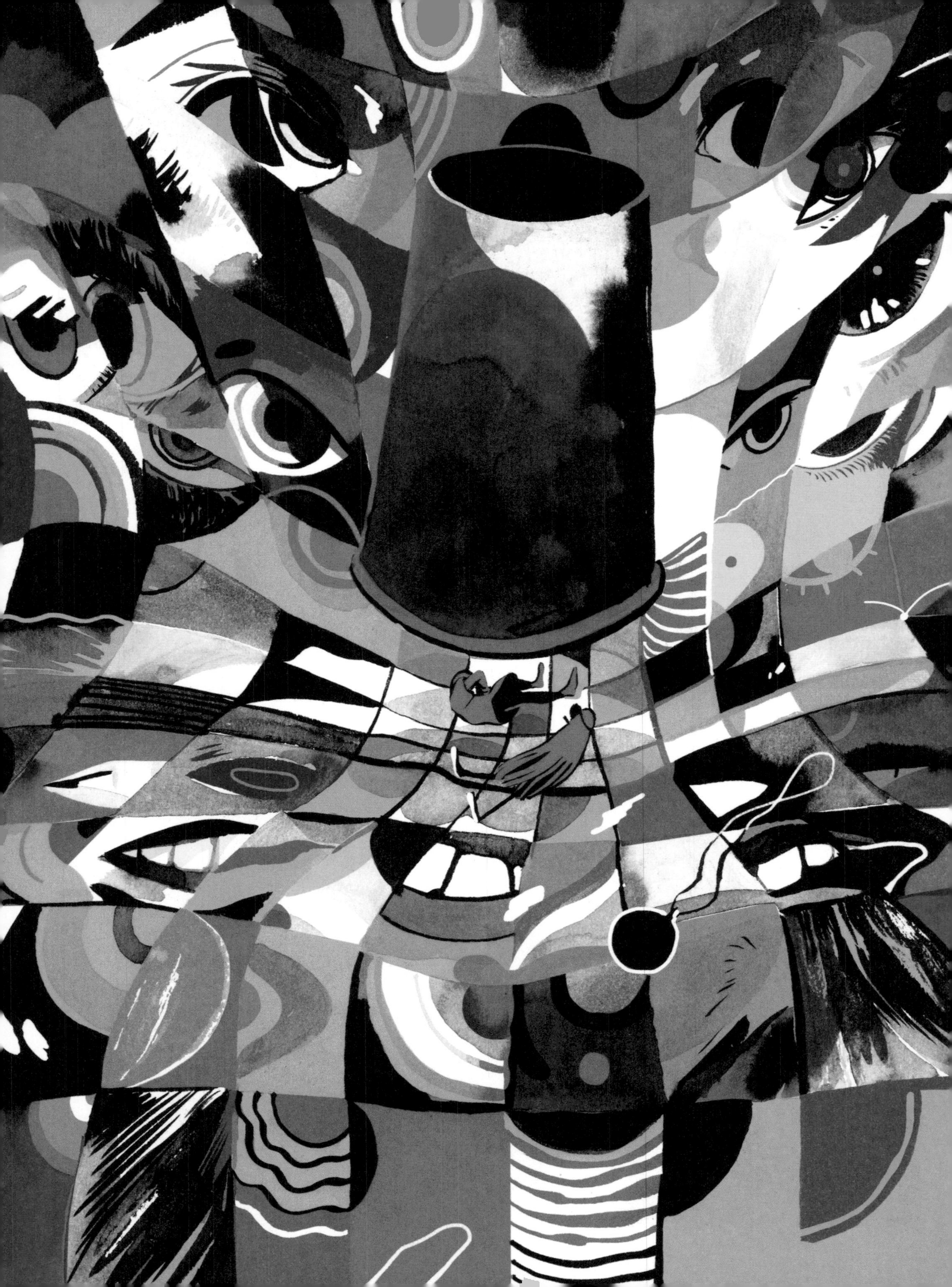

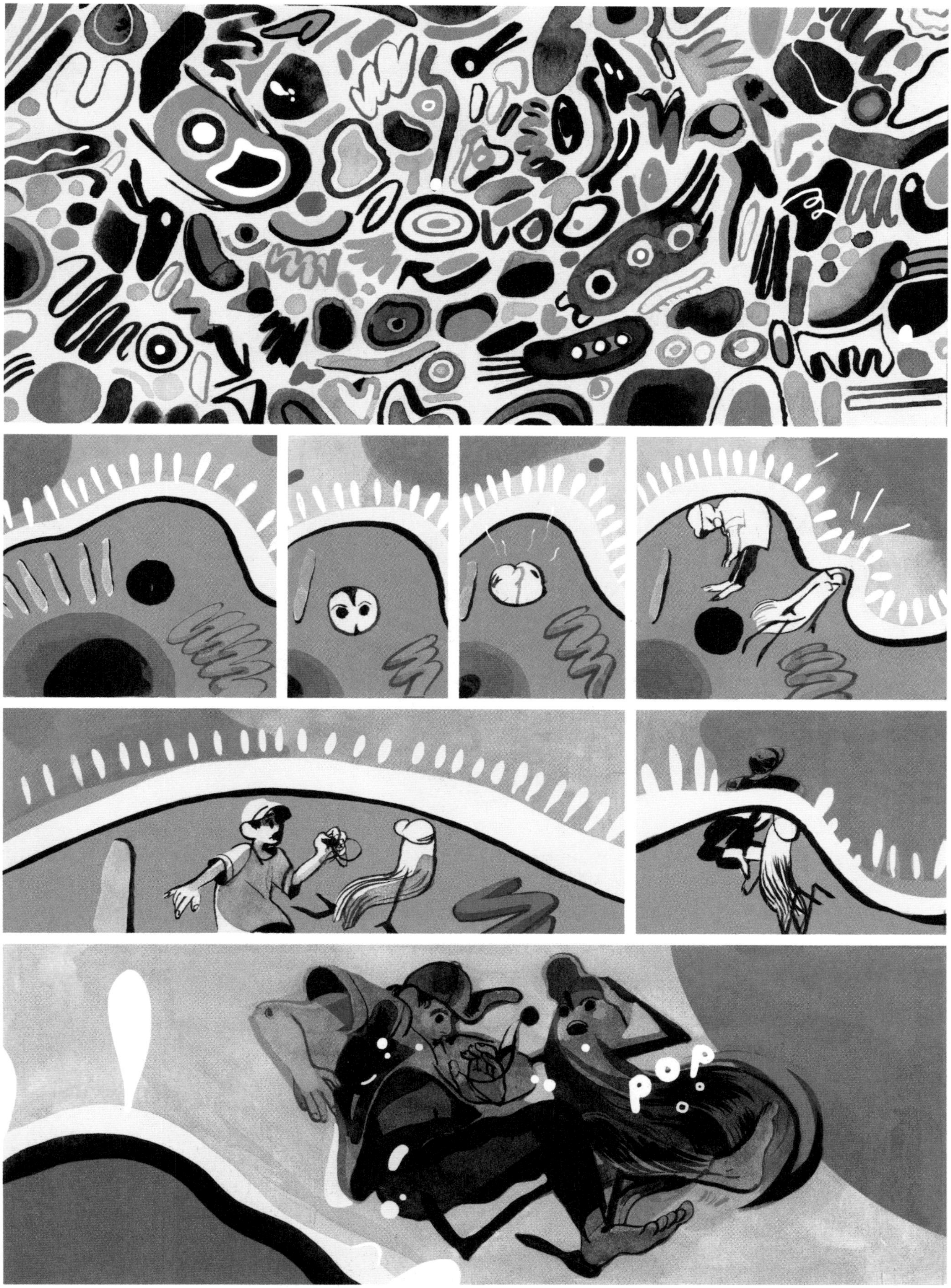
POP

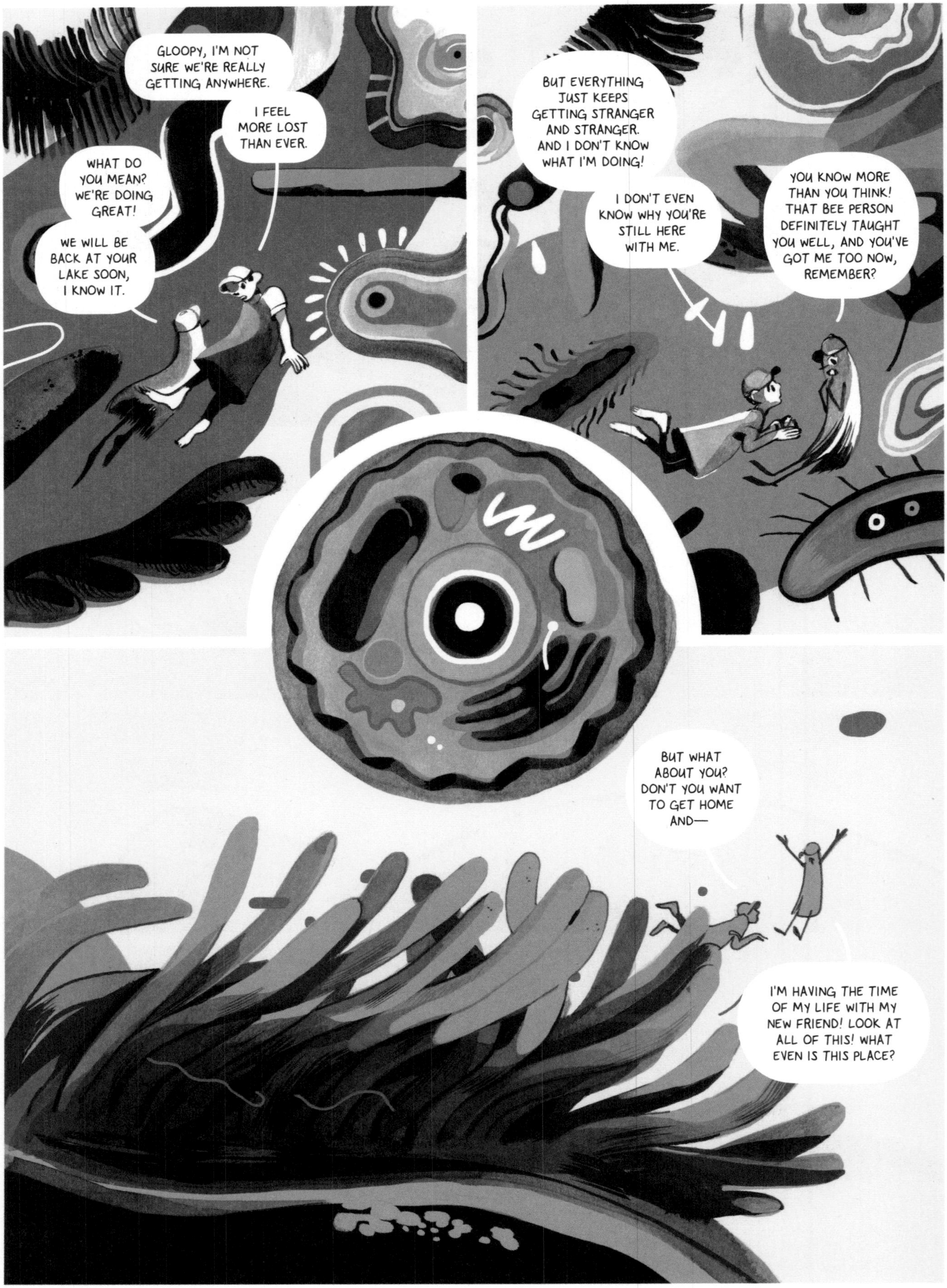
GLOOPY, I'M NOT SURE WE'RE REALLY GETTING ANYWHERE.
I FEEL MORE LOST THAN EVER.
WHAT DO YOU MEAN? WE'RE DOING GREAT!
WE WILL BE BACK AT YOUR LAKE SOON, I KNOW IT.
BUT EVERYTHING JUST KEEPS GETTING STRANGER AND STRANGER. AND I DON'T KNOW WHAT I'M DOING!
I DON'T EVEN KNOW WHY YOU'RE STILL HERE WITH ME.
YOU KNOW MORE THAN YOU THINK! THAT BEE PERSON DEFINITELY TAUGHT YOU WELL, AND YOU'VE GOT ME TOO NOW, REMEMBER?
BUT WHAT ABOUT YOU? DON'T YOU WANT TO GET HOME AND—
I'M HAVING THE TIME OF MY LIFE WITH MY NEW FRIEND! LOOK AT ALL OF THIS! WHAT EVEN IS THIS PLACE?

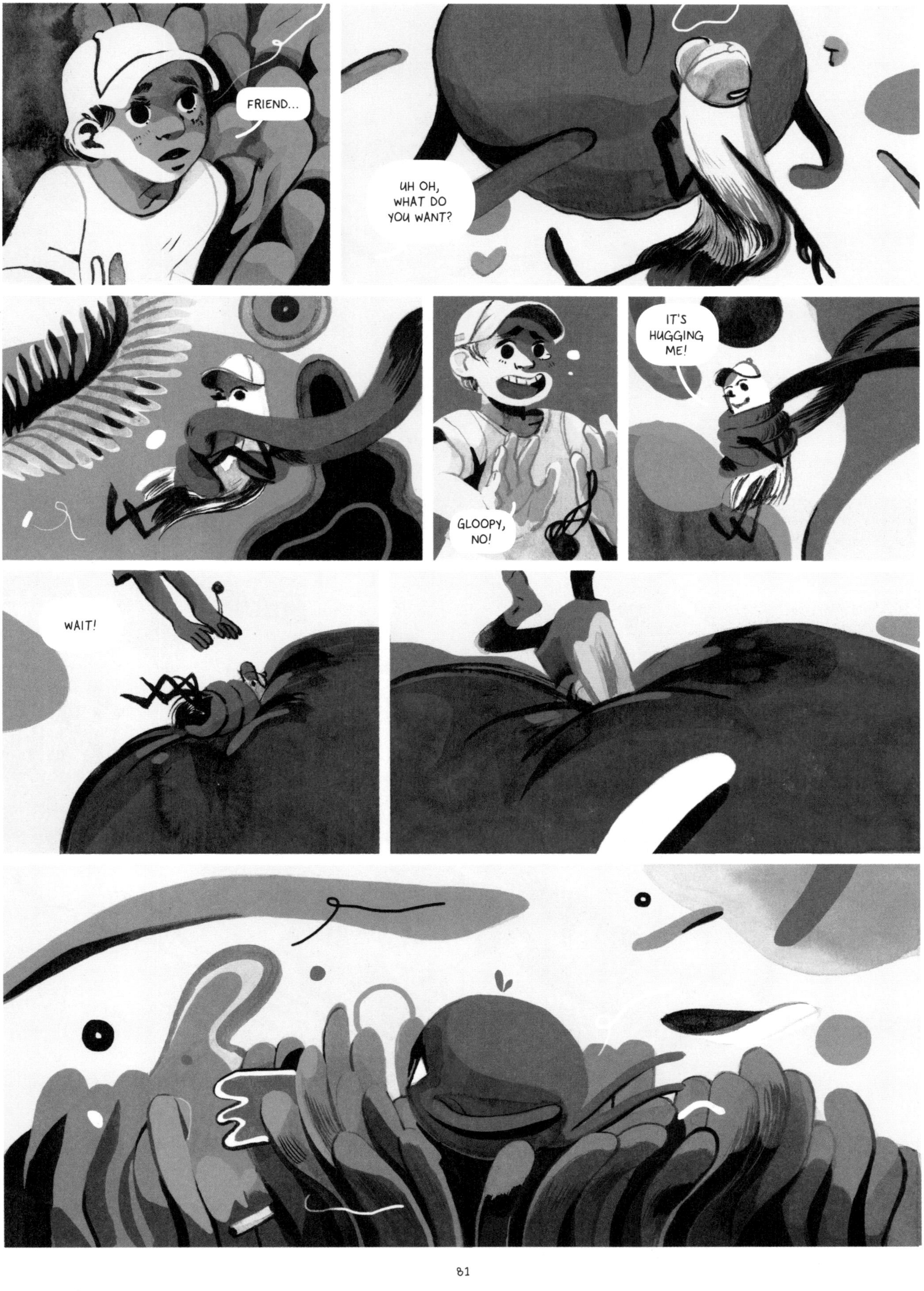
FRIEND...
UH OH, WHAT DO YOU WANT?
IT'S HUGGING ME!
GLOOPY, NO!
WAIT!

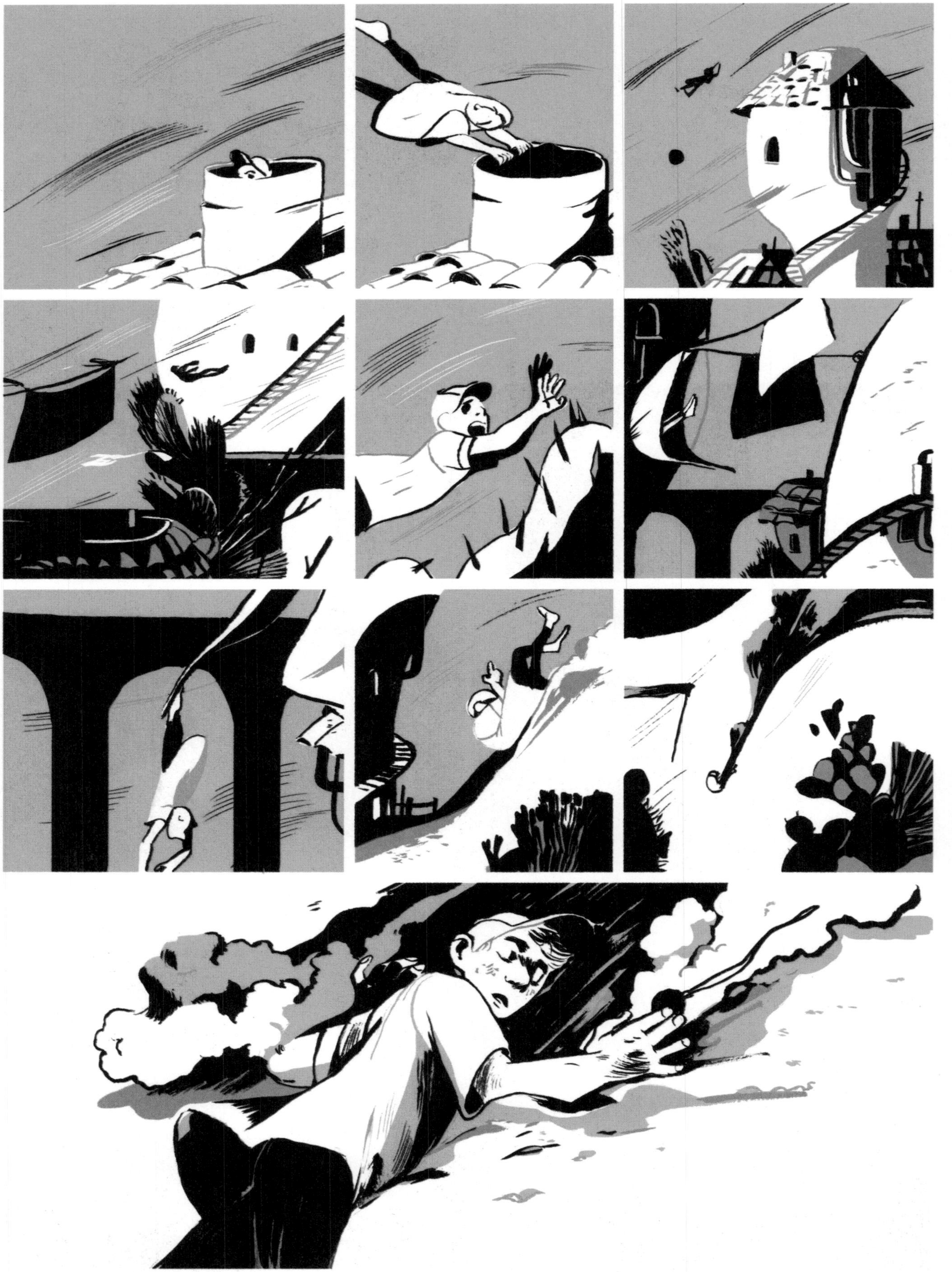

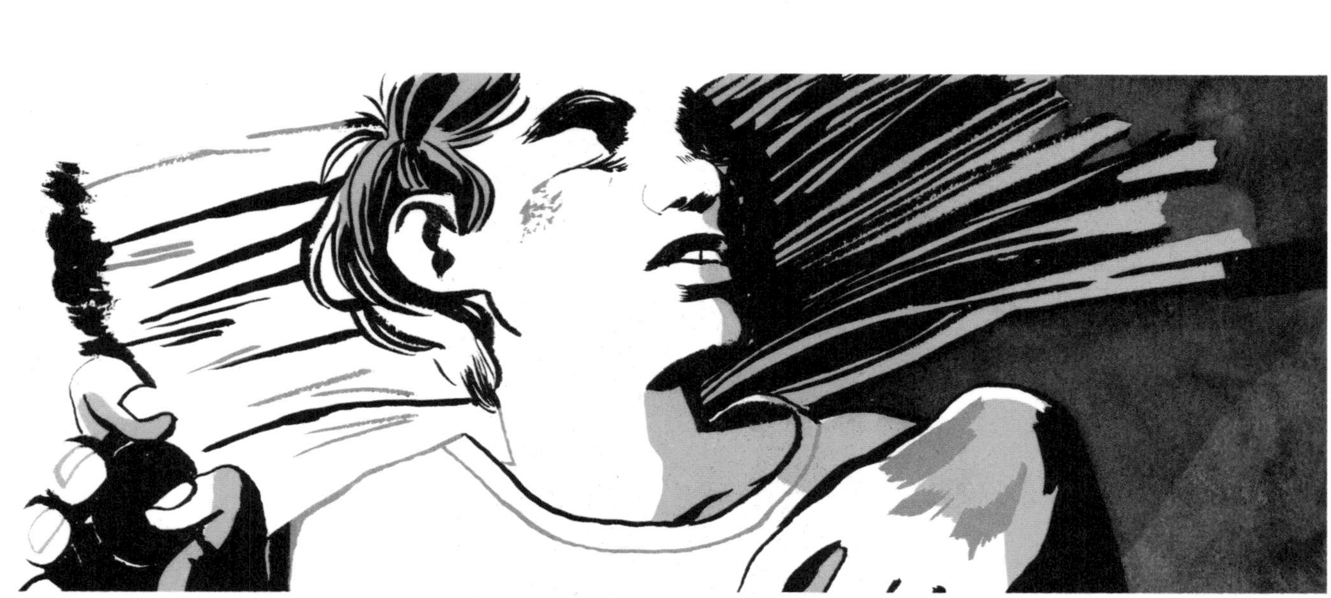

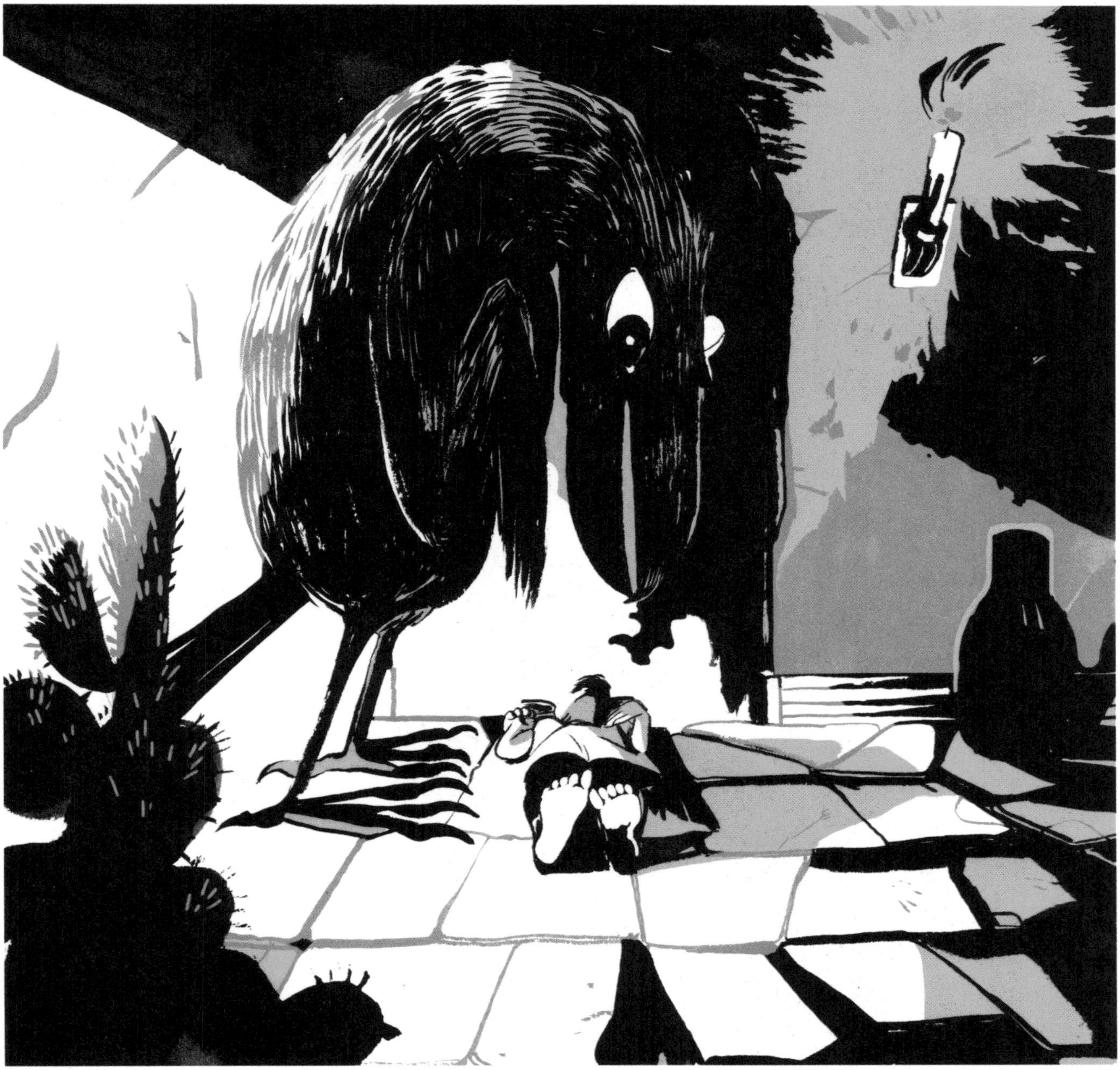

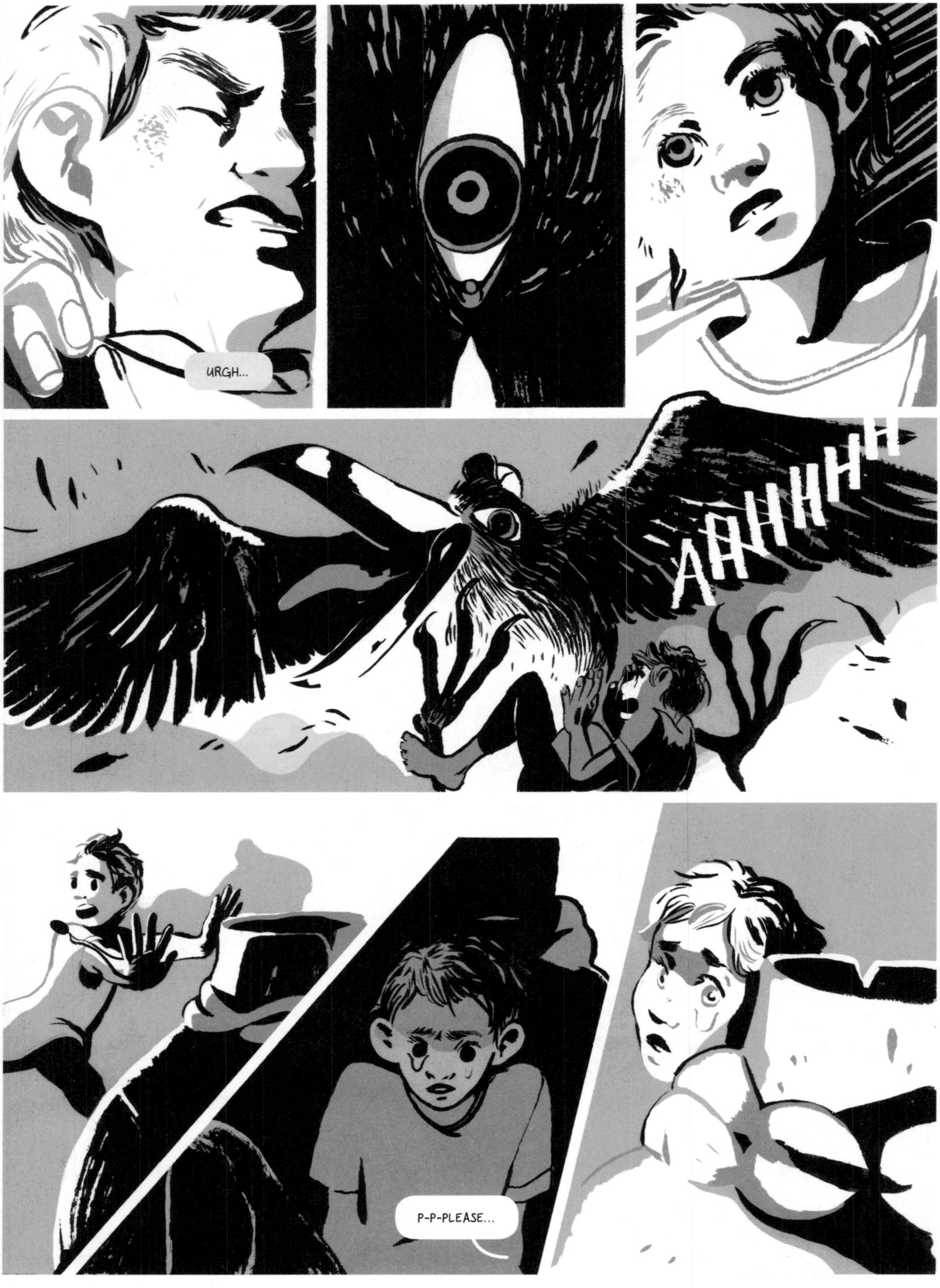
URGH...
AAHHHHH
P-P-PLEASE...

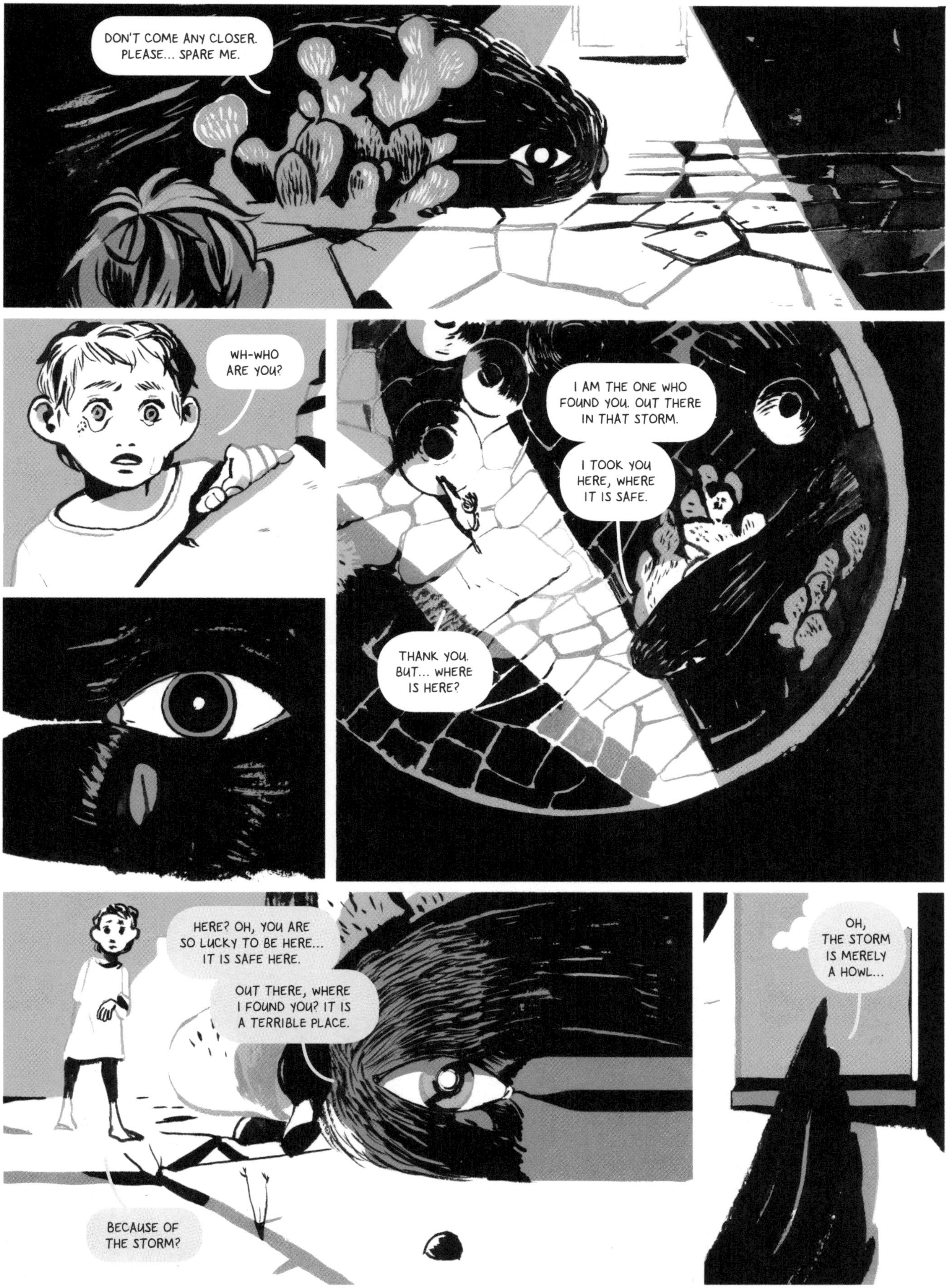
DON'T COME ANY CLOSER. PLEASE... SPARE ME.
WH-WHO ARE YOU?
I AM THE ONE WHO FOUND YOU. OUT THERE IN THAT STORM.
I TOOK YOU HERE, WHERE IT IS SAFE.
THANK YOU. BUT... WHERE IS HERE?
HERE? OH, YOU ARE SO LUCKY TO BE HERE... IT IS SAFE HERE.
OUT THERE, WHERE I FOUND YOU? IT IS A TERRIBLE PLACE.
BECAUSE OF THE STORM?
OH, THE STORM IS MERELY A HOWL...

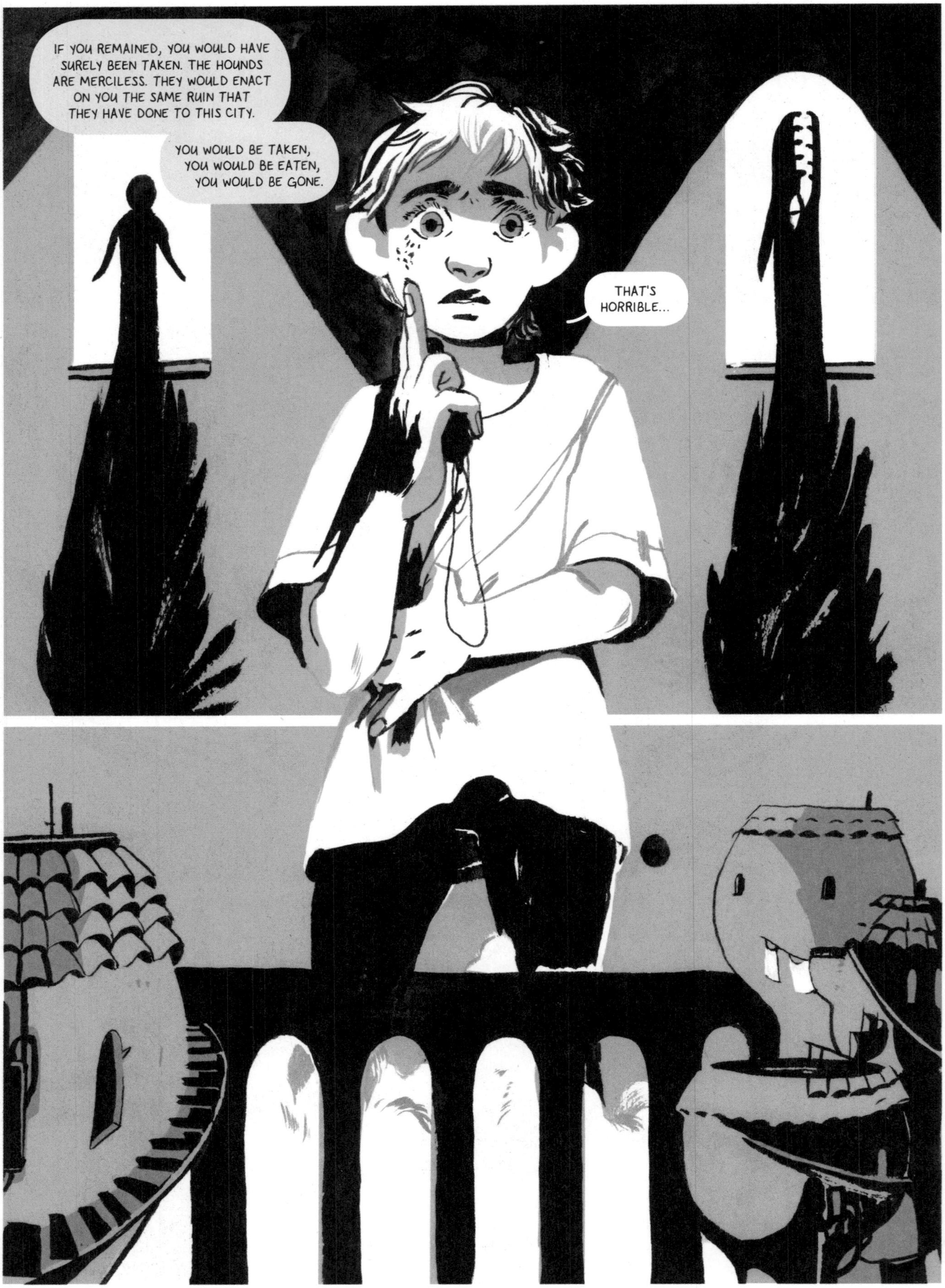
IF YOU REMAINED, YOU WOULD HAVE SURELY BEEN TAKEN. THE HOUNDS ARE MERCILESS. THEY WOULD ENACT ON YOU THE SAME RUIN THAT THEY HAVE DONE TO THIS CITY.
YOU WOULD BE TAKEN, YOU WOULD BE EATEN, YOU WOULD BE GONE.
THAT'S HORRIBLE...

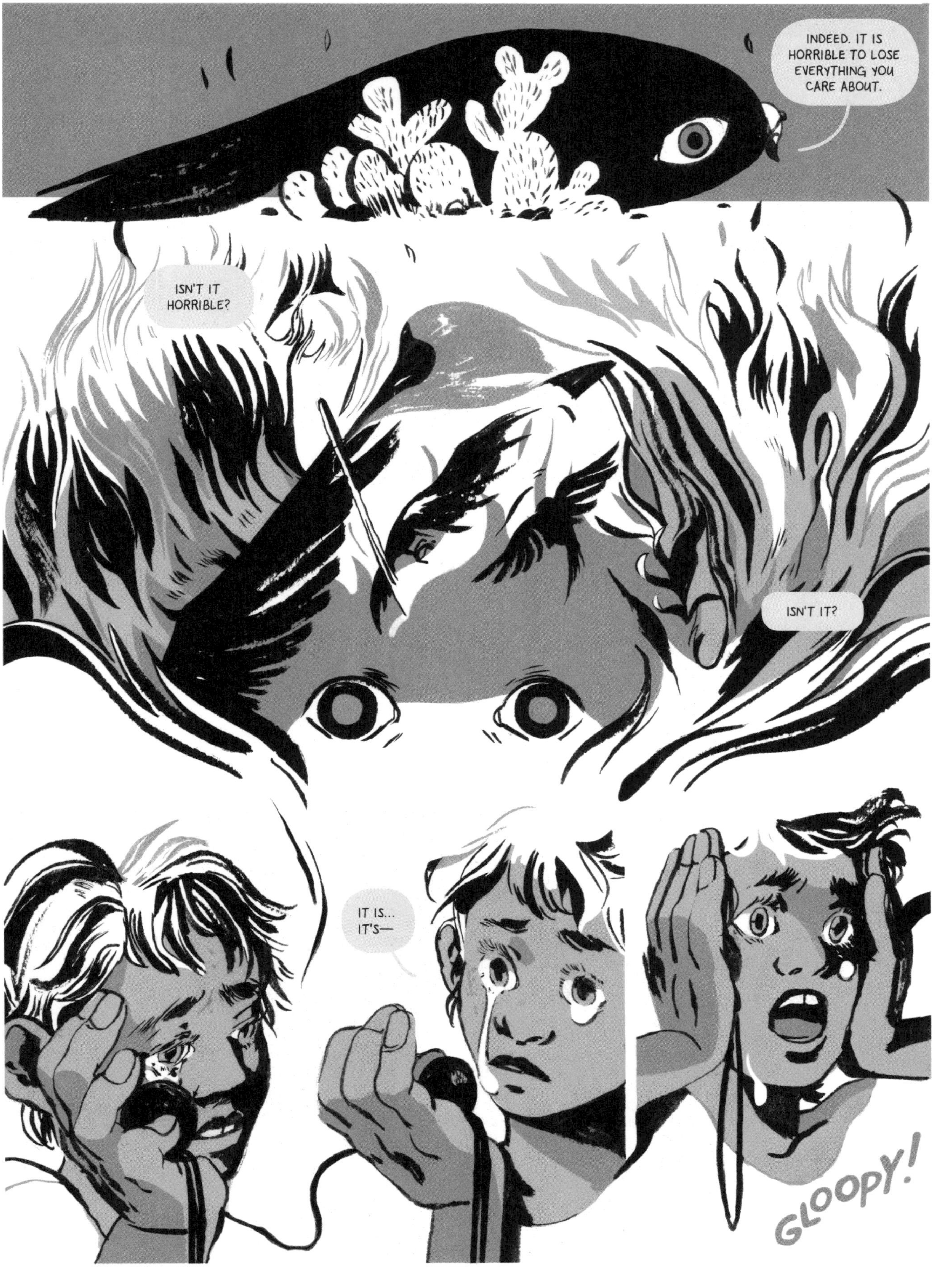
INDEED. IT IS HORRIBLE TO LOSE EVERYTHING YOU CARE ABOUT.
ISN'T IT HORRIBLE?
ISN'T IT?
IT IS... IT'S—
GLOOPY!

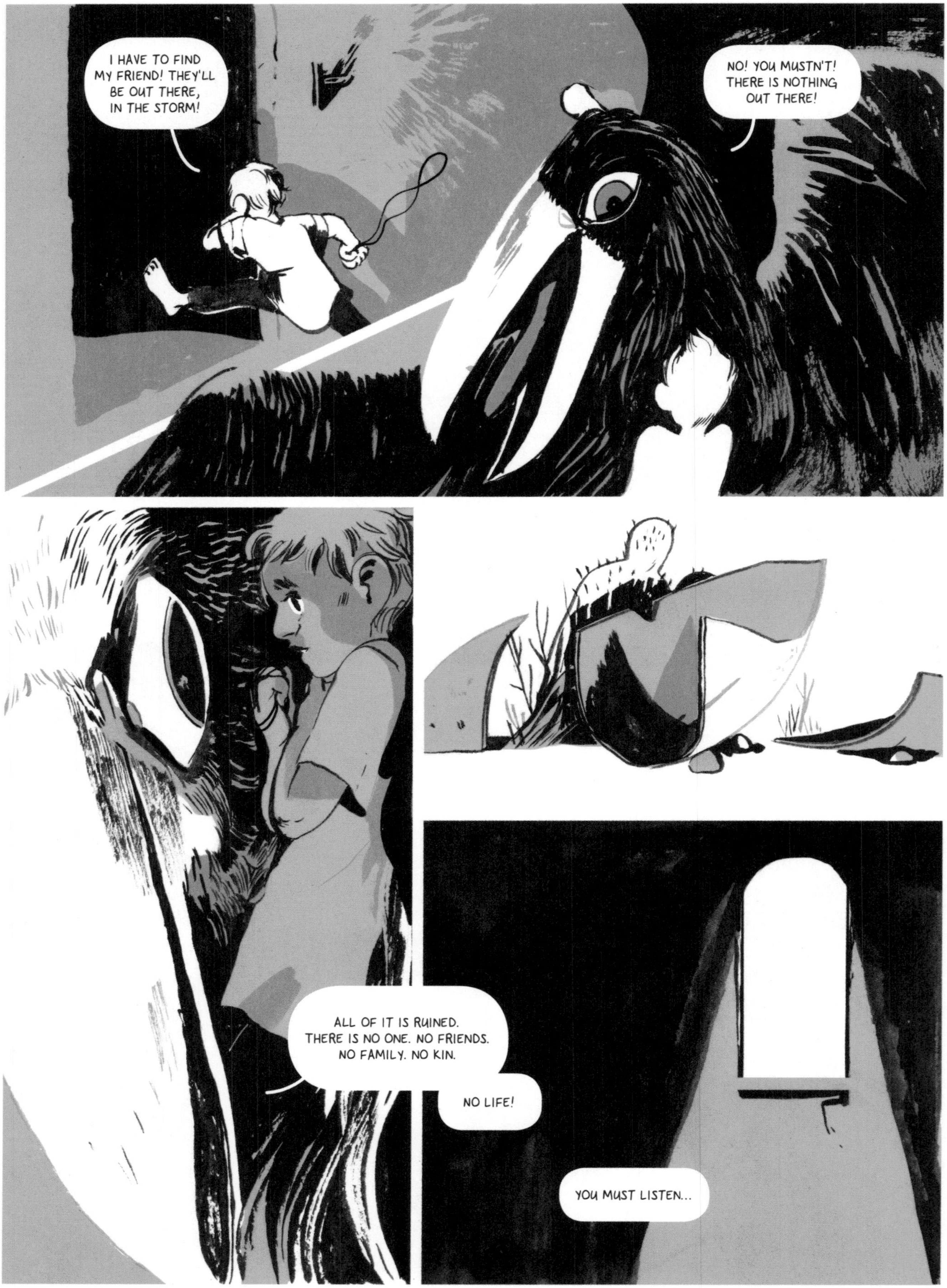
I HAVE TO FIND MY FRIEND! THEY'LL BE OUT THERE, IN THE STORM!
NO! YOU MUSTN'T! THERE IS NOTHING OUT THERE!
ALL OF IT IS RUINED. THERE IS NO ONE. NO FRIENDS. NO FAMILY. NO KIN.
NO LIFE!
YOU MUST LISTEN...

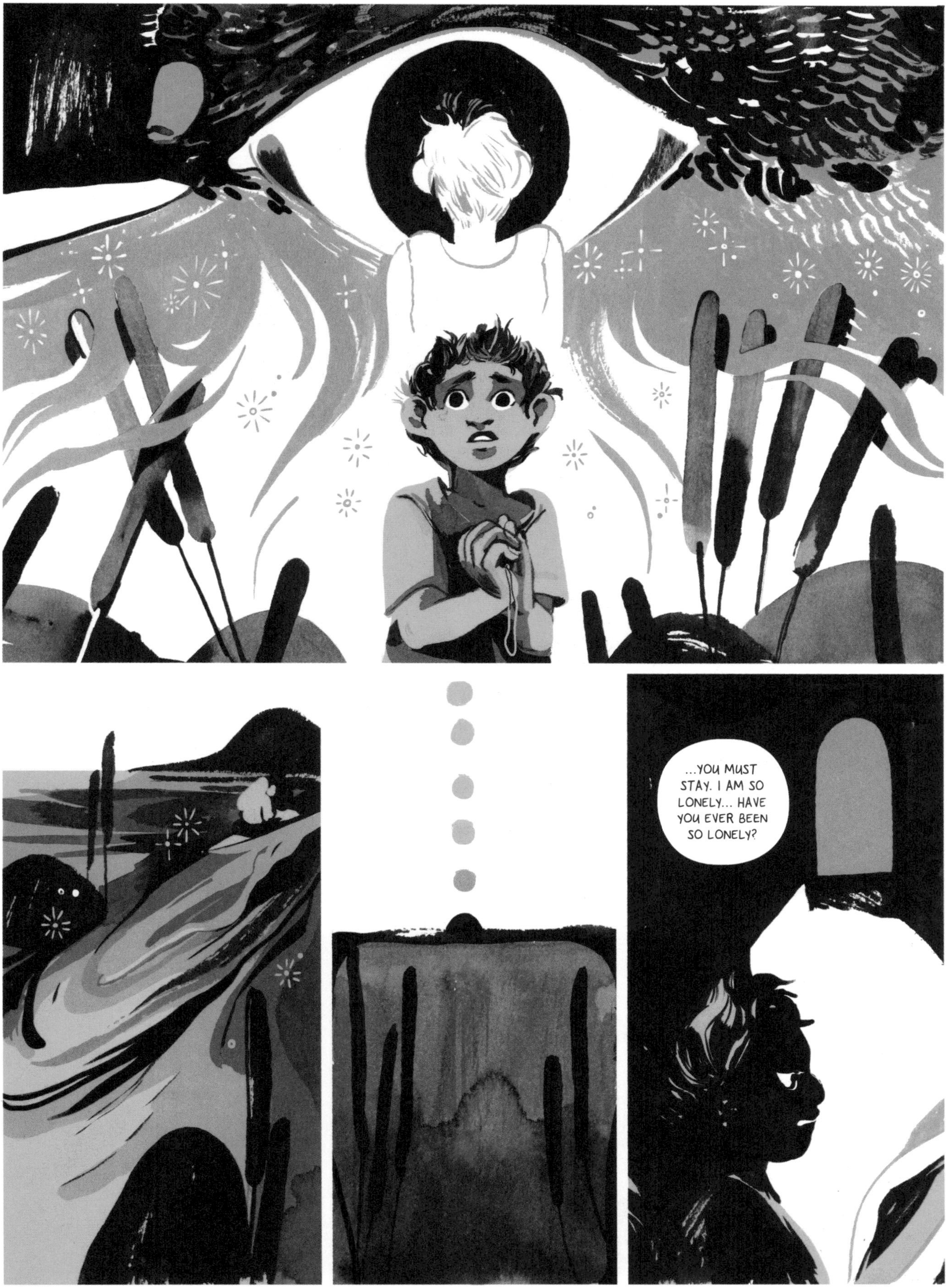
...YOU MUST STAY. I AM SO LONELY... HAVE YOU EVER BEEN SO LONELY?

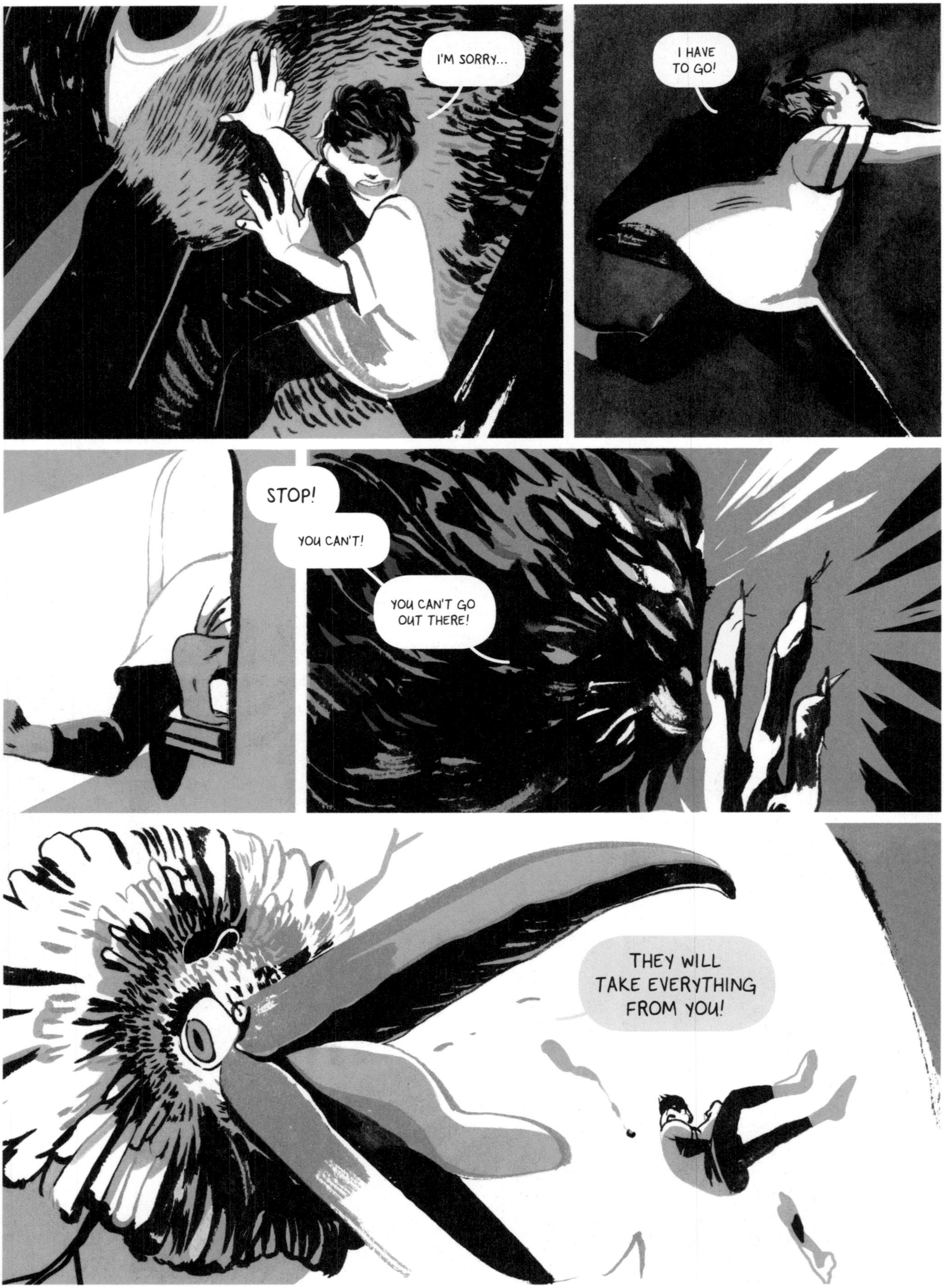
I'M SORRY...
I HAVE TO GO!
STOP!
YOU CAN'T!
YOU CAN'T GO OUT THERE!
THEY WILL TAKE EVERYTHING FROM YOU!

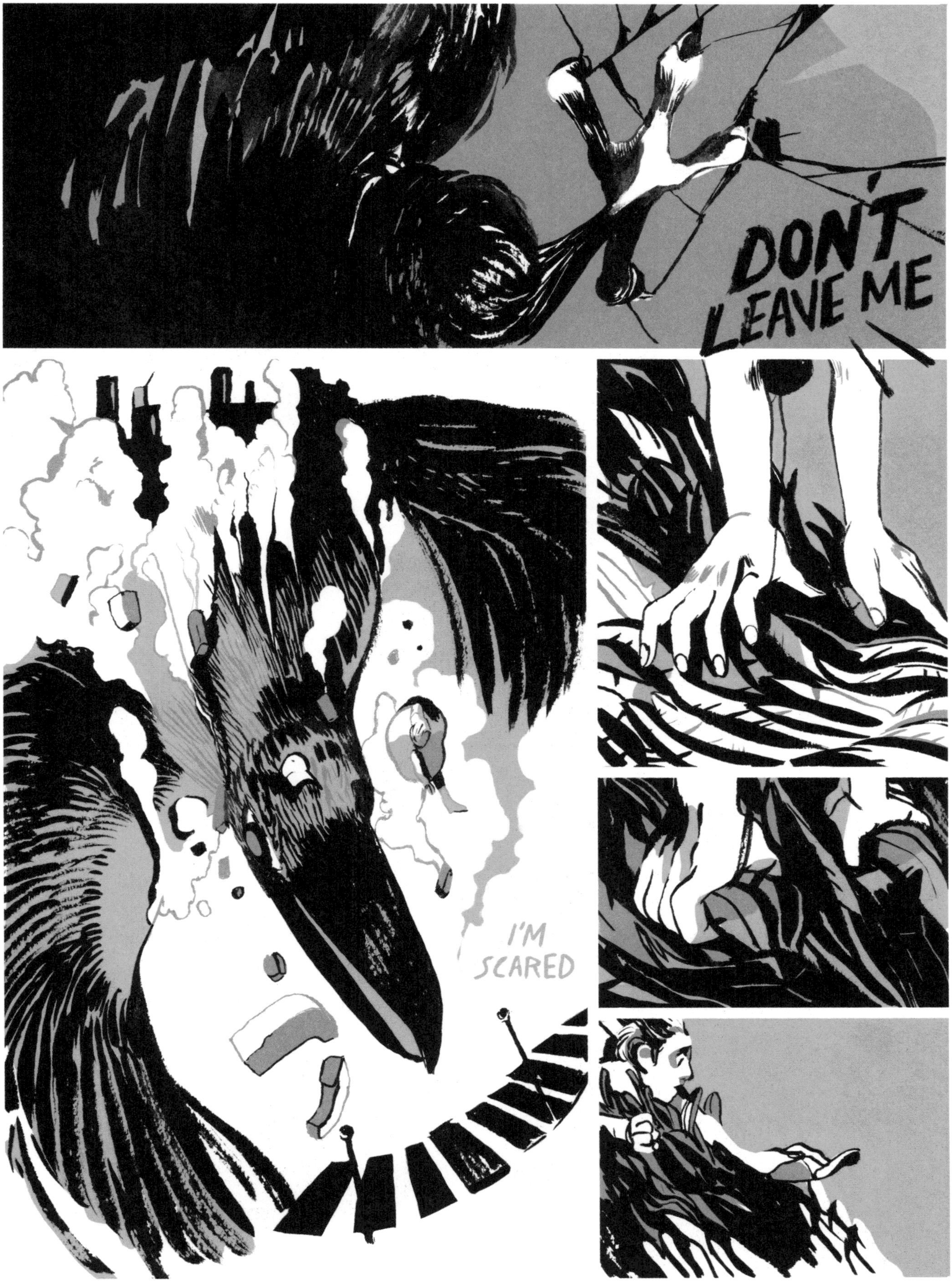
DON'T LEAVE ME
I'M SCARED

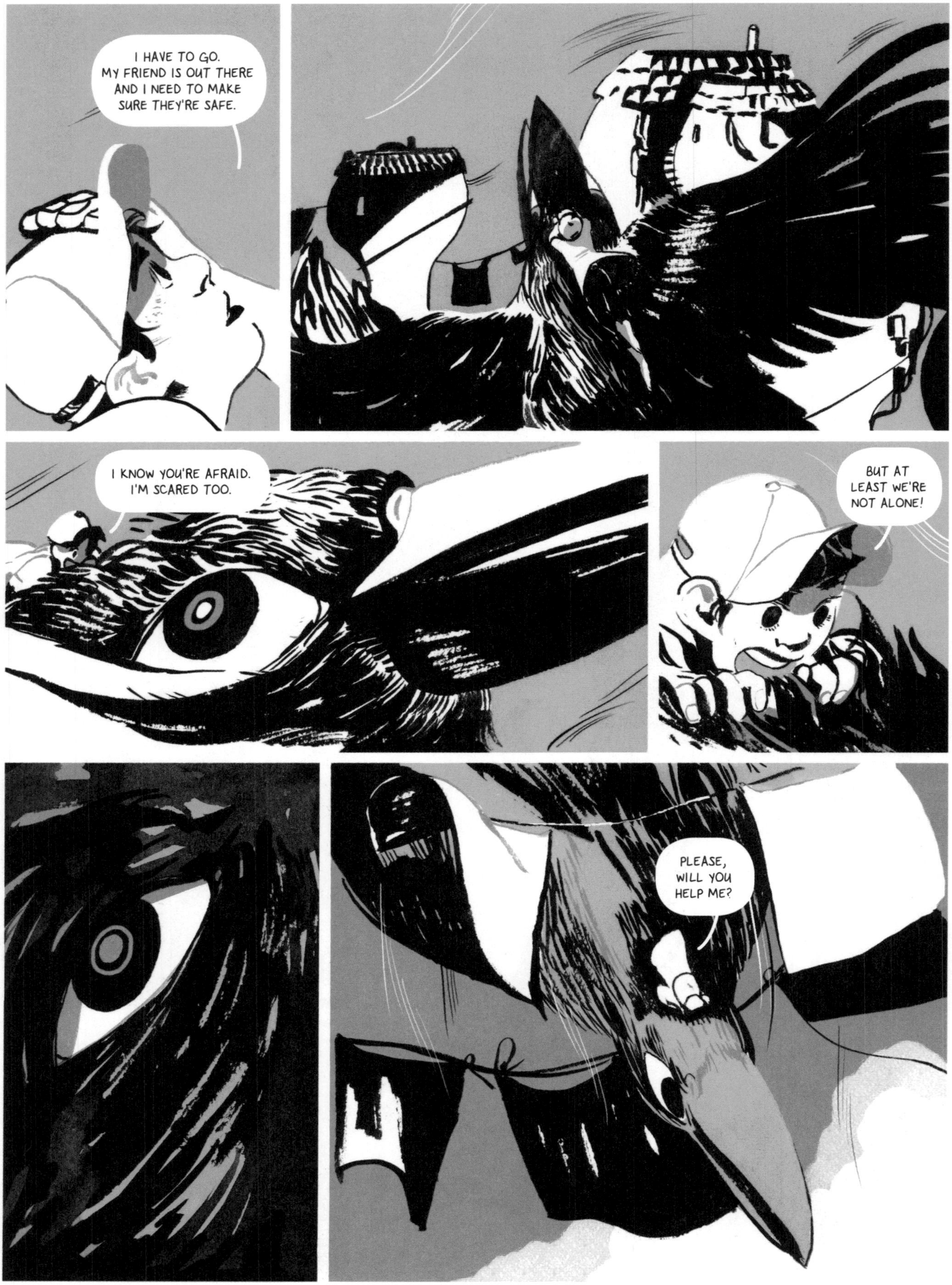
I HAVE TO GO.
MY FRIEND IS OUT THERE AND I NEED TO MAKE SURE THEY'RE SAFE.
I KNOW YOU'RE AFRAID. I'M SCARED TOO.
BUT AT LEAST WE'RE NOT ALONE!
PLEASE, WILL YOU HELP ME?

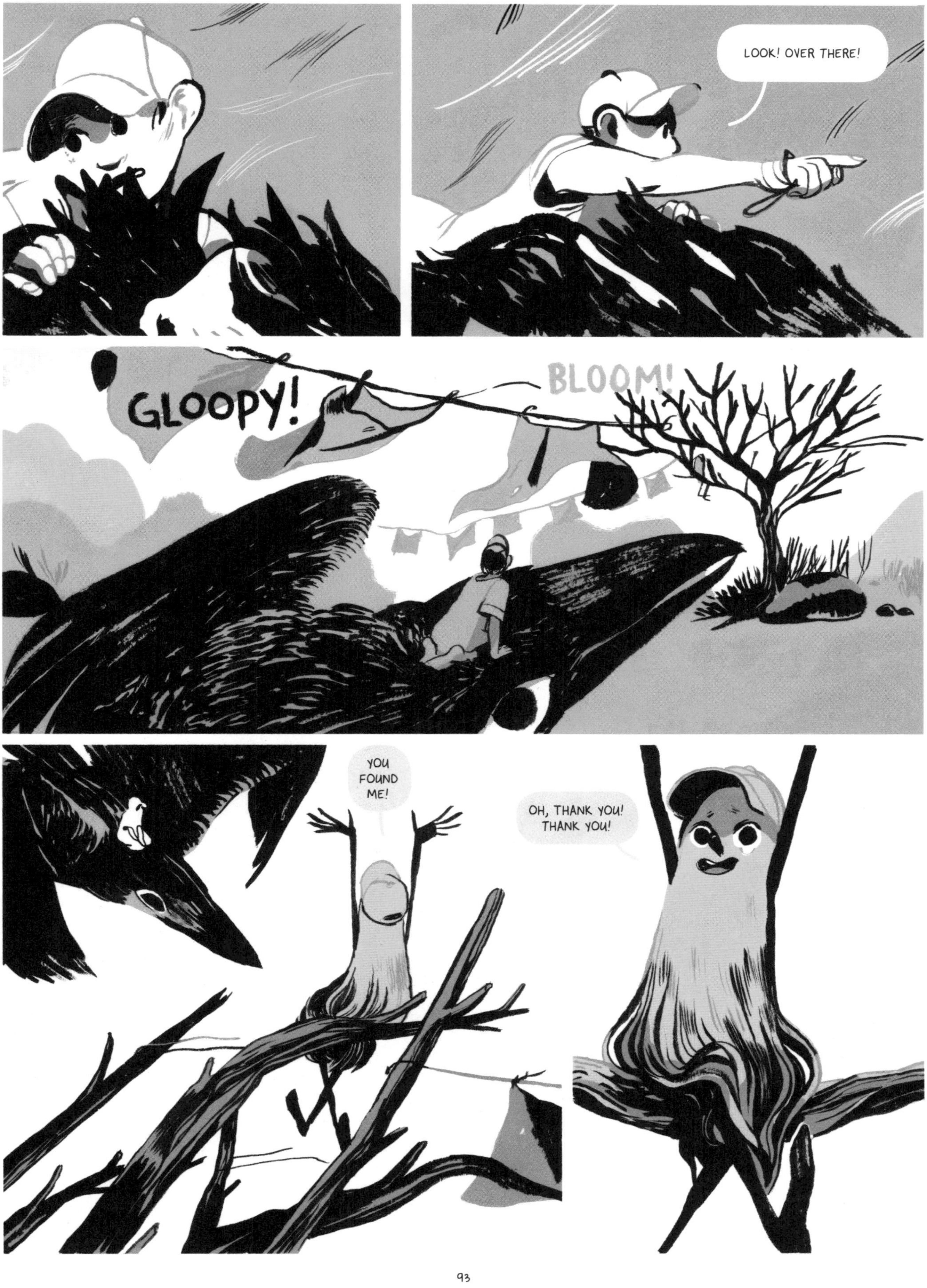
LOOK! OVER THERE!
GLOOPY!
BLOOM!
YOU FOUND ME!
OH, THANK YOU! THANK YOU!

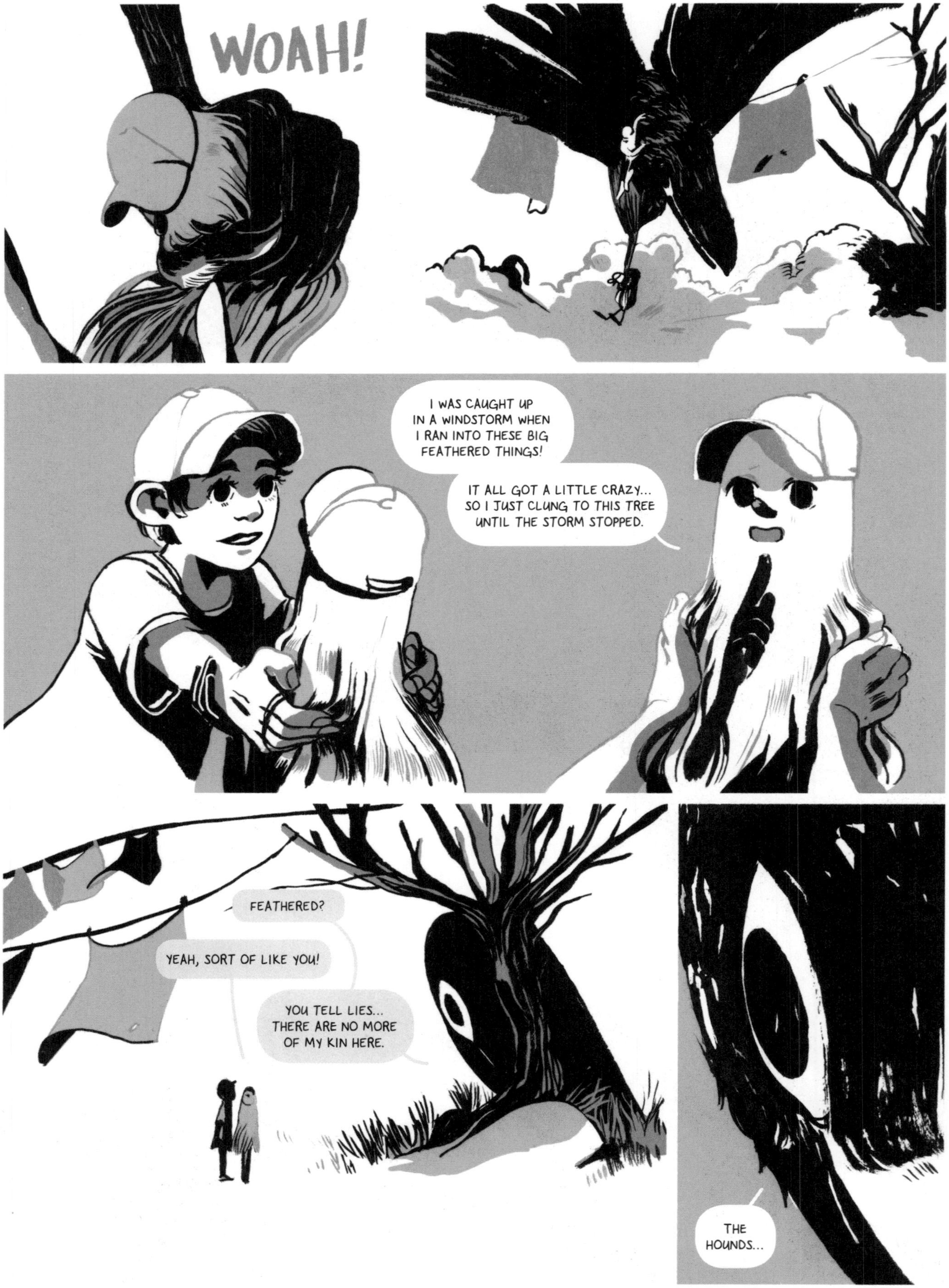
WOAH!
I WAS CAUGHT UP IN A WINDSTORM WHEN I RAN INTO THESE BIG FEATHERED THINGS!
IT ALL GOT A LITTLE CRAZY... SO I JUST CLUNG TO THIS TREE UNTIL THE STORM STOPPED.
FEATHERED?
YEAH, SORT OF LIKE YOU!
YOU TELL LIES... THERE ARE NO MORE OF MY KIN HERE.
THE HOUNDS...

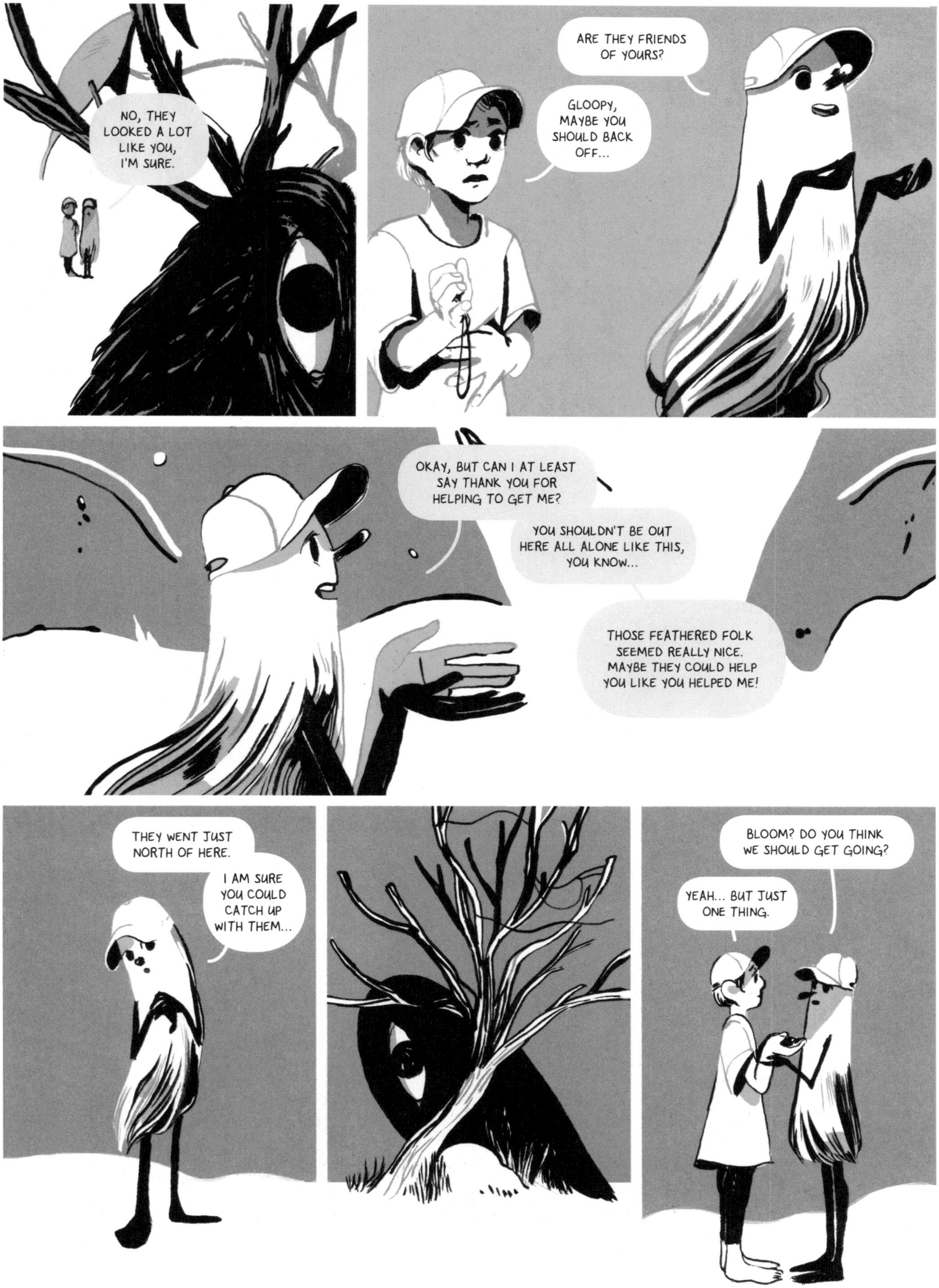
NO, THEY LOOKED A LOT LIKE YOU, I'M SURE.
ARE THEY FRIENDS OF YOURS?
GLOOPY, MAYBE YOU SHOULD BACK OFF...
OKAY, BUT CAN I AT LEAST SAY THANK YOU FOR HELPING TO GET ME?
YOU SHOULDN'T BE OUT HERE ALL ALONE LIKE THIS, YOU KNOW...
THOSE FEATHERED FOLK SEEMED REALLY NICE. MAYBE THEY COULD HELP YOU LIKE YOU HELPED ME!
THEY WENT JUST NORTH OF HERE.
I AM SURE YOU COULD CATCH UP WITH THEM...
BLOOM? DO YOU THINK WE SHOULD GET GOING?
YEAH... BUT JUST ONE THING.

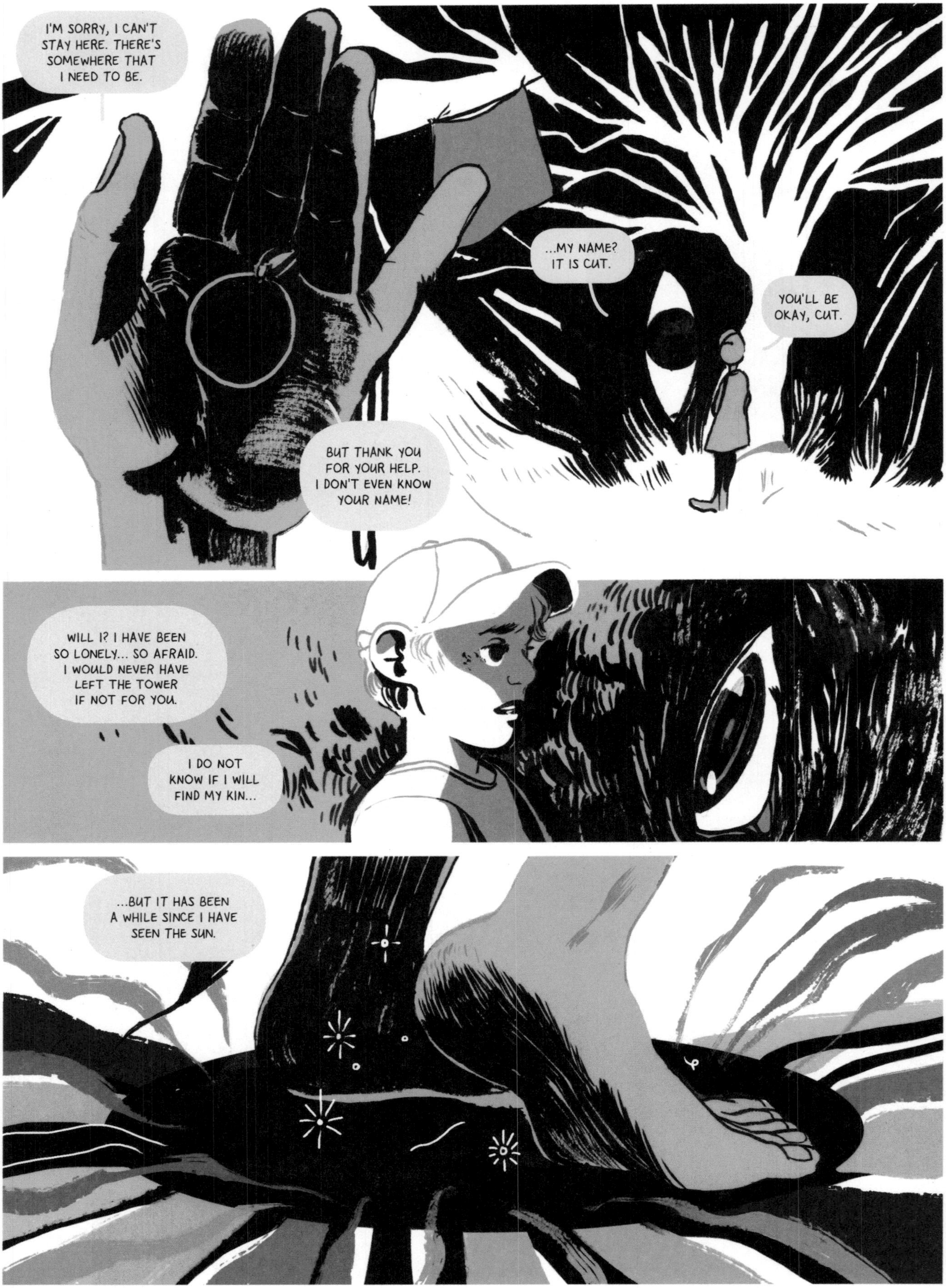
I'M SORRY, I CAN'T STAY HERE. THERE'S SOMEWHERE THAT I NEED TO BE.
BUT THANK YOU FOR YOUR HELP. I DON'T EVEN KNOW YOUR NAME!
...MY NAME? IT IS CUT.
YOU'LL BE OKAY, CUT.
WILL I? I HAVE BEEN SO LONELY... SO AFRAID. I WOULD NEVER HAVE LEFT THE TOWER IF NOT FOR YOU.
I DO NOT KNOW IF I WILL FIND MY KIN...
...BUT IT HAS BEEN A WHILE SINCE I HAVE SEEN THE SUN.

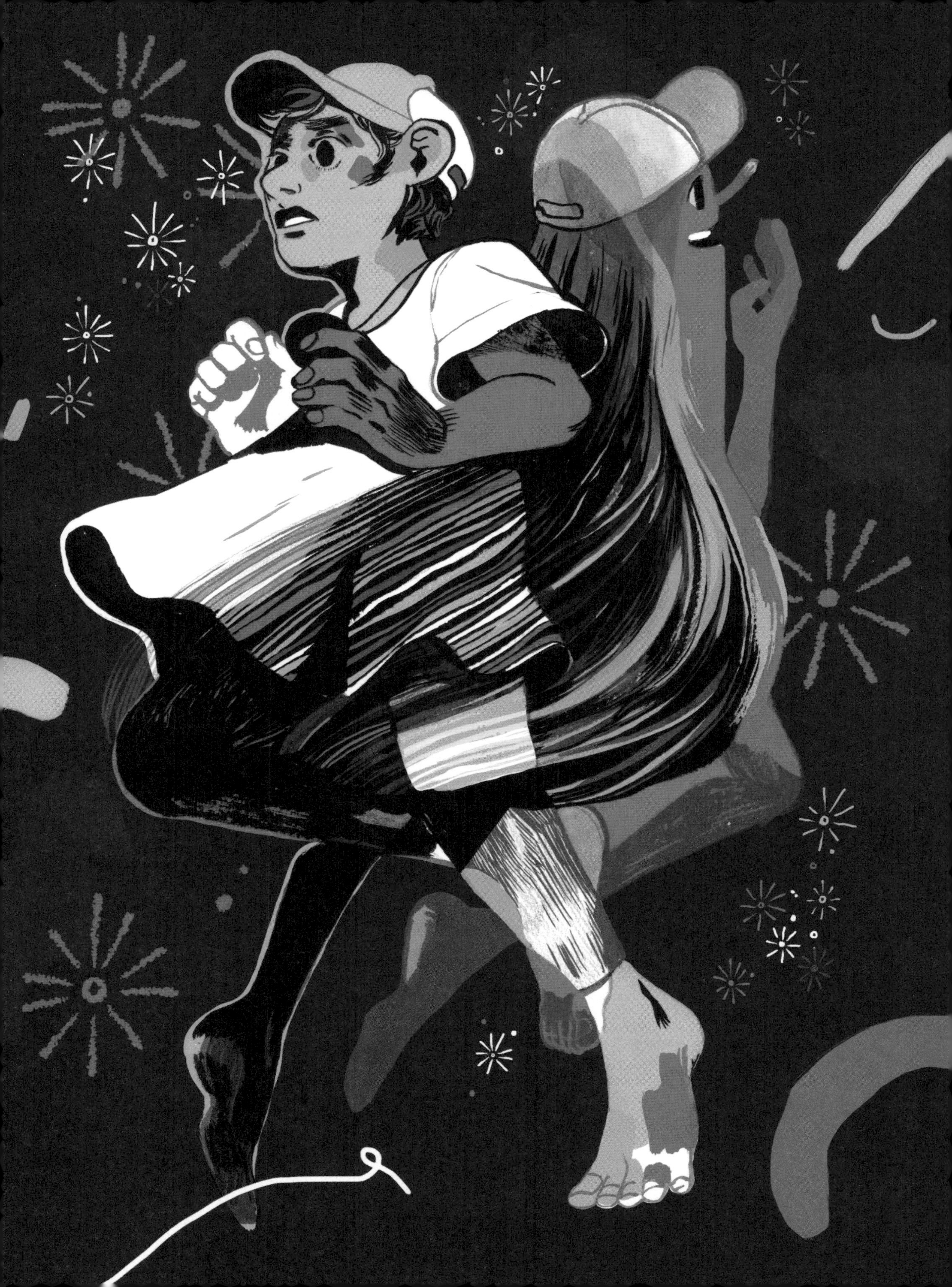

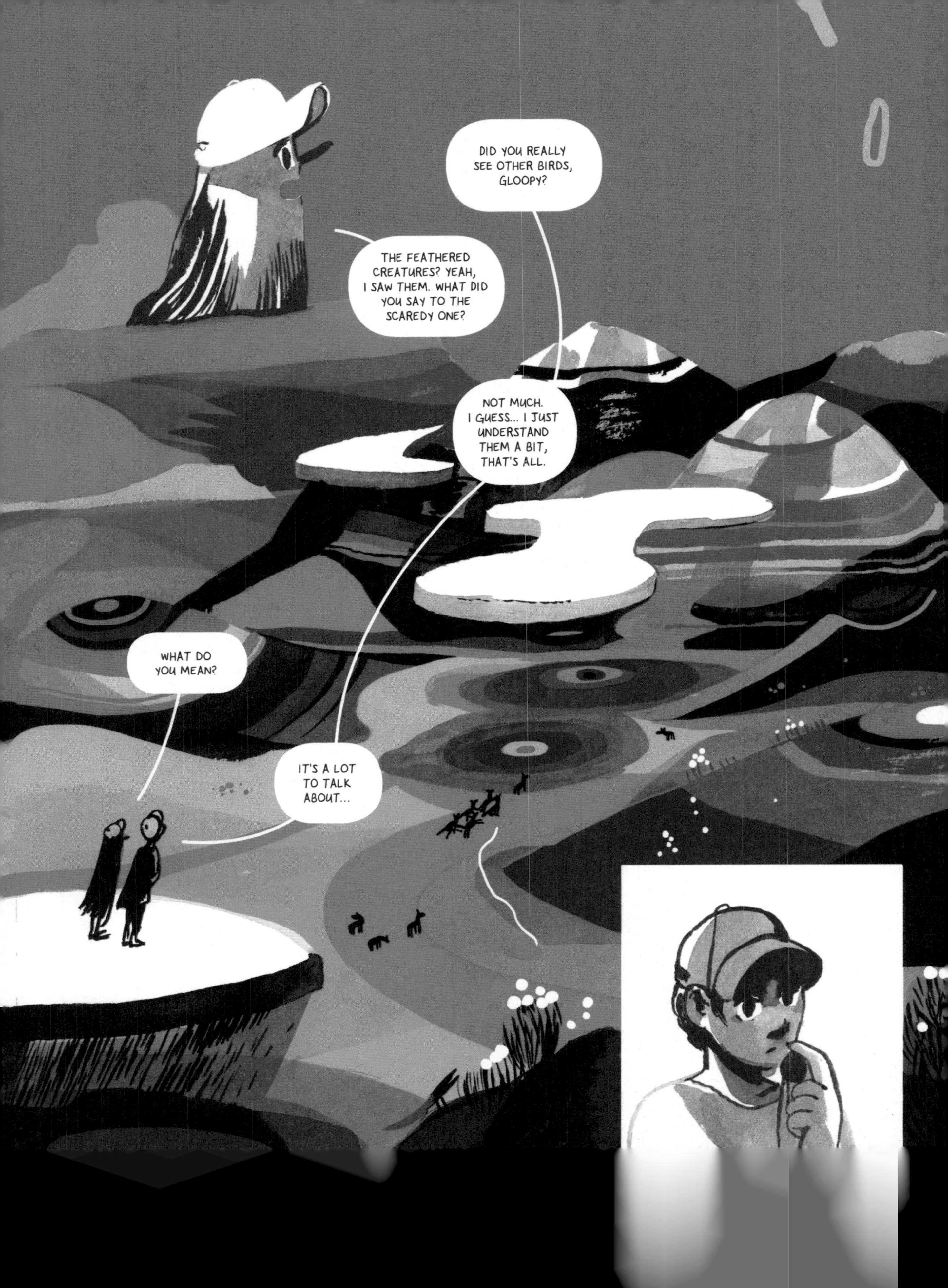
DID YOU REALLY SEE OTHER BIRDS, GLOOPY?
THE FEATHERED CREATURES? YEAH, I SAW THEM. WHAT DID YOU SAY TO THE SCAREDY ONE?
NOT MUCH. I GUESS... I JUST UNDERSTAND THEM A BIT, THAT'S ALL.
WHAT DO YOU MEAN?
IT'S A LOT TO TALK ABOUT...

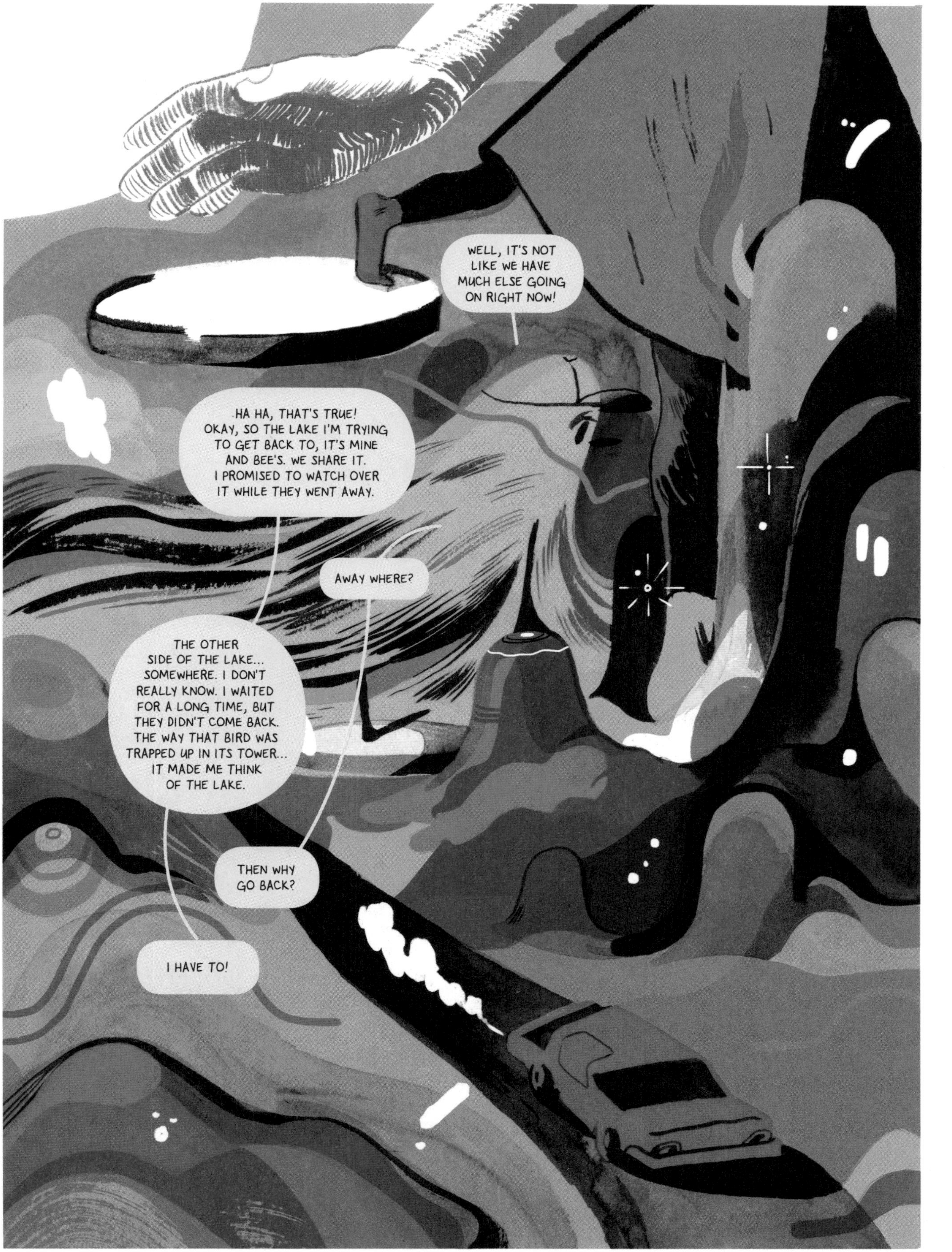
WELL, IT'S NOT LIKE WE HAVE MUCH ELSE GOING ON RIGHT NOW!
HA HA, THAT'S TRUE! OKAY, SO THE LAKE I'M TRYING TO GET BACK TO, IT'S MINE AND BEE'S. WE SHARE IT. I PROMISED TO WATCH OVER IT WHILE THEY WENT AWAY.
AWAY WHERE?
THE OTHER SIDE OF THE LAKE... SOMEWHERE. I DON'T REALLY KNOW. I WAITED FOR A LONG TIME, BUT THEY DIDN'T COME BACK. THE WAY THAT BIRD WAS TRAPPED UP IN ITS TOWER... IT MADE ME THINK OF THE LAKE.
THEN WHY GO BACK?
I HAVE TO!

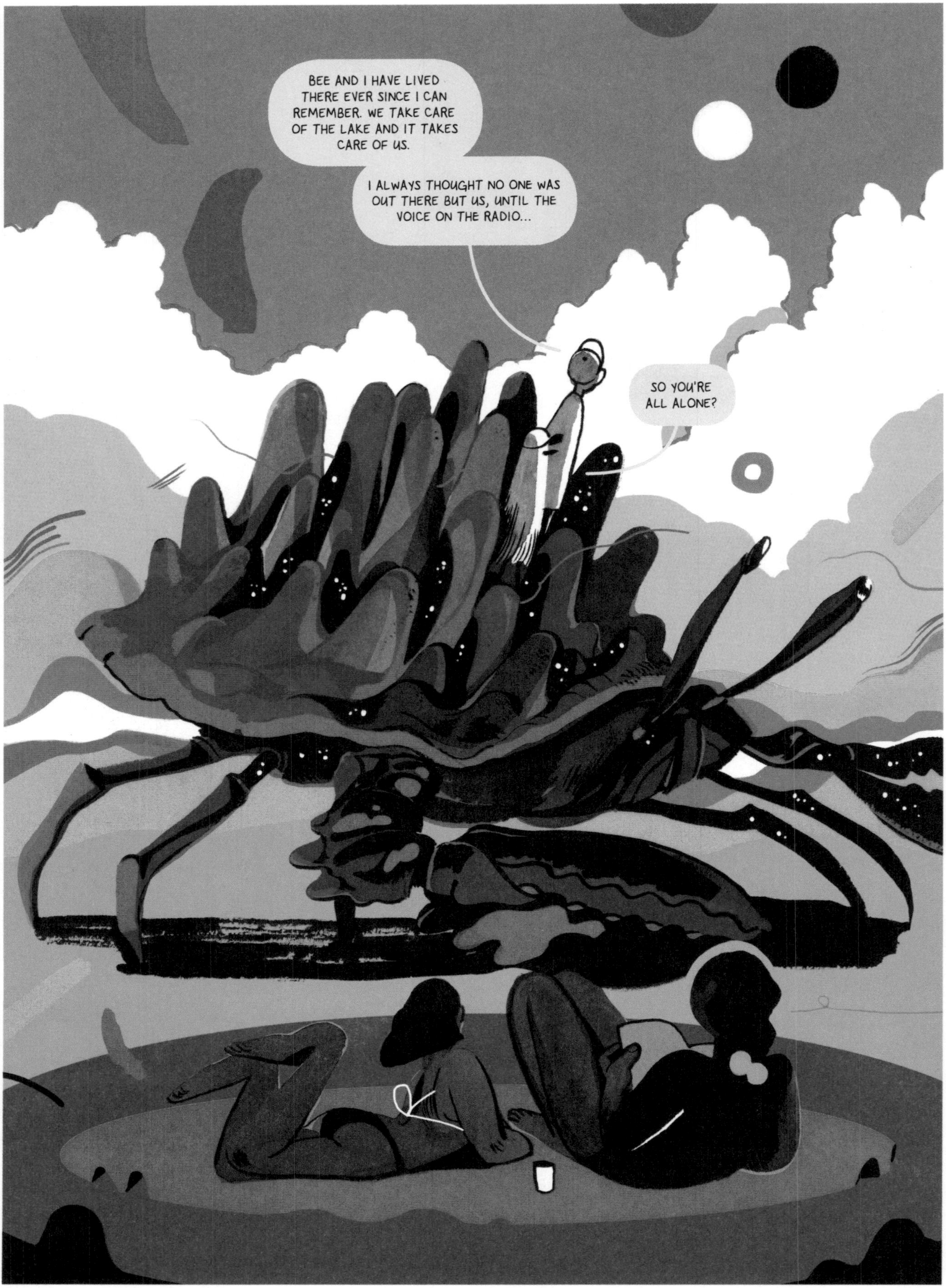
BEE AND I HAVE LIVED THERE EVER SINCE I CAN REMEMBER. WE TAKE CARE OF THE LAKE AND IT TAKES CARE OF US.
I ALWAYS THOUGHT NO ONE WAS OUT THERE BUT US, UNTIL THE VOICE ON THE RADIO...
SO YOU'RE ALL ALONE?

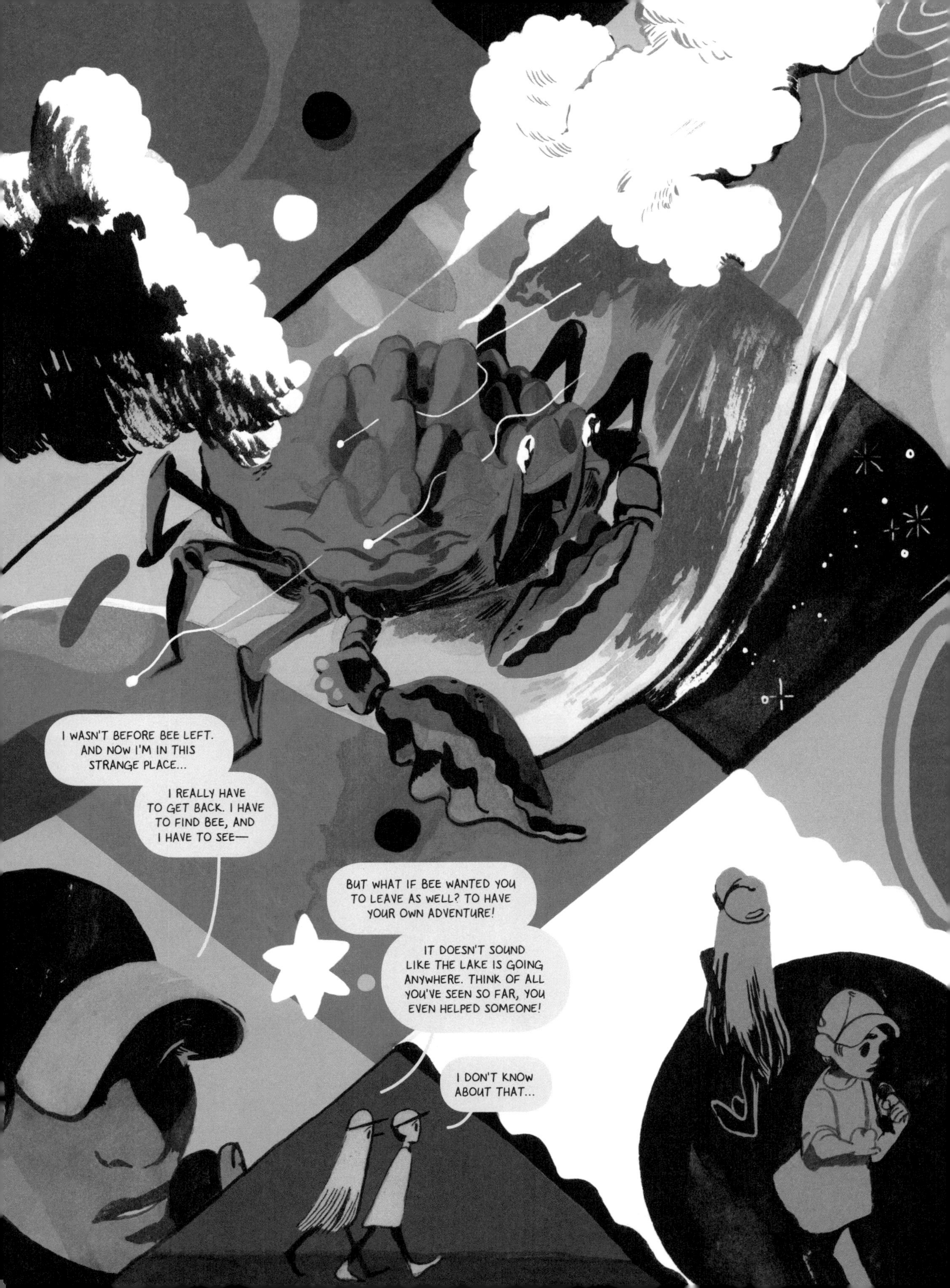
I WASN'T BEFORE BEE LEFT. AND NOW I'M IN THIS STRANGE PLACE...
I REALLY HAVE TO GET BACK. I HAVE TO FIND BEE, AND I HAVE TO SEE—
BUT WHAT IF BEE WANTED YOU TO LEAVE AS WELL? TO HAVE YOUR OWN ADVENTURE!
IT DOESN'T SOUND LIKE THE LAKE IS GOING ANYWHERE. THINK OF ALL YOU'VE SEEN SO FAR, YOU EVEN HELPED SOMEONE!
I DON'T KNOW ABOUT THAT...

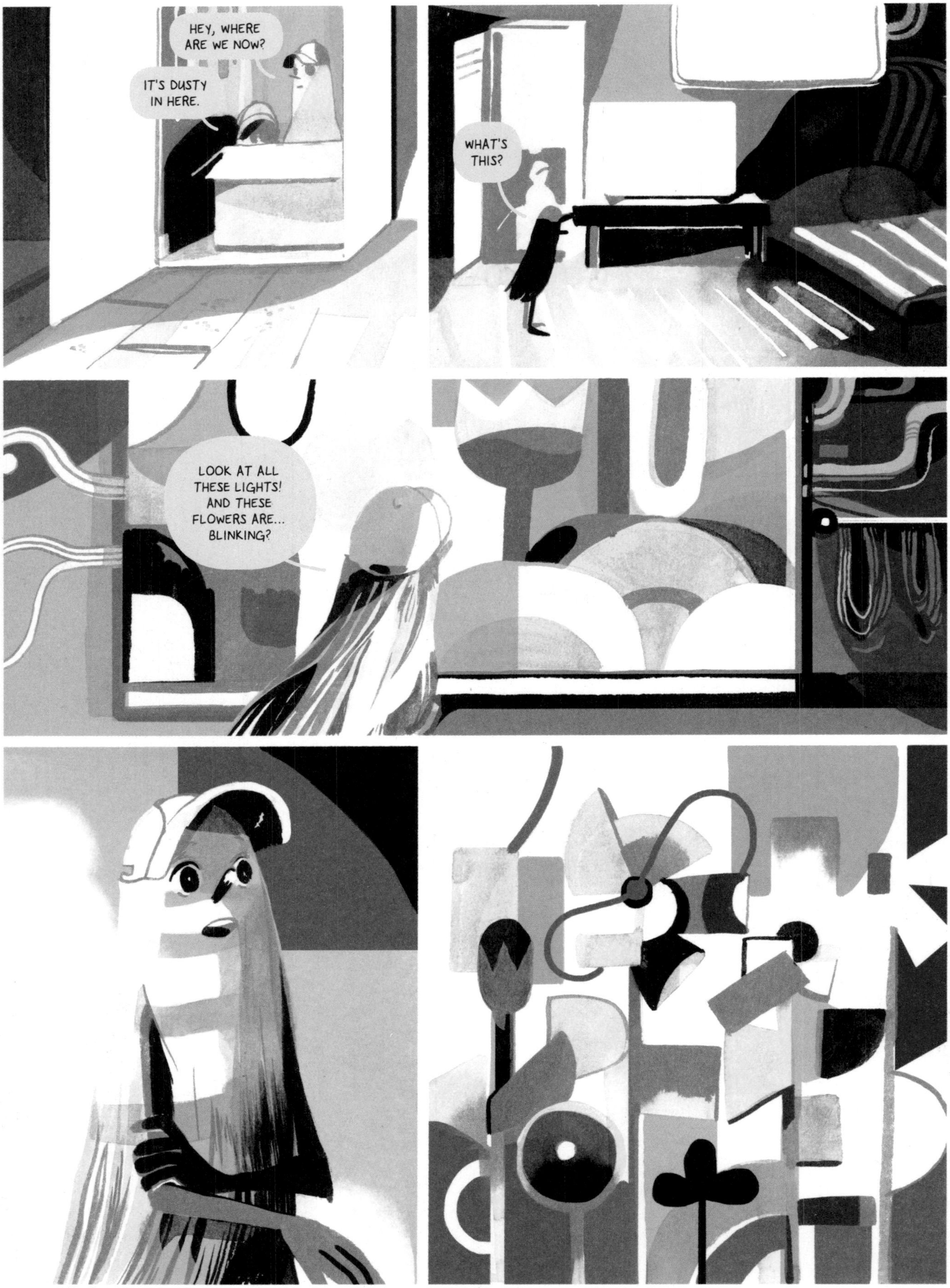
HEY, WHERE ARE WE NOW?
IT'S DUSTY IN HERE.
WHAT'S THIS?
LOOK AT ALL THESE LIGHTS! AND THESE FLOWERS ARE... BLINKING?

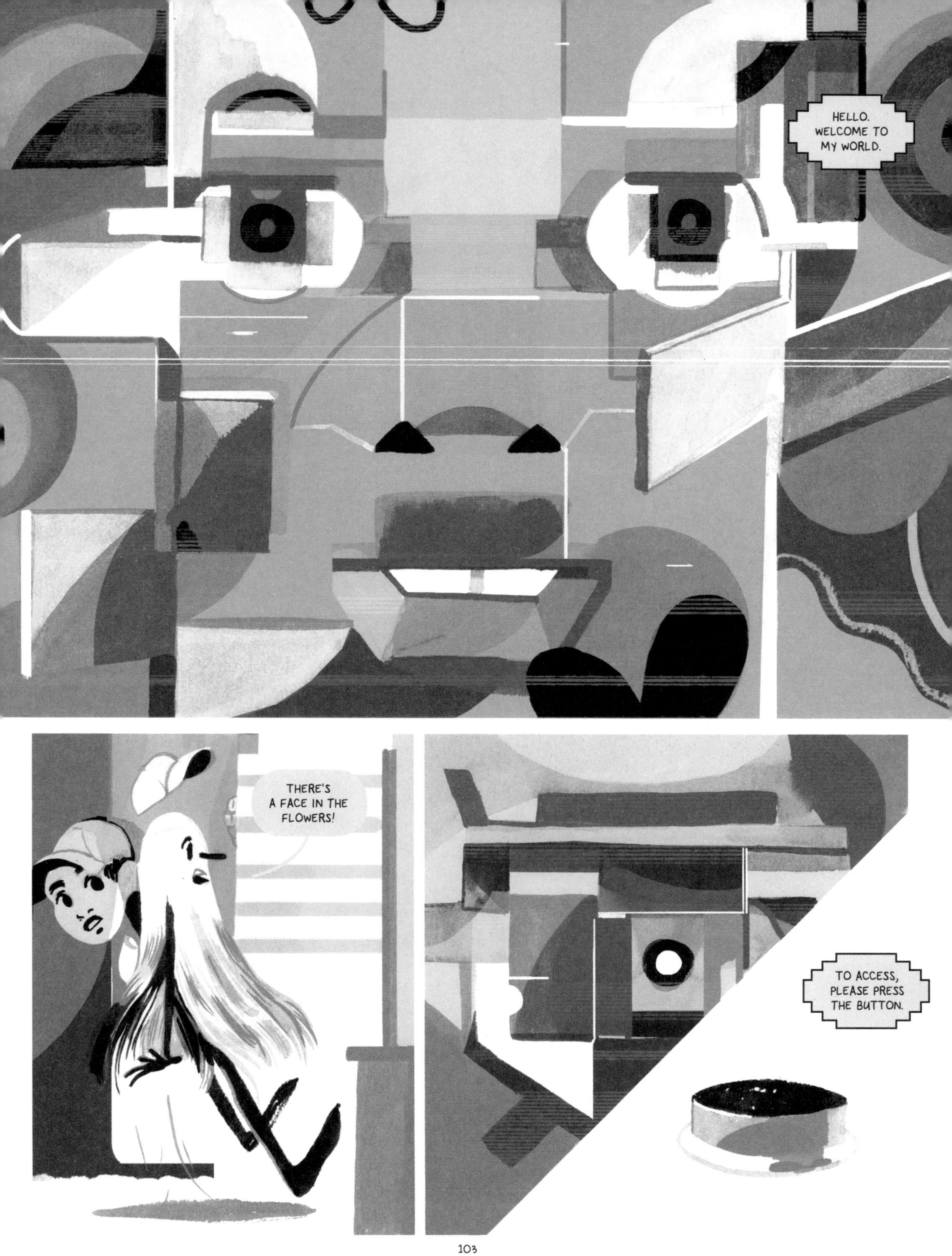
HELLO. WELCOME TO MY WORLD.
THERE'S A FACE IN THE FLOWERS!
TO ACCESS, PLEASE PRESS THE BUTTON.

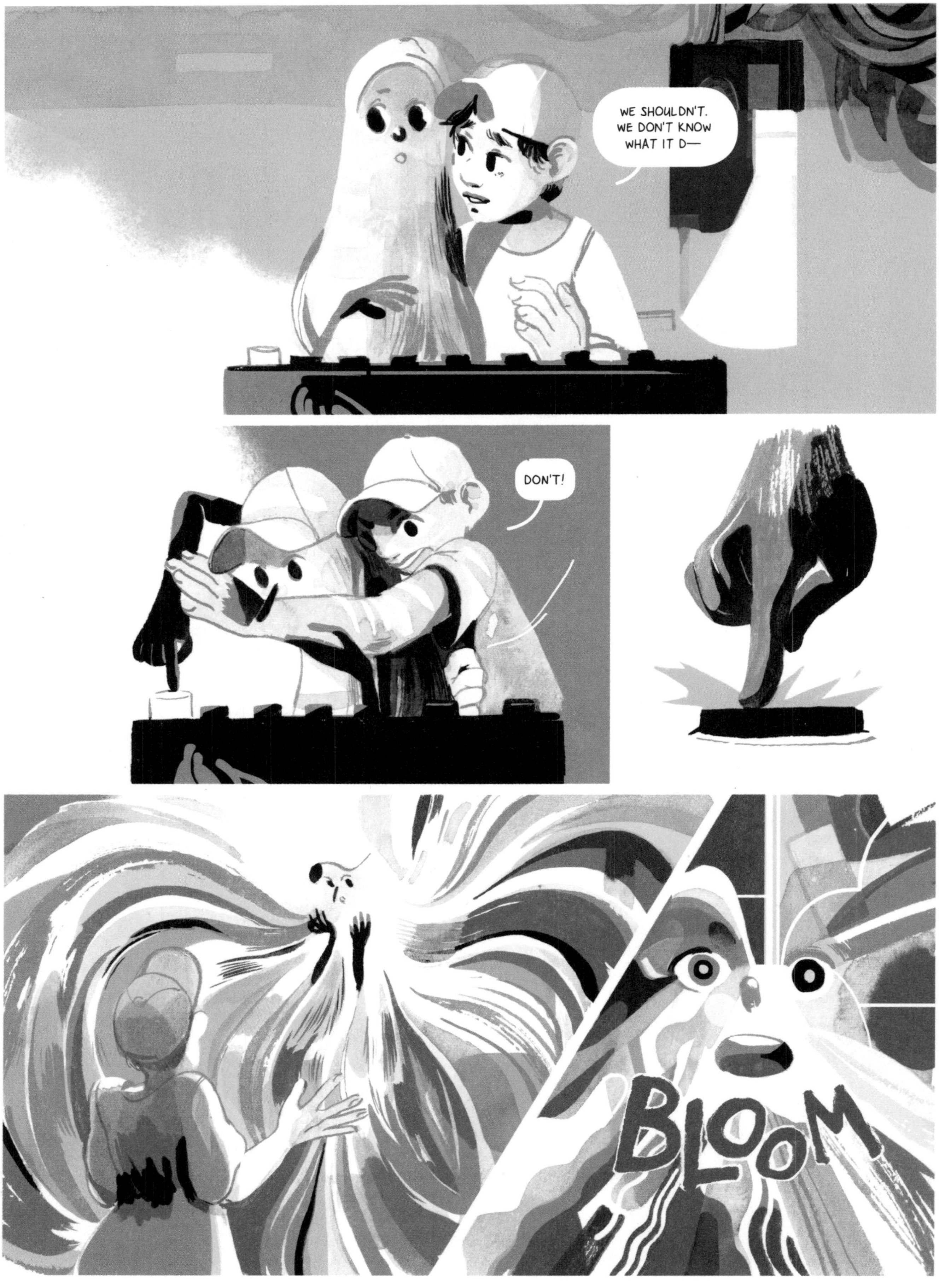
WE SHOULDN'T.
WE DON'T KNOW
WHAT IT D—
DON'T!
BLOOM

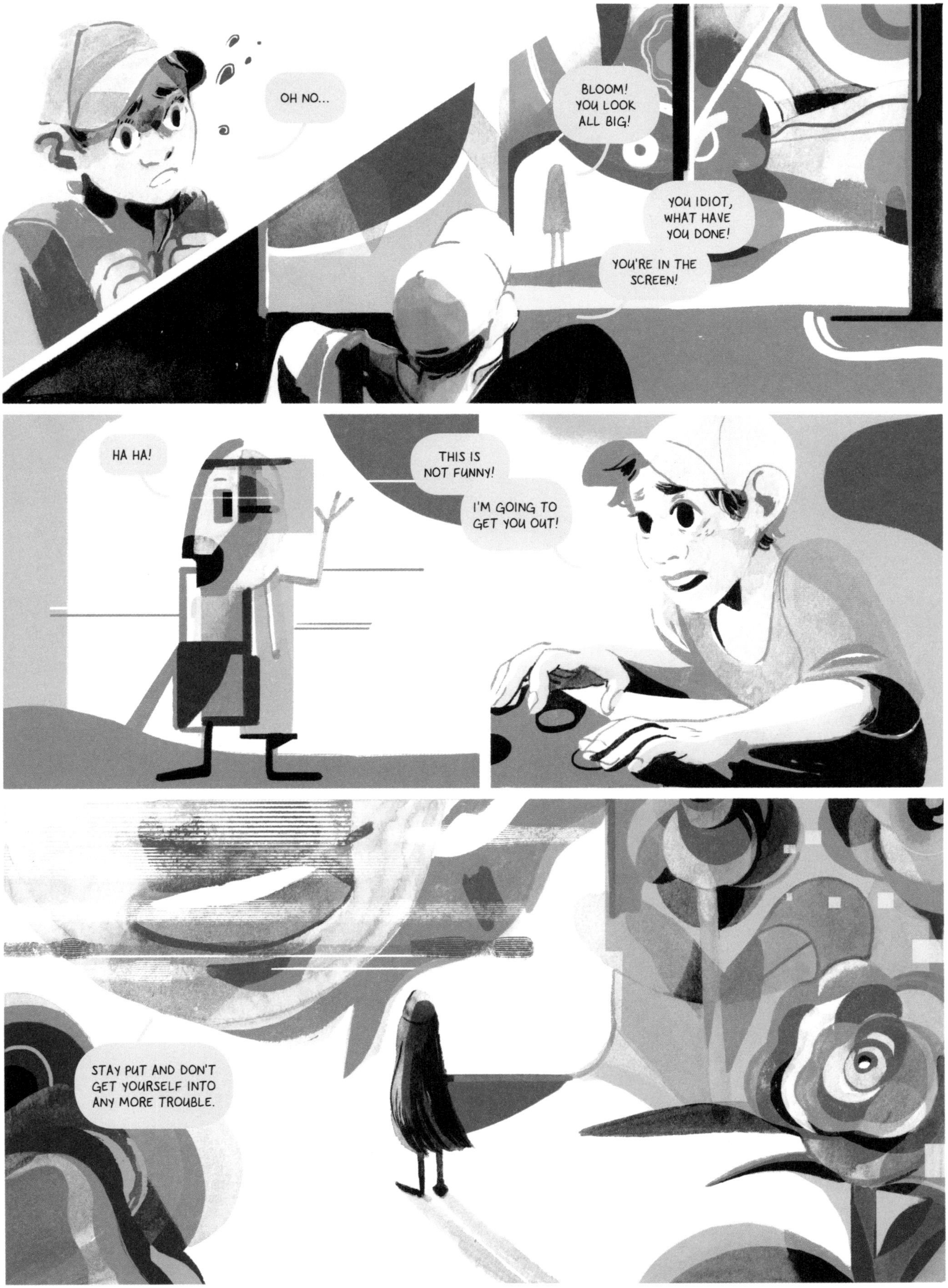
OH NO...
BLOOM! YOU LOOK ALL BIG!
YOU IDIOT, WHAT HAVE YOU DONE!
YOU'RE IN THE SCREEN!
HA HA!
THIS IS NOT FUNNY!
I'M GOING TO GET YOU OUT!
STAY PUT AND DON'T GET YOURSELF INTO ANY MORE TROUBLE.

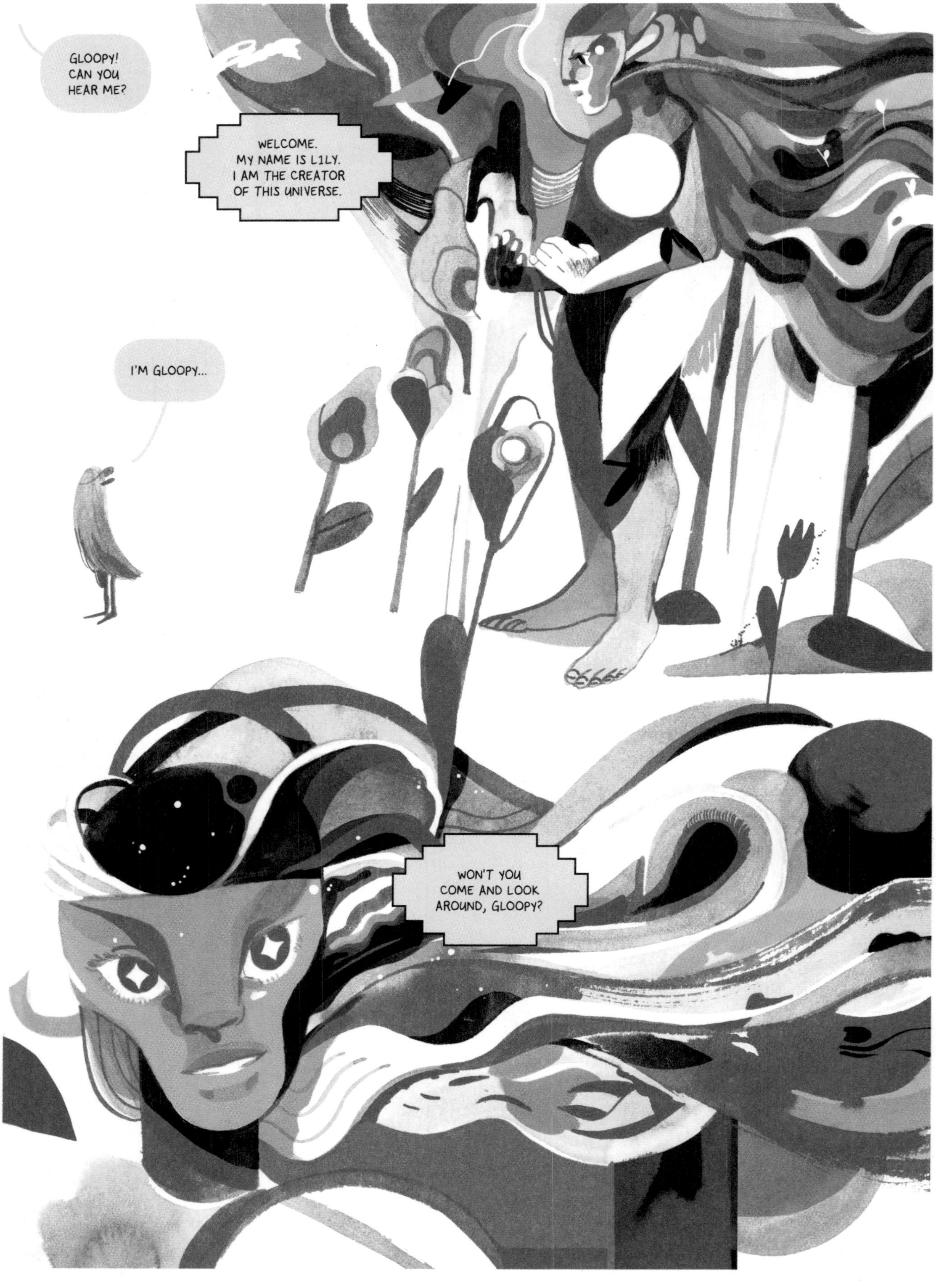
GLOOPY! CAN YOU HEAR ME?
WELCOME. MY NAME IS L1LY. I AM THE CREATOR OF THIS UNIVERSE.
I'M GLOOPY...
WON'T YOU COME AND LOOK AROUND, GLOOPY?

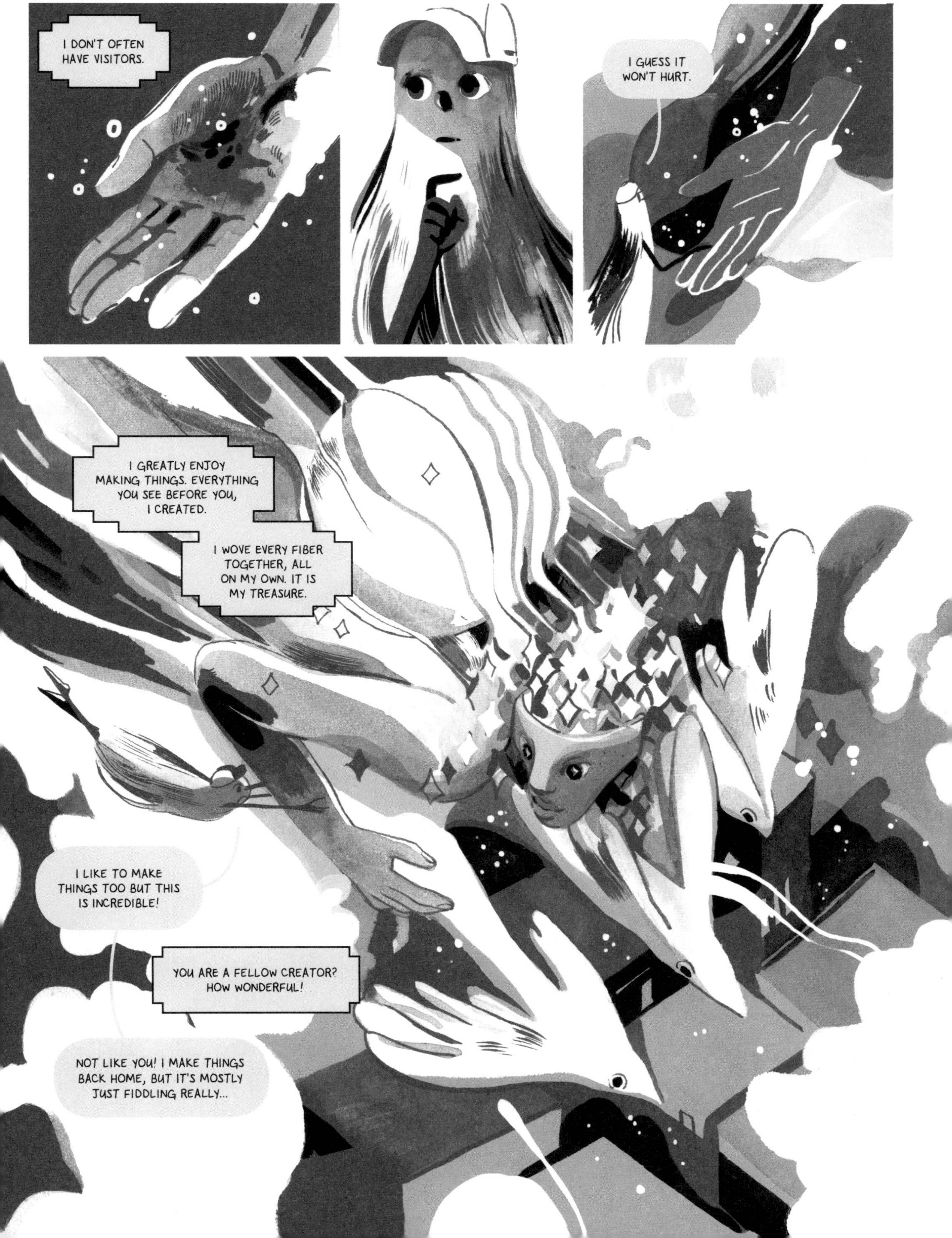
I DON'T OFTEN HAVE VISITORS.
I GUESS IT WON'T HURT.
I GREATLY ENJOY MAKING THINGS. EVERYTHING YOU SEE BEFORE YOU, I CREATED.
I WOVE EVERY FIBER TOGETHER, ALL ON MY OWN. IT IS MY TREASURE.
I LIKE TO MAKE THINGS TOO BUT THIS IS INCREDIBLE!
YOU ARE A FELLOW CREATOR? HOW WONDERFUL!
NOT LIKE YOU! I MAKE THINGS BACK HOME, BUT IT'S MOSTLY JUST FIDDLING REALLY...

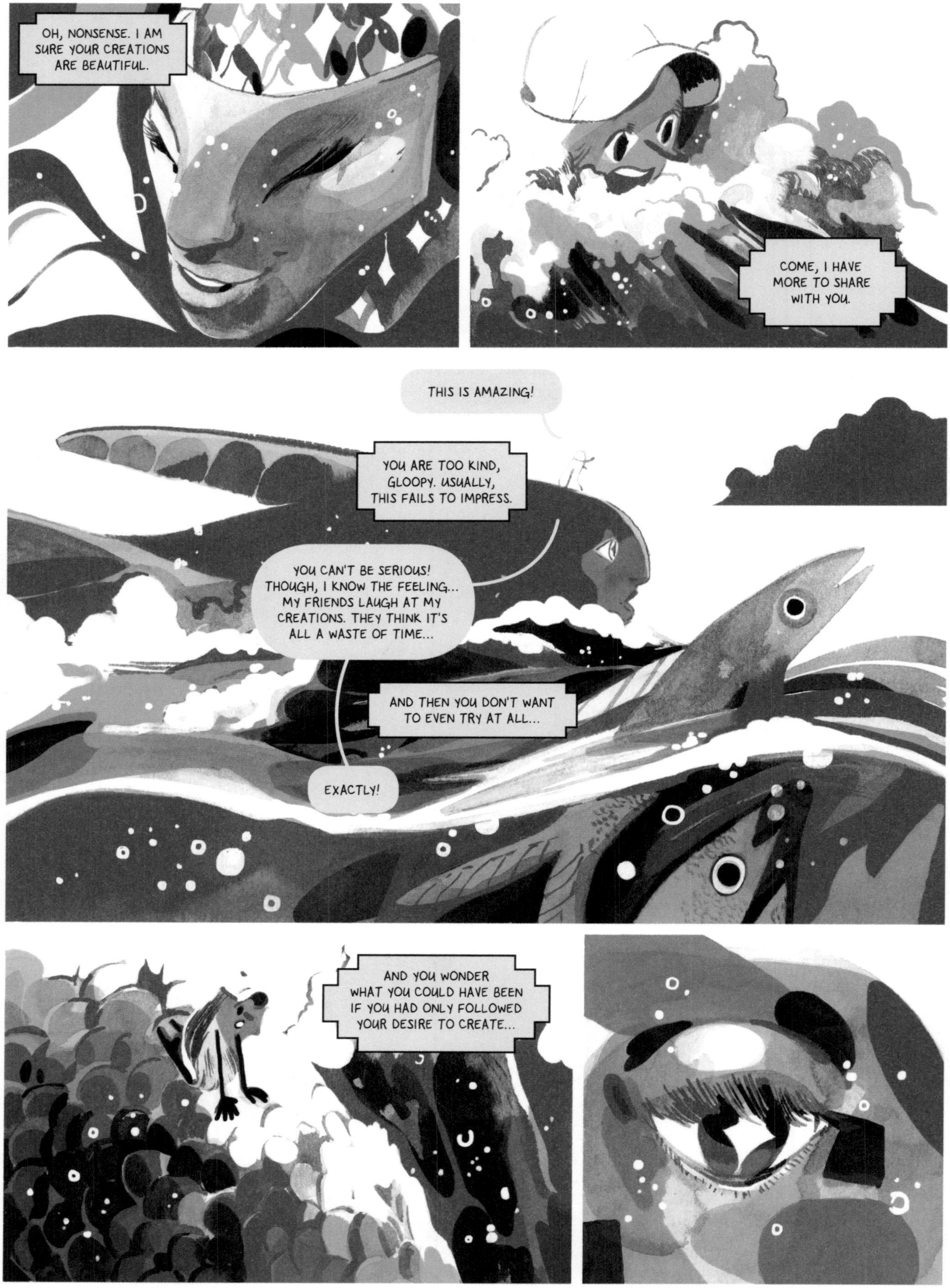
OH, NONSENSE. I AM SURE YOUR CREATIONS ARE BEAUTIFUL.
COME, I HAVE MORE TO SHARE WITH YOU.
THIS IS AMAZING!
YOU ARE TOO KIND, GLOOPY. USUALLY, THIS FAILS TO IMPRESS.
YOU CAN'T BE SERIOUS! THOUGH, I KNOW THE FEELING... MY FRIENDS LAUGH AT MY CREATIONS. THEY THINK IT'S ALL A WASTE OF TIME...
AND THEN YOU DON'T WANT TO EVEN TRY AT ALL...
EXACTLY!
AND YOU WONDER WHAT YOU COULD HAVE BEEN IF YOU HAD ONLY FOLLOWED YOUR DESIRE TO CREATE...

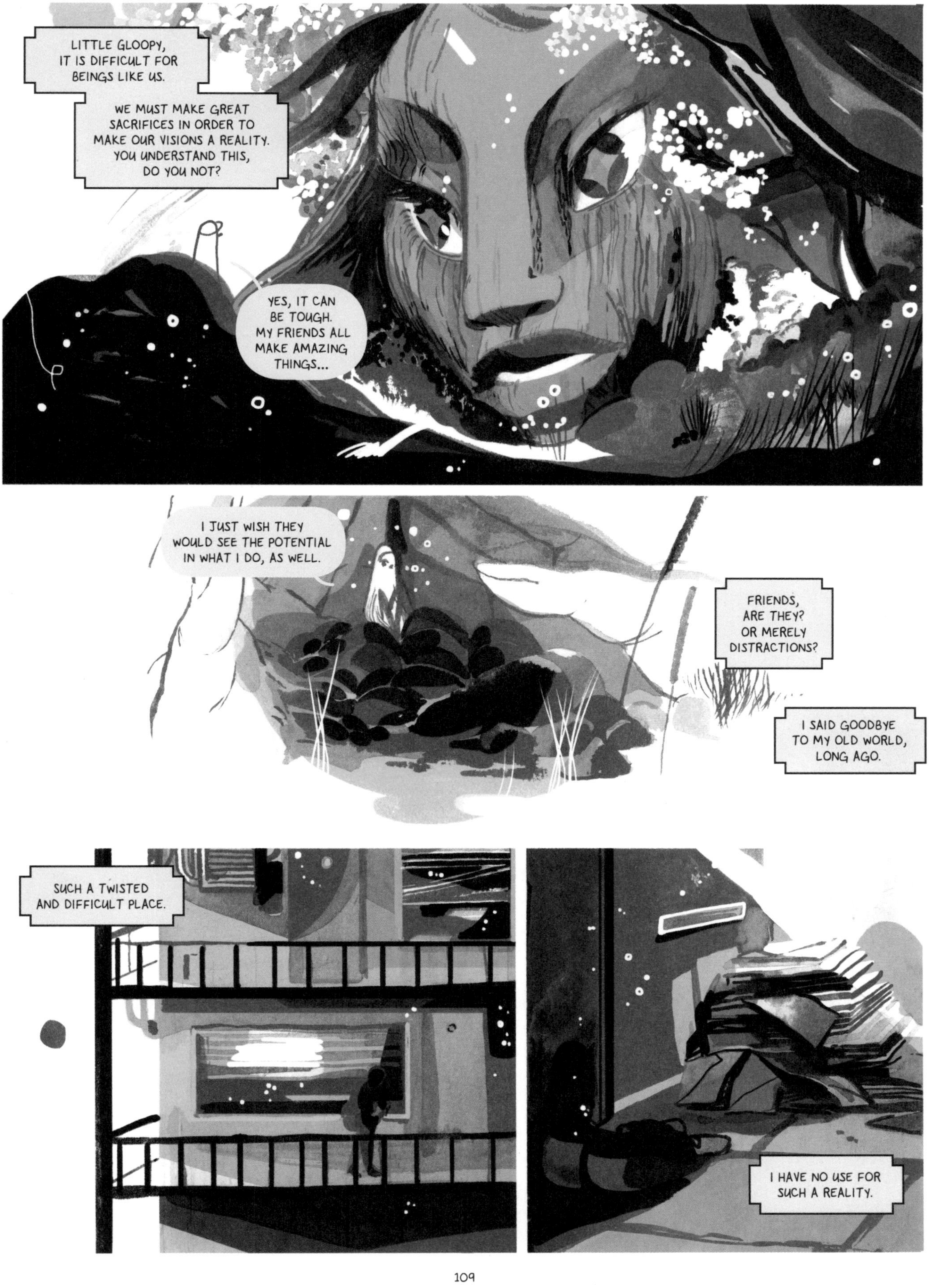
LITTLE GLOOPY,
IT IS DIFFICULT FOR
BEINGS LIKE US.
WE MUST MAKE GREAT
SACRIFICES IN ORDER TO
MAKE OUR VISIONS A REALITY.
YOU UNDERSTAND THIS,
DO YOU NOT?
YES, IT CAN
BE TOUGH.
MY FRIENDS ALL
MAKE AMAZING
THINGS...
I JUST WISH THEY
WOULD SEE THE POTENTIAL
IN WHAT I DO, AS WELL.
FRIENDS,
ARE THEY?
OR MERELY
DISTRACTIONS?
I SAID GOODBYE
TO MY OLD WORLD,
LONG AGO.
SUCH A TWISTED
AND DIFFICULT PLACE.
I HAVE NO USE FOR
SUCH A REALITY.

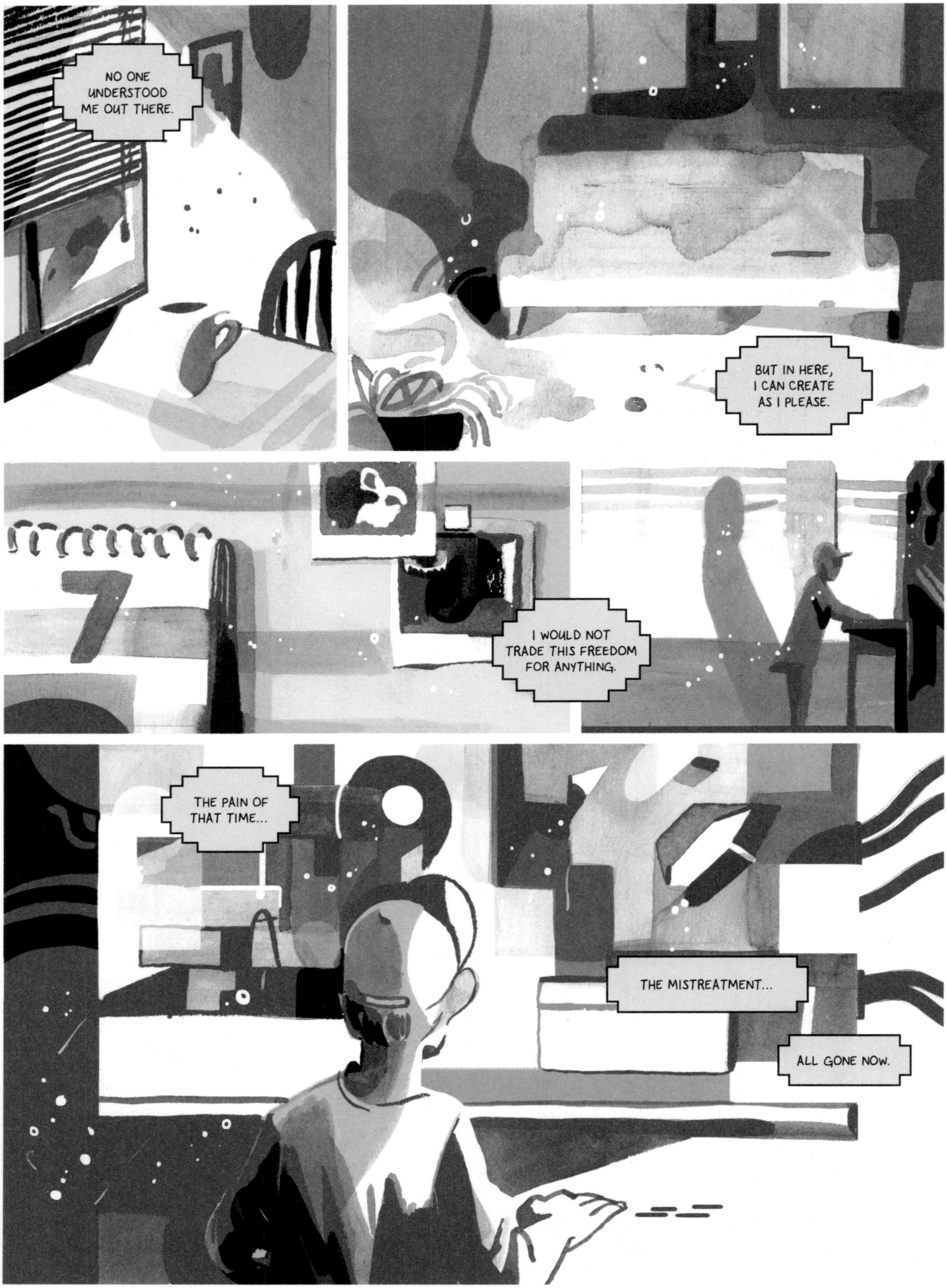
NO ONE UNDERSTOOD ME OUT THERE.
BUT IN HERE, I CAN CREATE AS I PLEASE.
I WOULD NOT TRADE THIS FREEDOM FOR ANYTHING.
THE PAIN OF THAT TIME...
THE MISTREATMENT...
ALL GONE NOW.

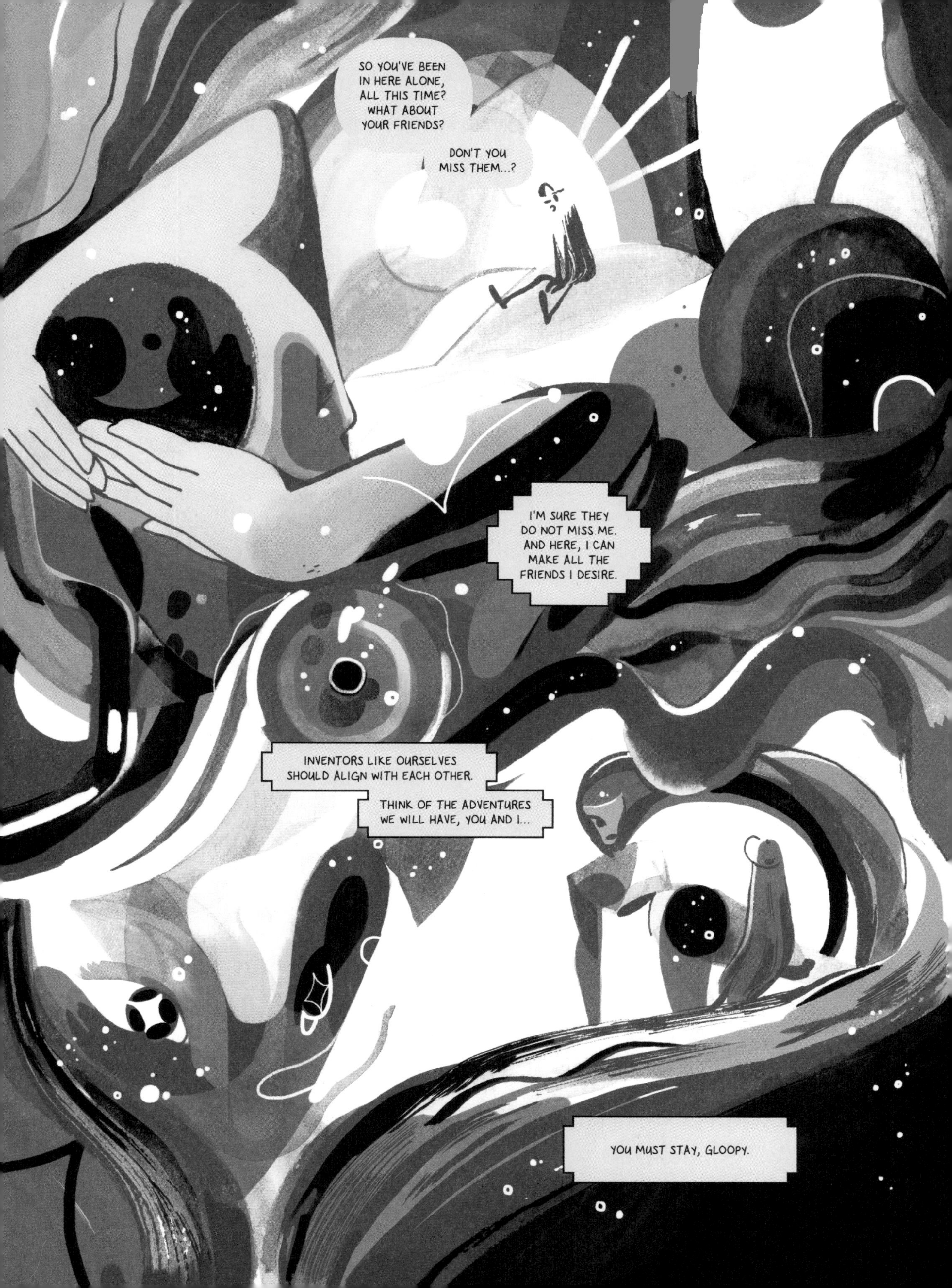
SO YOU'VE BEEN IN HERE ALONE, ALL THIS TIME? WHAT ABOUT YOUR FRIENDS?
DON'T YOU MISS THEM...?
I'M SURE THEY DO NOT MISS ME. AND HERE, I CAN MAKE ALL THE FRIENDS I DESIRE.
INVENTORS LIKE OURSELVES SHOULD ALIGN WITH EACH OTHER.
THINK OF THE ADVENTURES WE WILL HAVE, YOU AND I...
YOU MUST STAY, GLOOPY.

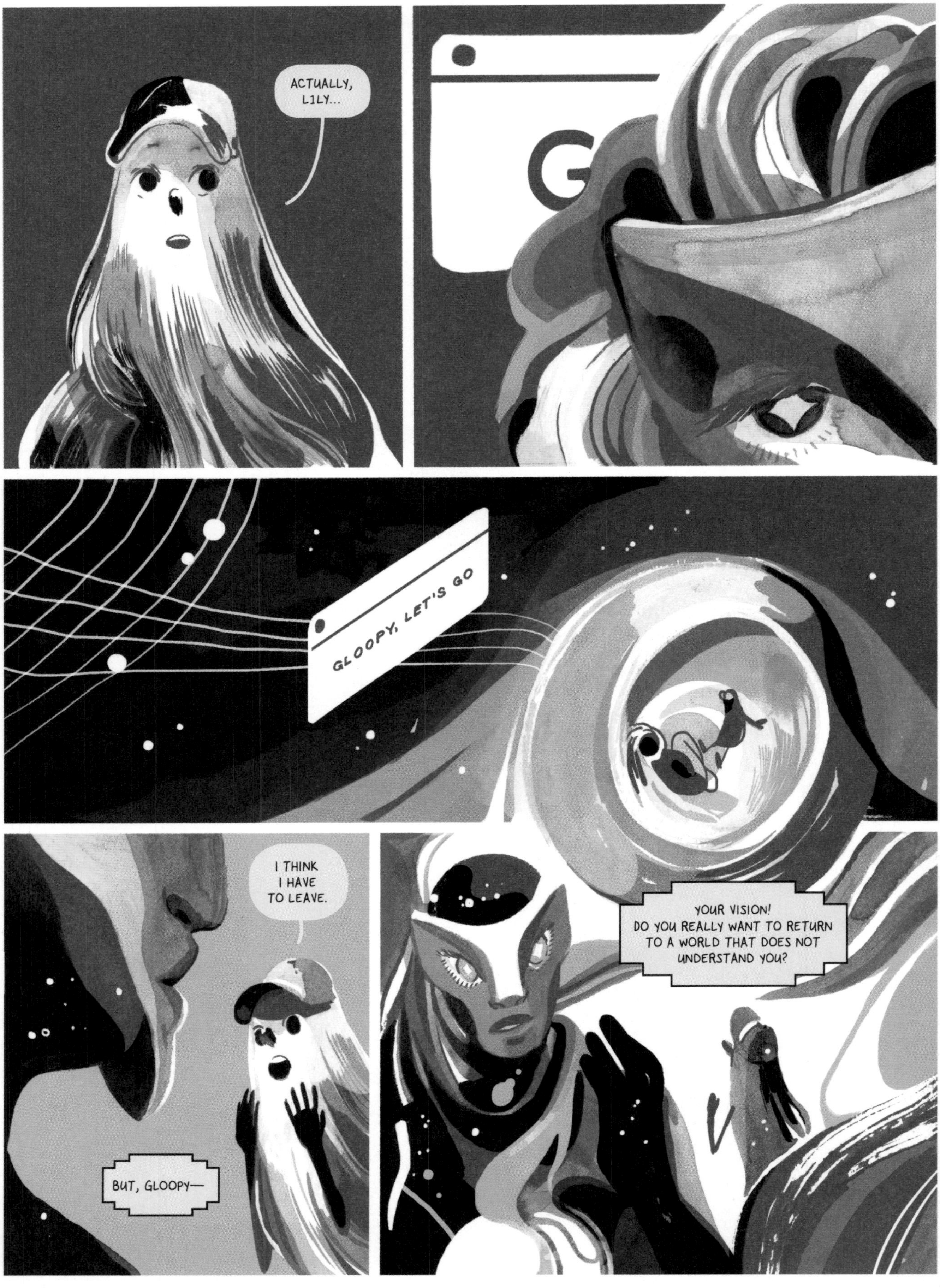
ACTUALLY, L1LY...
G
GLOOPY, LET'S GO
I THINK I HAVE TO LEAVE.
BUT, GLOOPY—
YOUR VISION! DO YOU REALLY WANT TO RETURN TO A WORLD THAT DOES NOT UNDERSTAND YOU?

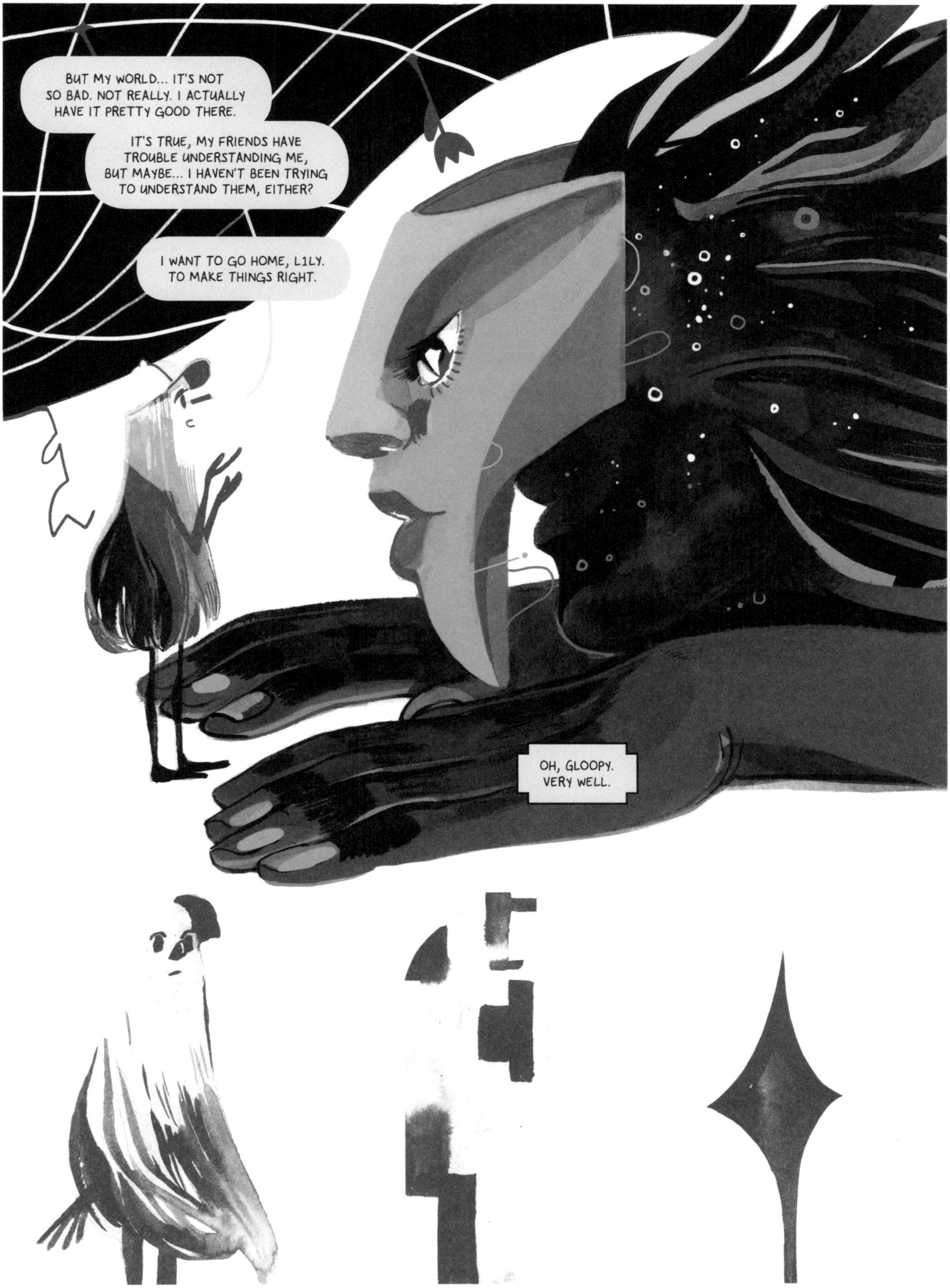
BUT MY WORLD... IT'S NOT SO BAD. NOT REALLY. I ACTUALLY HAVE IT PRETTY GOOD THERE.
IT'S TRUE, MY FRIENDS HAVE TROUBLE UNDERSTANDING ME, BUT MAYBE... I HAVEN'T BEEN TRYING TO UNDERSTAND THEM, EITHER?
I WANT TO GO HOME, L1LY. TO MAKE THINGS RIGHT.
OH, GLOOPY. VERY WELL.

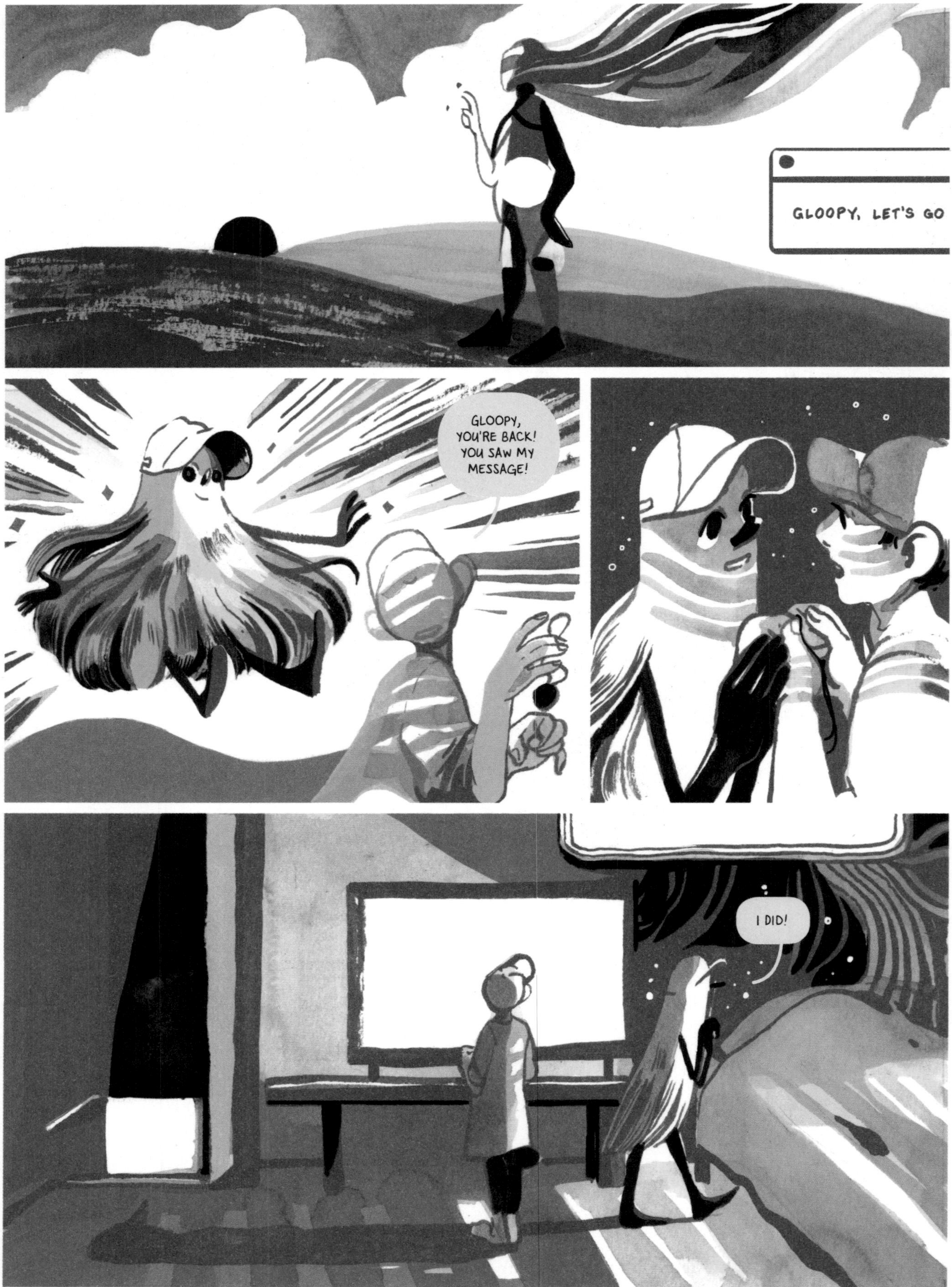
GLOOPY, LET'S GO
GLOOPY, YOU'RE BACK! YOU SAW MY MESSAGE!
I DID!

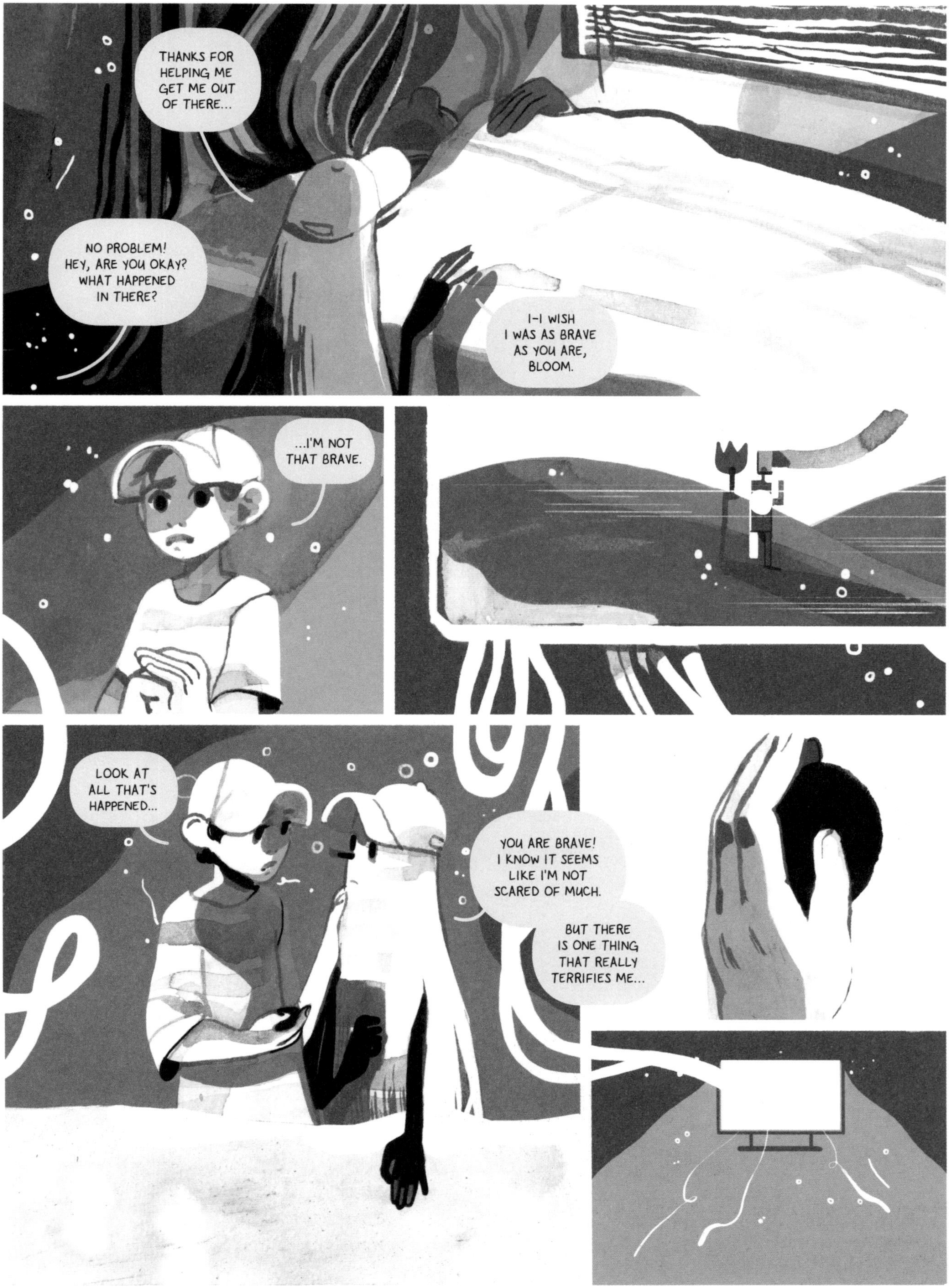
THANKS FOR HELPING ME GET ME OUT OF THERE...
NO PROBLEM! HEY, ARE YOU OKAY? WHAT HAPPENED IN THERE?
I-I WISH I WAS AS BRAVE AS YOU ARE, BLOOM.
...I'M NOT THAT BRAVE.
LOOK AT ALL THAT'S HAPPENED...
YOU ARE BRAVE! I KNOW IT SEEMS LIKE I'M NOT SCARED OF MUCH.
BUT THERE IS ONE THING THAT REALLY TERRIFIES ME...

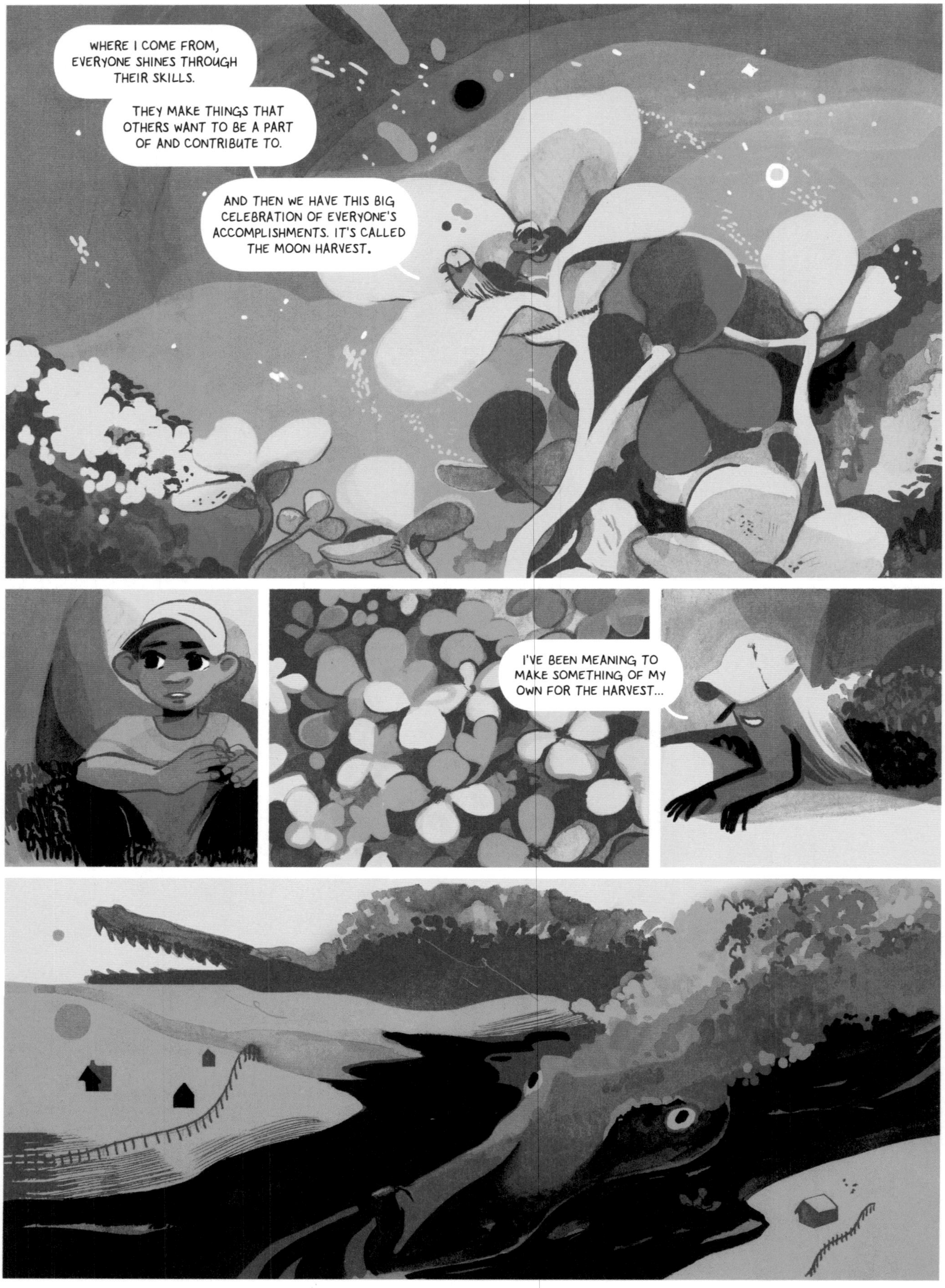
WHERE I COME FROM, EVERYONE SHINES THROUGH THEIR SKILLS.
THEY MAKE THINGS THAT OTHERS WANT TO BE A PART OF AND CONTRIBUTE TO.
AND THEN WE HAVE THIS BIG CELEBRATION OF EVERYONE'S ACCOMPLISHMENTS. IT'S CALLED THE MOON HARVEST.
I'VE BEEN MEANING TO MAKE SOMETHING OF MY OWN FOR THE HARVEST...

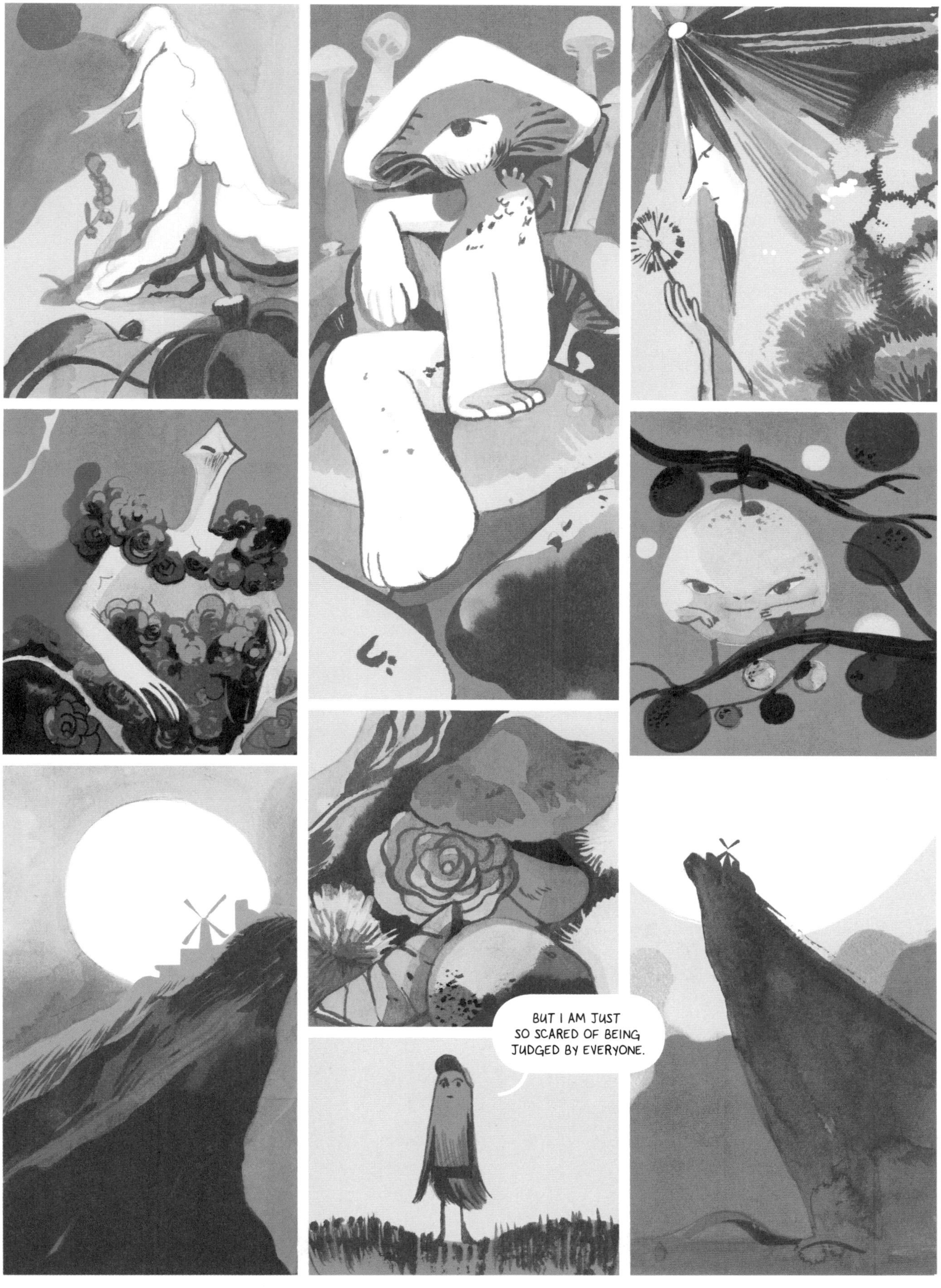
BUT I AM JUST SO SCARED OF BEING JUDGED BY EVERYONE.

I JUST CAN'T SEE ANYTHING I MAKE WORKING OUT.

I'VE TRIED TO HELP OTHERS WITH THEIR WORK, BUT I REALLY WANT TO MAKE SOMETHING OF MY OWN!

I DON'T THINK I'LL EVER REALLY BE ACCEPTED.

HOW DO YOU KNOW THAT?

I'M SURE YOUR FRIENDS KNOW THERE'S SO MUCH MORE TO YOU THAN WHAT YOU MAKE.

THANKS BLOOM, BUT I'M NOT SO SURE...

...I GUESS THAT'S THE LEAST OF MY PROBLEMS RIGHT NOW, THOUGH!

LET'S GET GOING!

WE'VE GOTTA GET YOU BACK TO THAT LAKE!

NOT AGAIN!

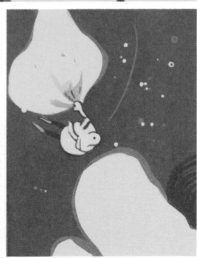

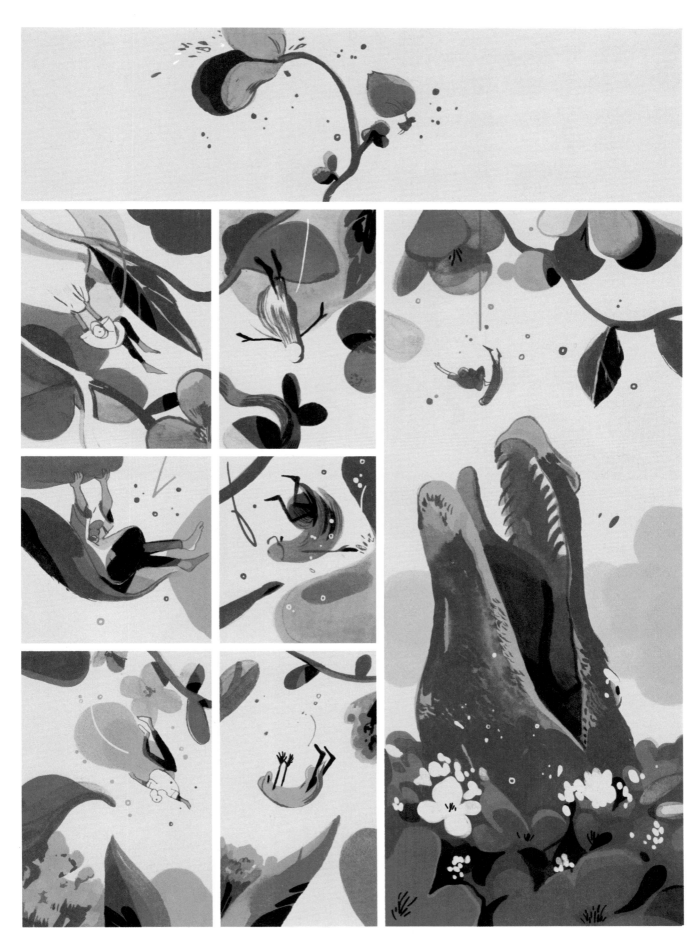

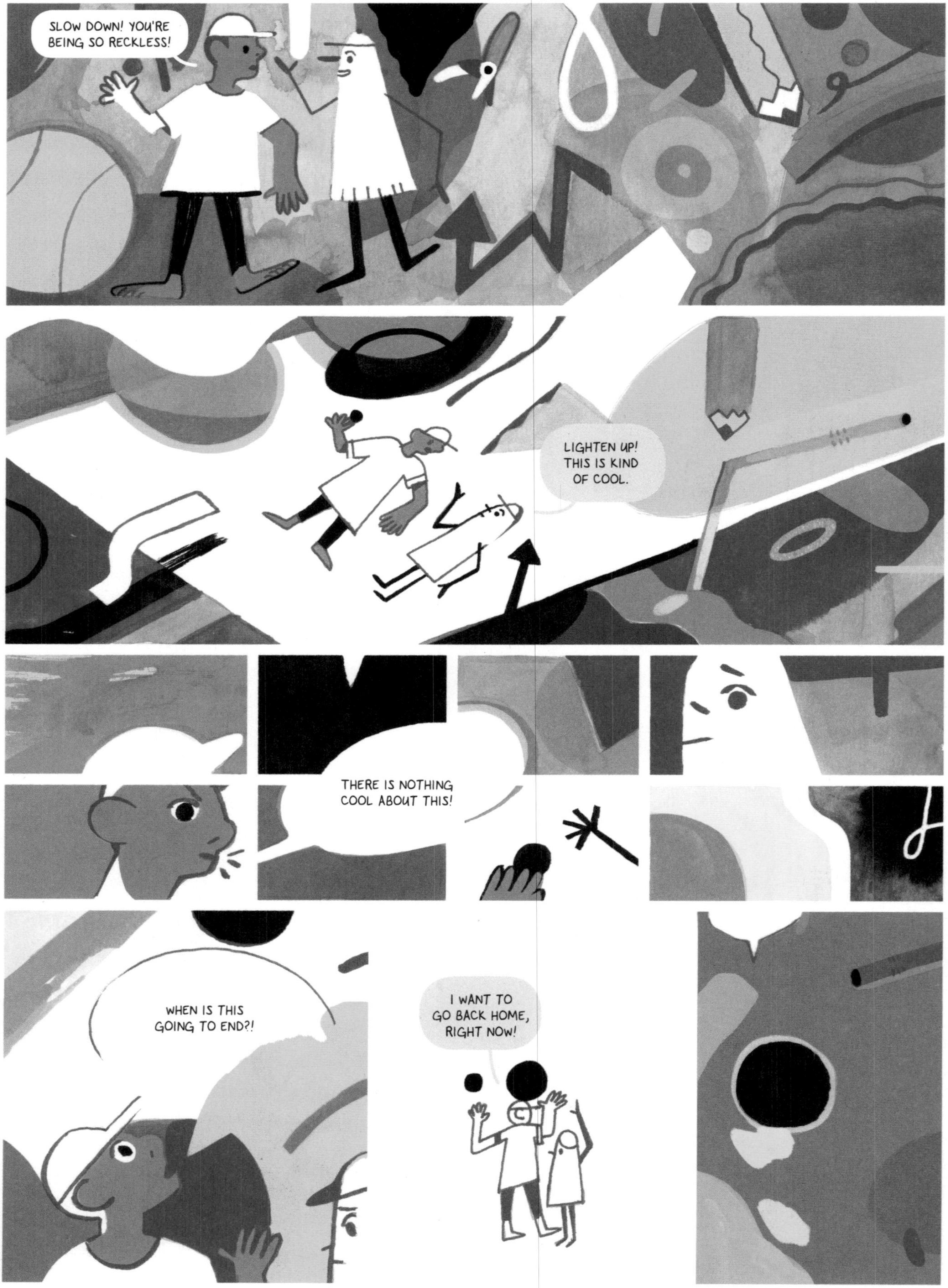
SLOW DOWN! YOU'RE BEING SO RECKLESS!
LIGHTEN UP! THIS IS KIND OF COOL.
THERE IS NOTHING COOL ABOUT THIS!
WHEN IS THIS GOING TO END?!
I WANT TO GO BACK HOME, RIGHT NOW!

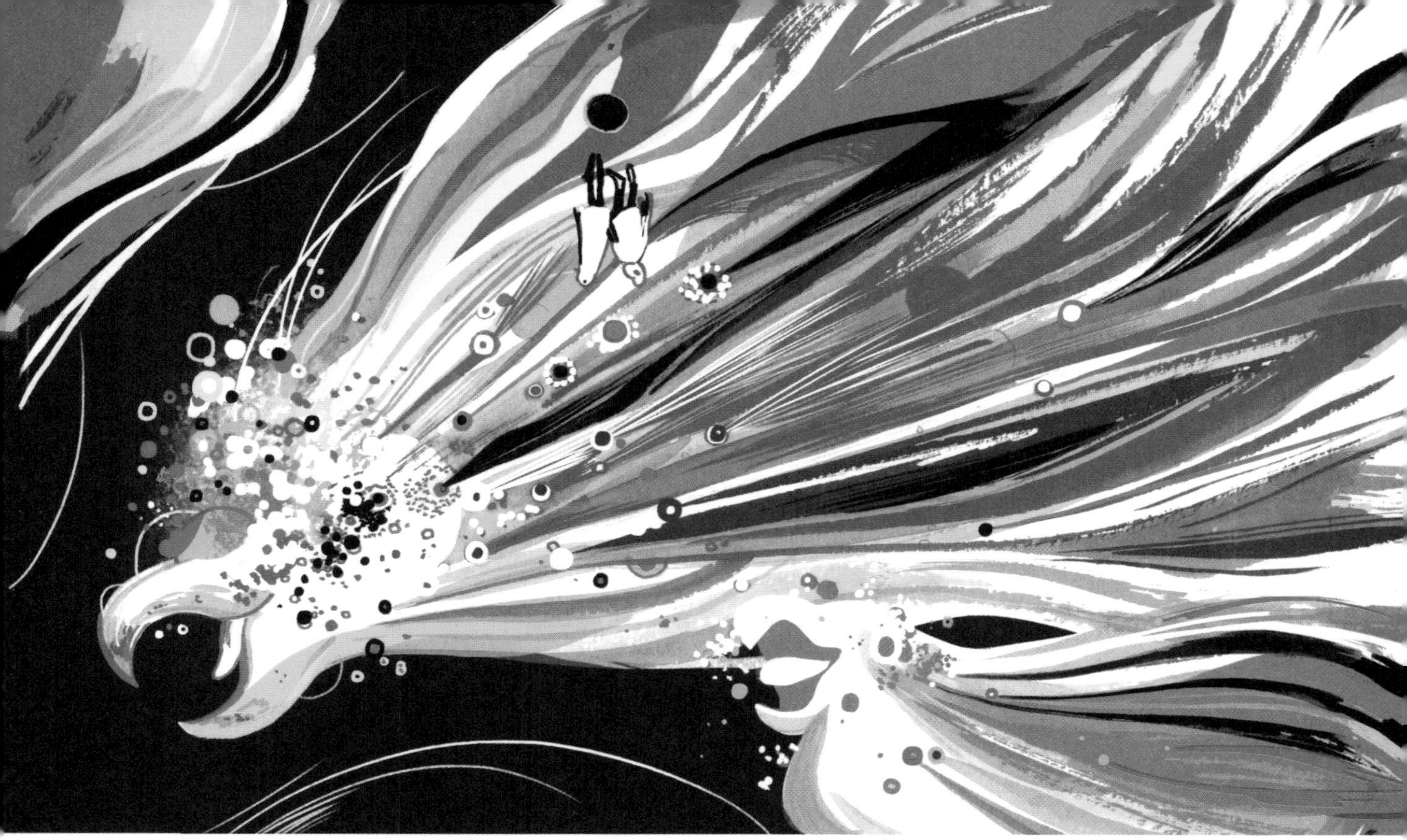

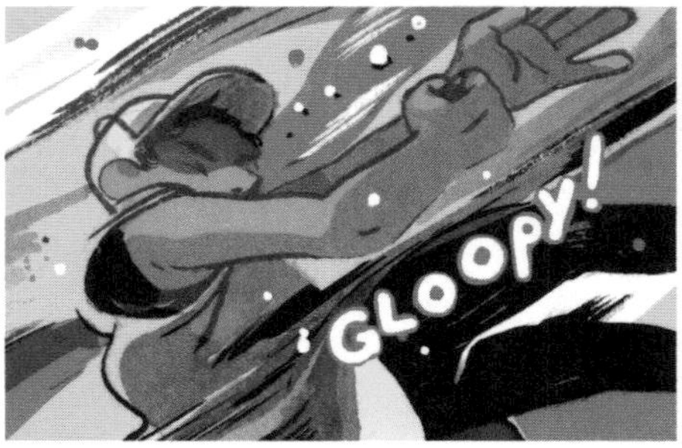
GLOOPY!

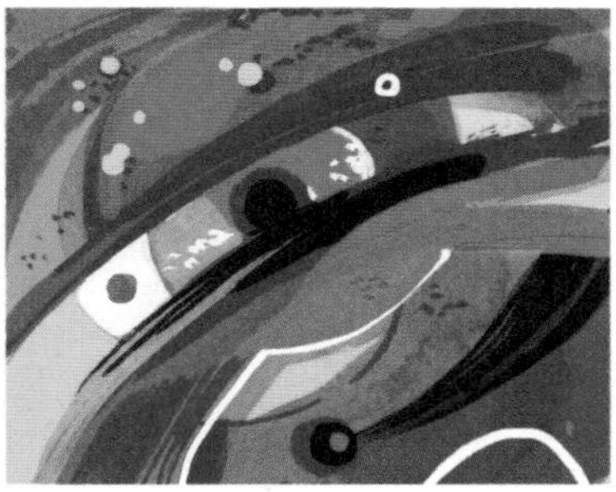

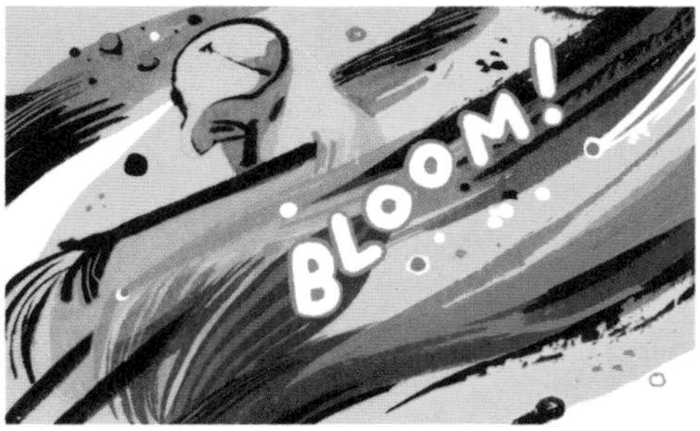
BLOOM!

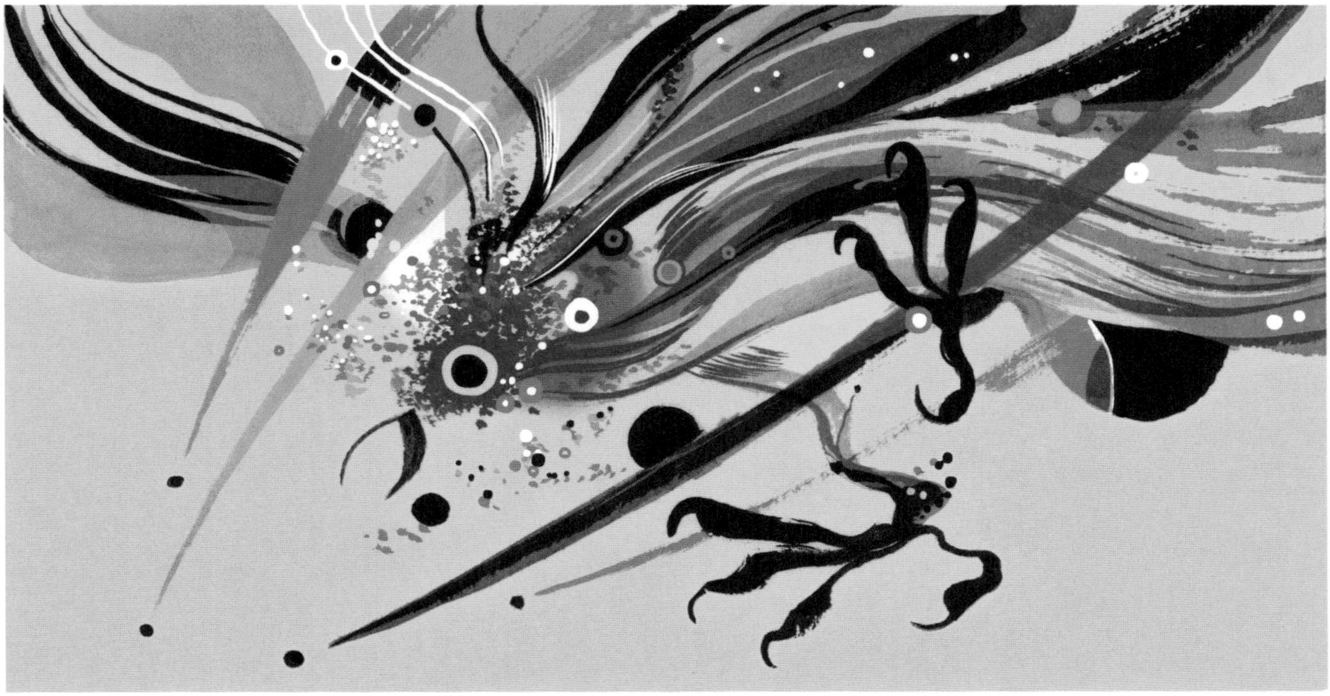

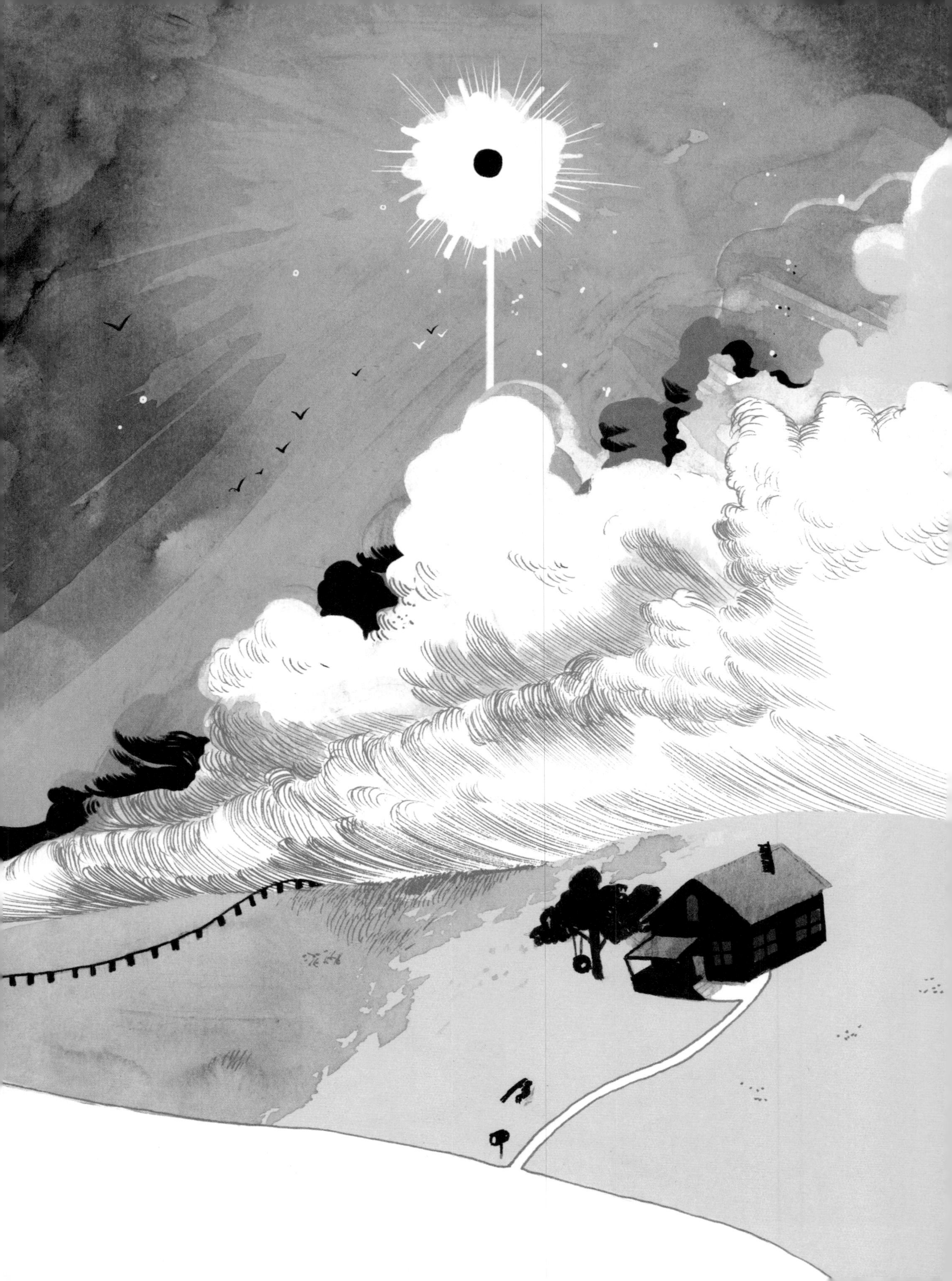

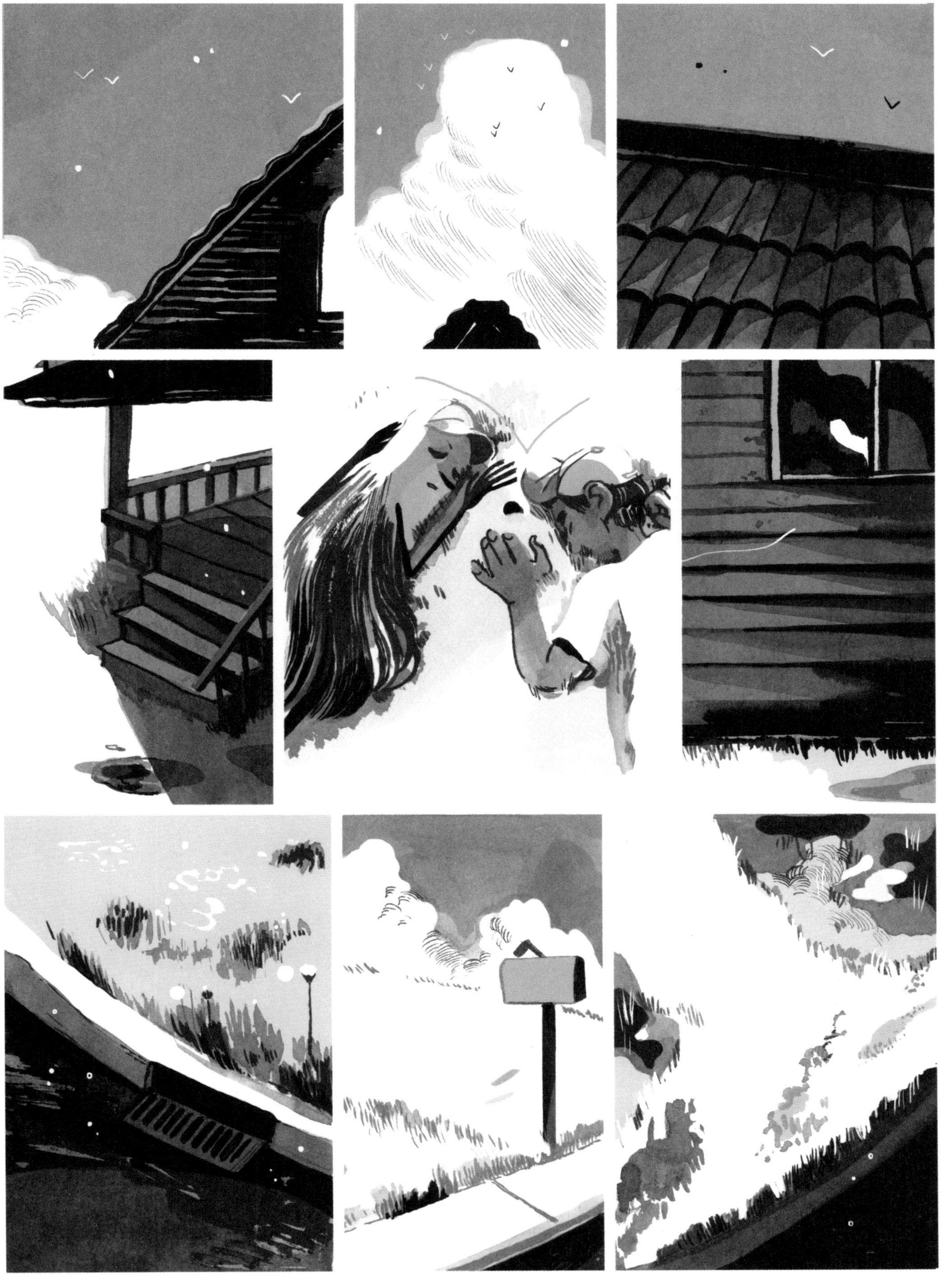

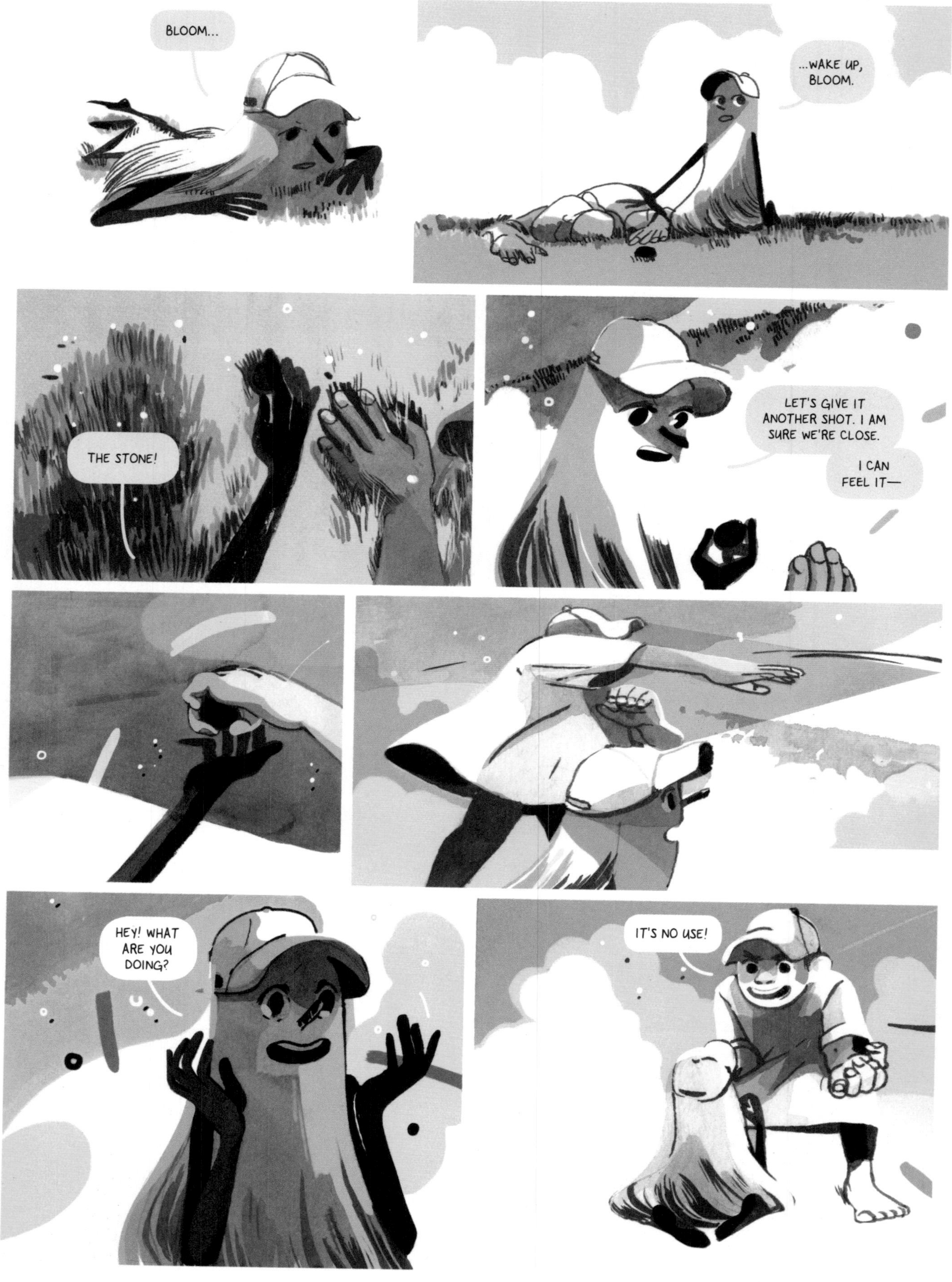
BLOOM...
...WAKE UP, BLOOM.
THE STONE!
LET'S GIVE IT ANOTHER SHOT. I AM SURE WE'RE CLOSE.
I CAN FEEL IT—
HEY! WHAT ARE YOU DOING?
IT'S NO USE!

WE KEEP TRYING, BUT LET'S BE HONEST.

WE HAVE NO IDEA HOW TO GET BACK. I SHOULD NEVER HAVE LEFT IN THE FIRST PLACE. AND NOW I'VE THROWN AWAY THE LAST THING BEE GAVE TO ME. AGAIN.

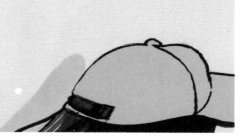

DON'T GO CHASING AFTER THAT STUPID STONE!

THERE'S NO POINT! WE'RE STUCK HERE.

IF YOU WANT TO KEEP GOING, FINE. BUT I'M DONE.

HOW WILL WE EVER KNOW IF WE JUST STOP TRYING?

ISN'T THIS THING IMPORTANT TO YOU?

ARE YOU??

YOU KEEP GETTING US INTO MORE TROUBLE AND YOU DON'T SEEM TO CARE ABOUT GETTING HOME!

LISTEN TO ME, I'M YOUR FRIEND.

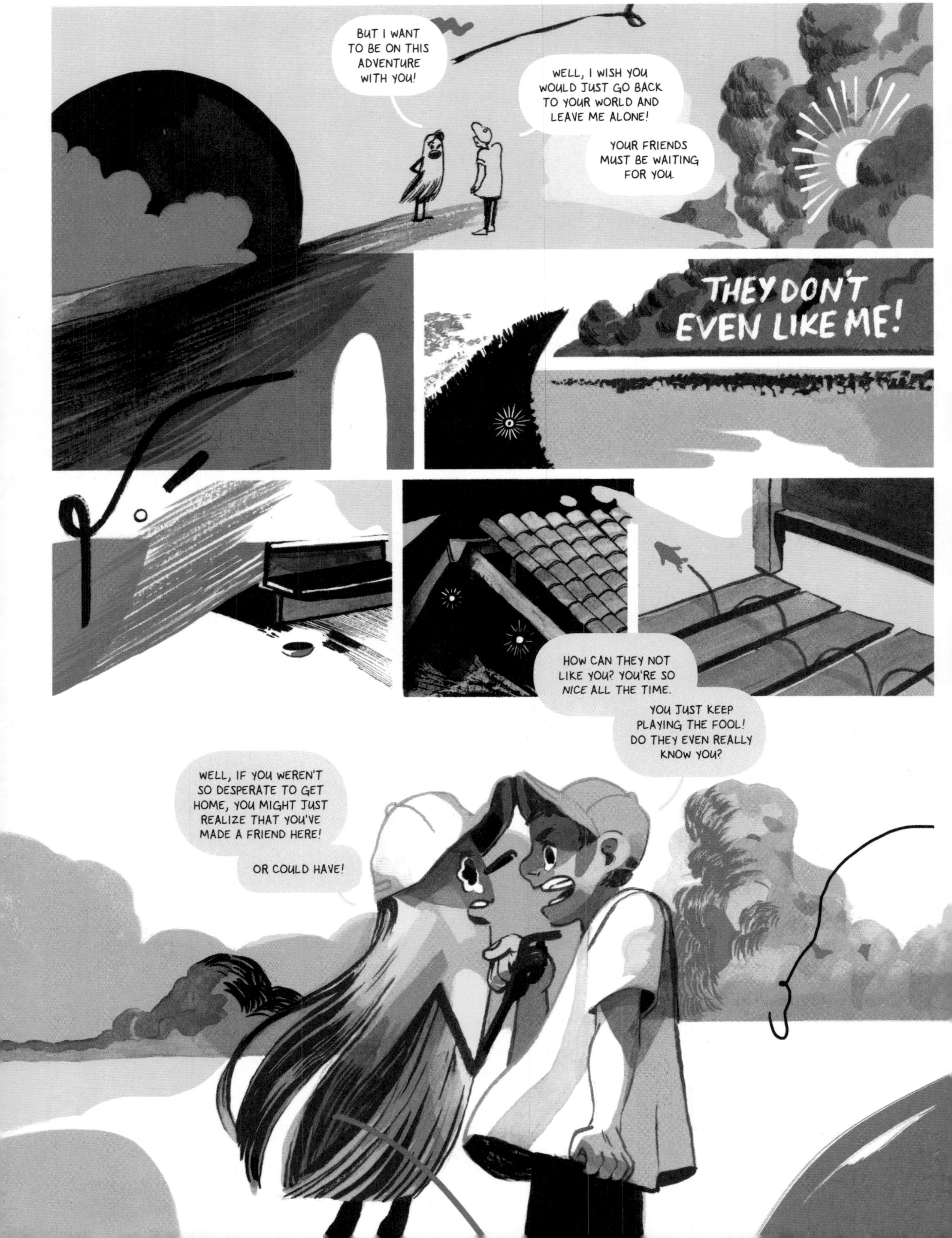
BUT I WANT TO BE ON THIS ADVENTURE WITH YOU!
WELL, I WISH YOU WOULD JUST GO BACK TO YOUR WORLD AND LEAVE ME ALONE!
YOUR FRIENDS MUST BE WAITING FOR YOU.
THEY DON'T EVEN LIKE ME!
HOW CAN THEY NOT LIKE YOU? YOU'RE SO *NICE* ALL THE TIME.
YOU JUST KEEP PLAYING THE FOOL! DO THEY EVEN REALLY KNOW YOU?
WELL, IF YOU WEREN'T SO DESPERATE TO GET HOME, YOU MIGHT JUST REALIZE THAT YOU'VE MADE A FRIEND HERE!
OR COULD HAVE!

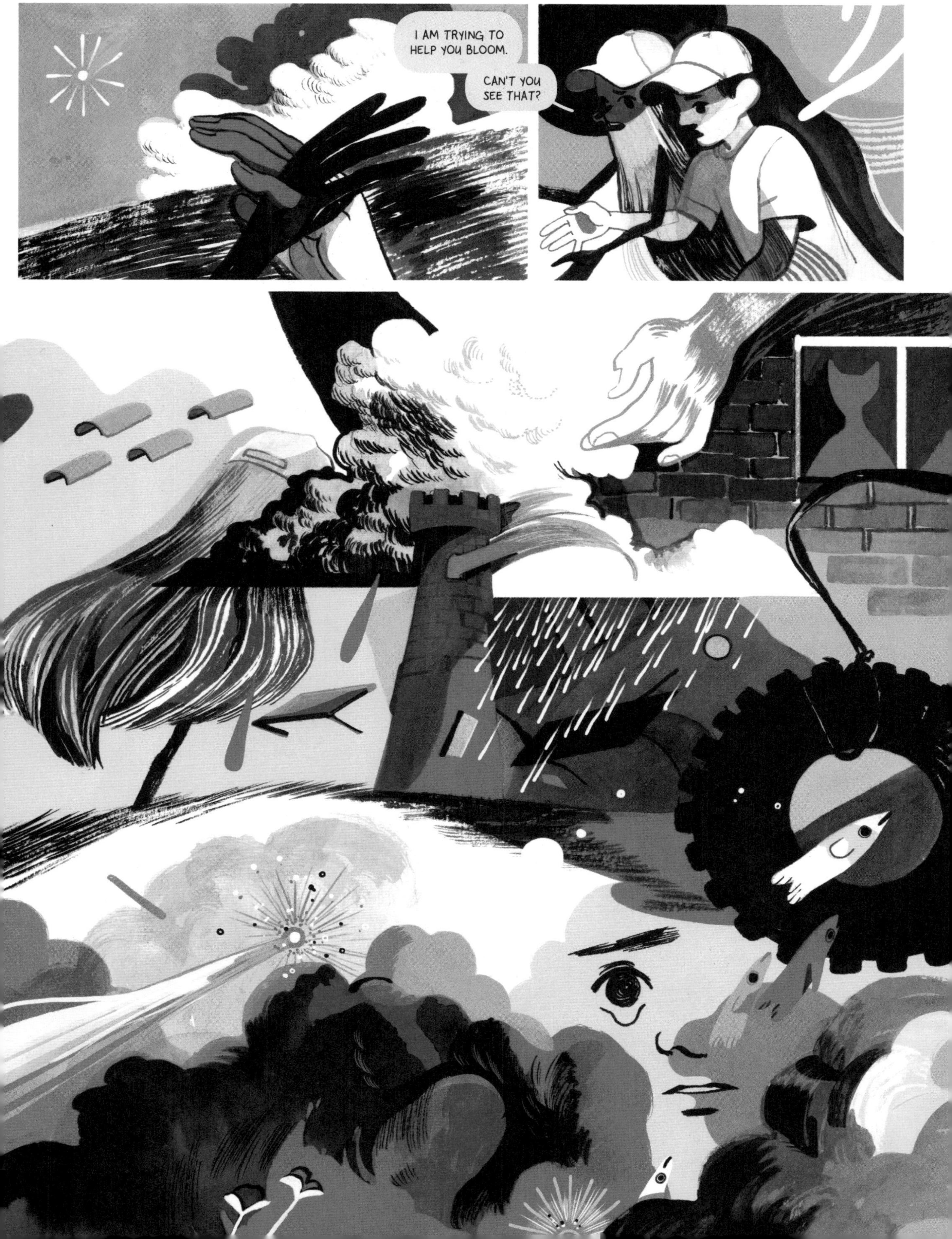
I AM TRYING TO HELP YOU BLOOM.
CAN'T YOU SEE THAT?

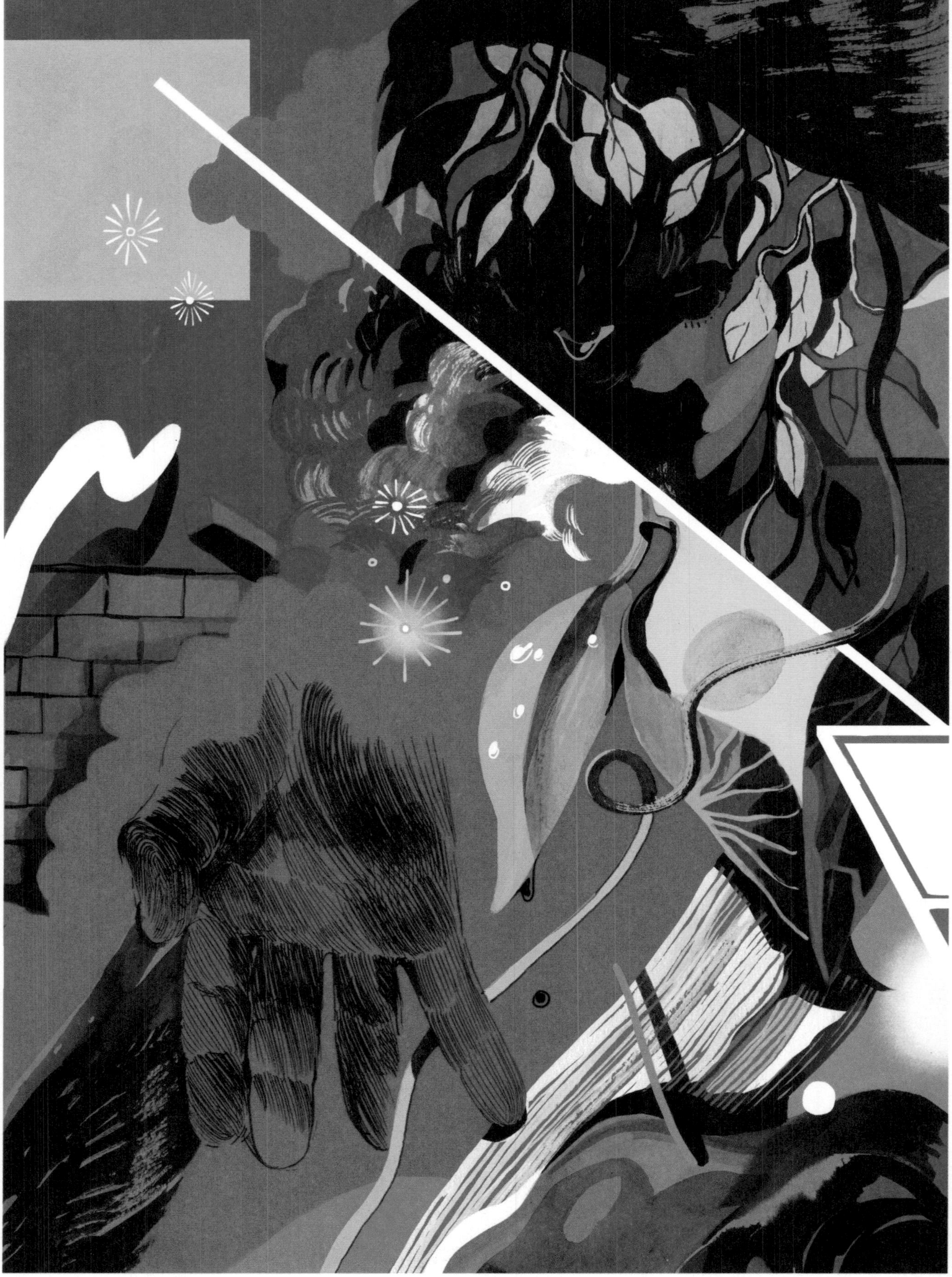

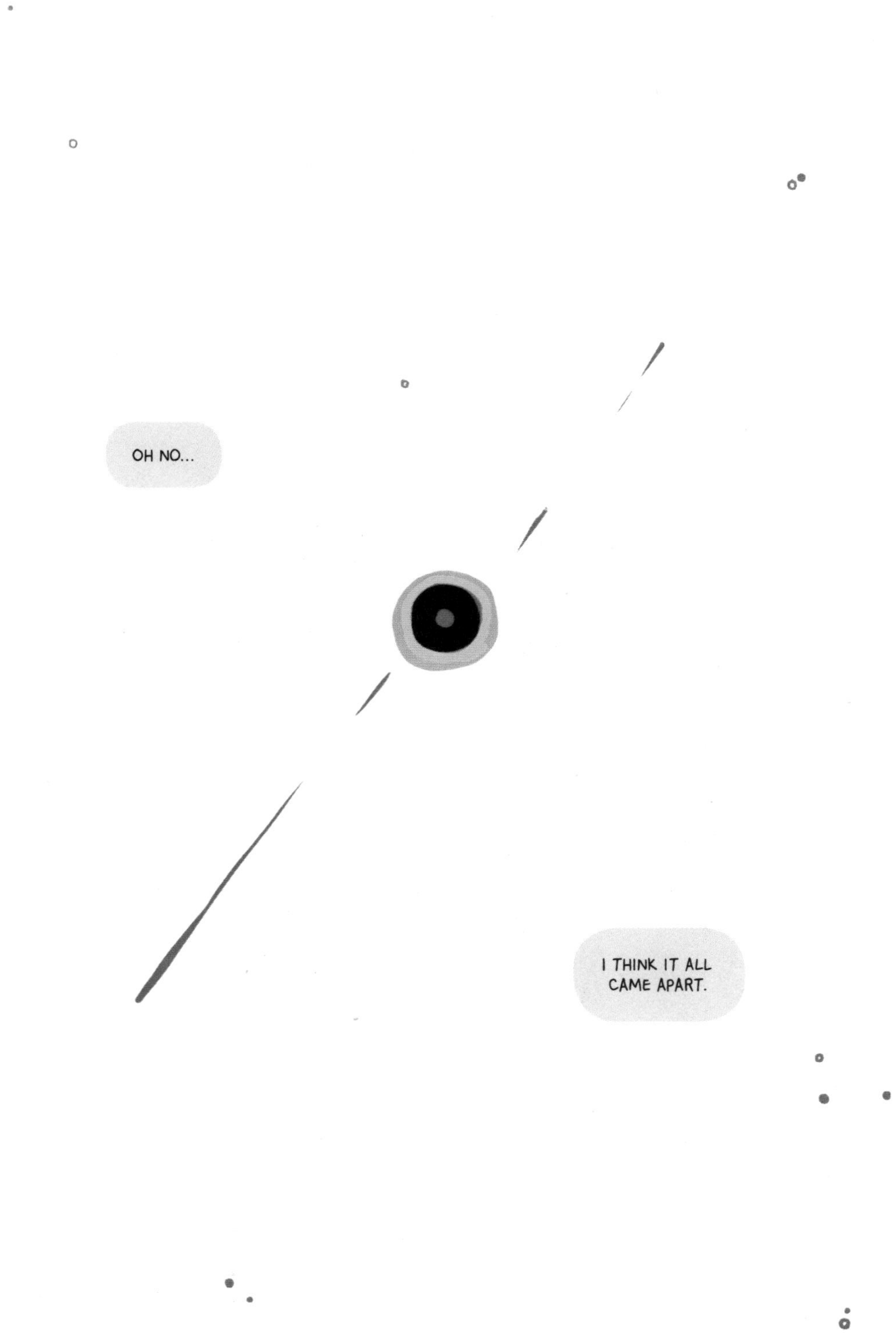
OH NO...
I THINK IT ALL CAME APART.

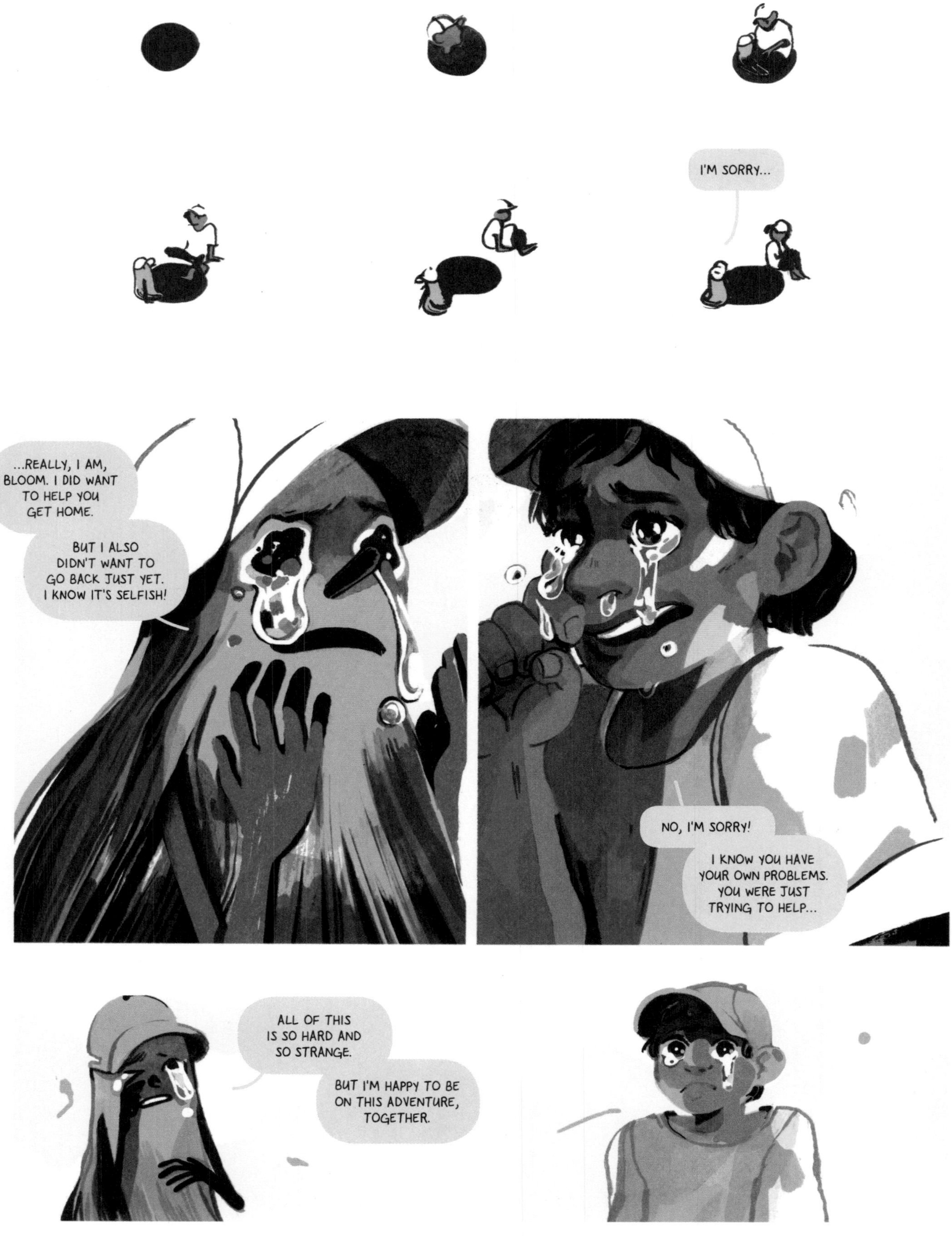
I'M SORRY...
...REALLY, I AM, BLOOM. I DID WANT TO HELP YOU GET HOME.
BUT I ALSO DIDN'T WANT TO GO BACK JUST YET. I KNOW IT'S SELFISH!
NO, I'M SORRY!
I KNOW YOU HAVE YOUR OWN PROBLEMS. YOU WERE JUST TRYING TO HELP...
ALL OF THIS IS SO HARD AND SO STRANGE.
BUT I'M HAPPY TO BE ON THIS ADVENTURE, TOGETHER.

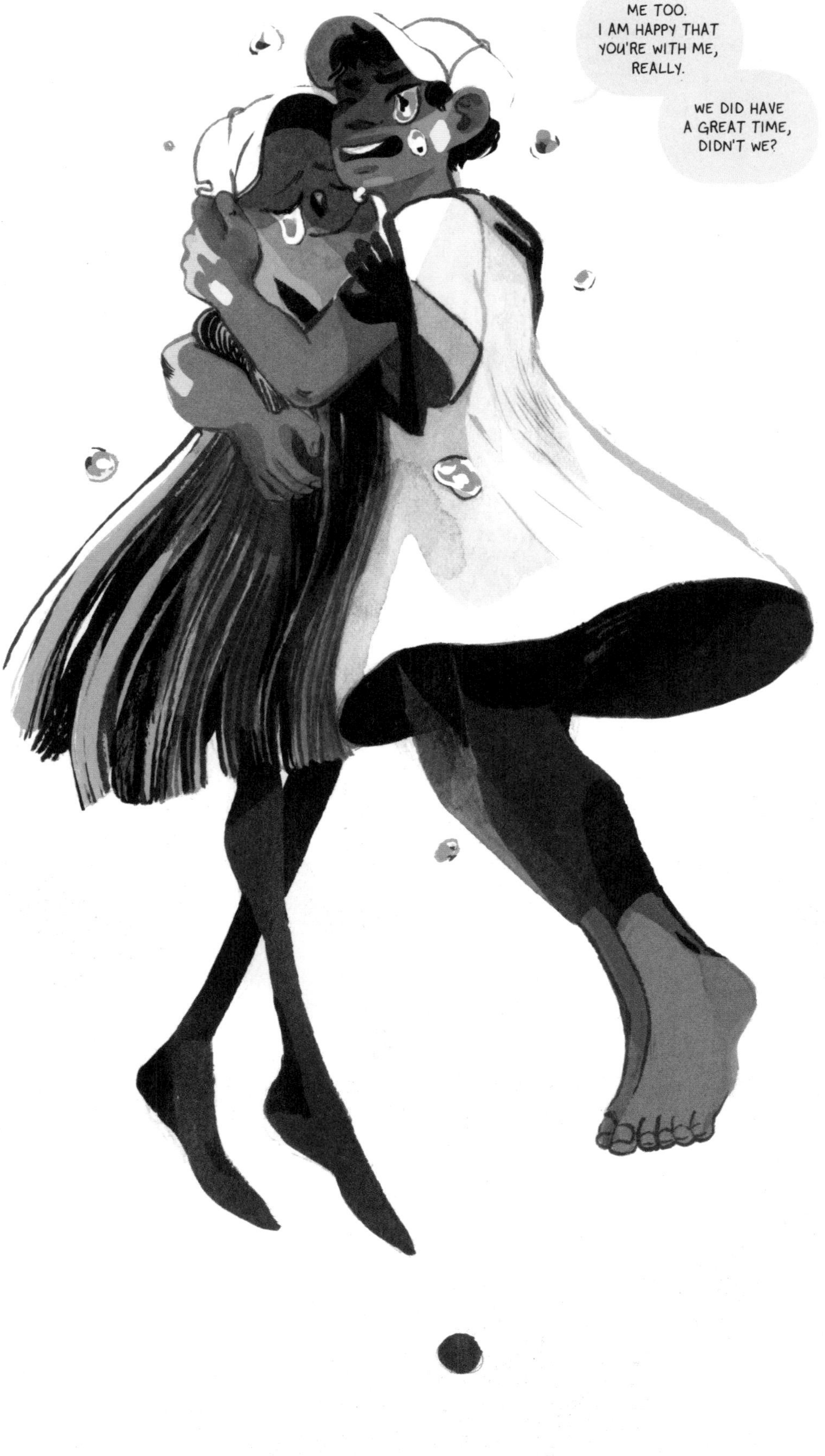
ME TOO. I AM HAPPY THAT YOU'RE WITH ME, REALLY.
WE DID HAVE A GREAT TIME, DIDN'T WE?

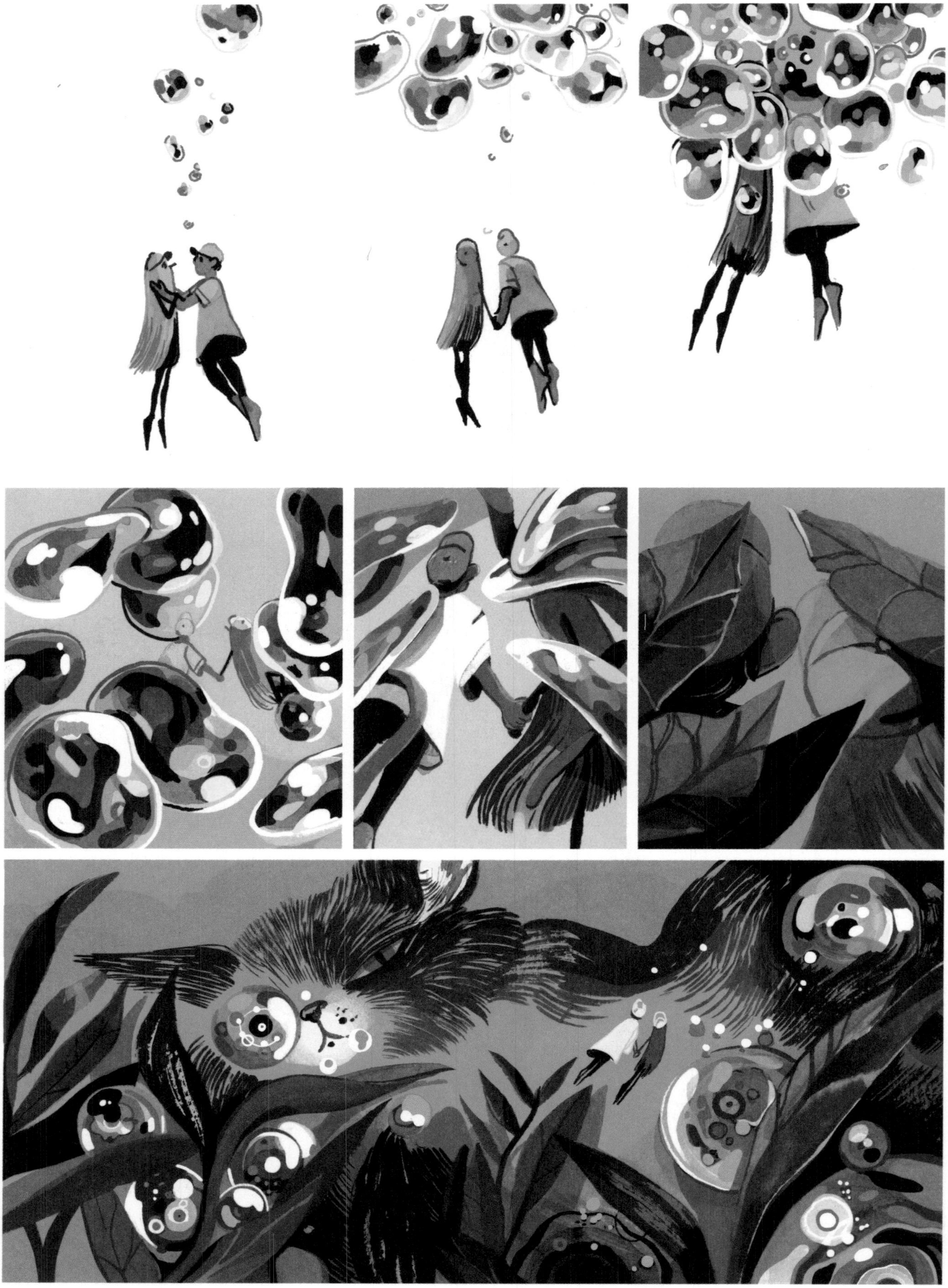

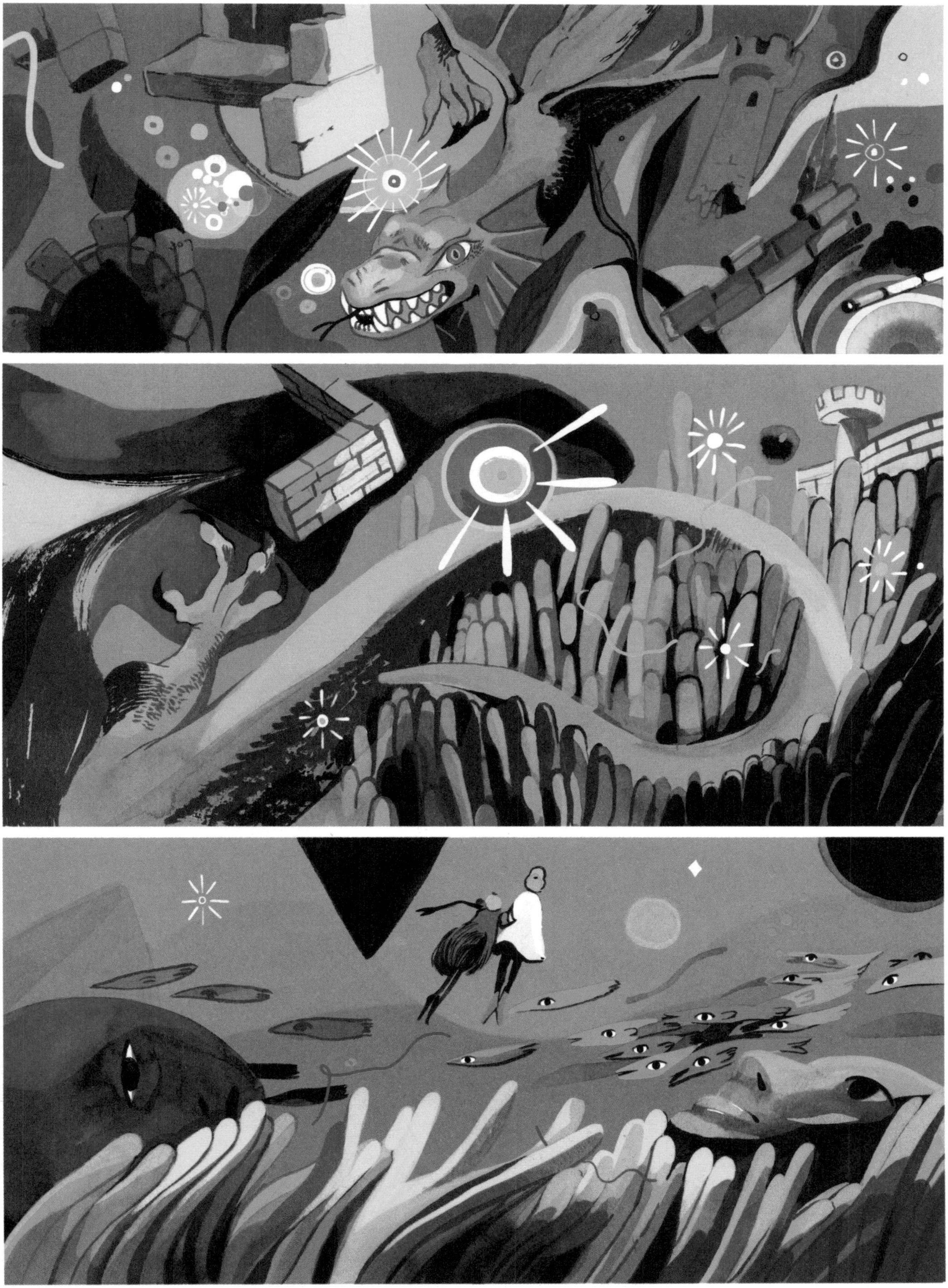

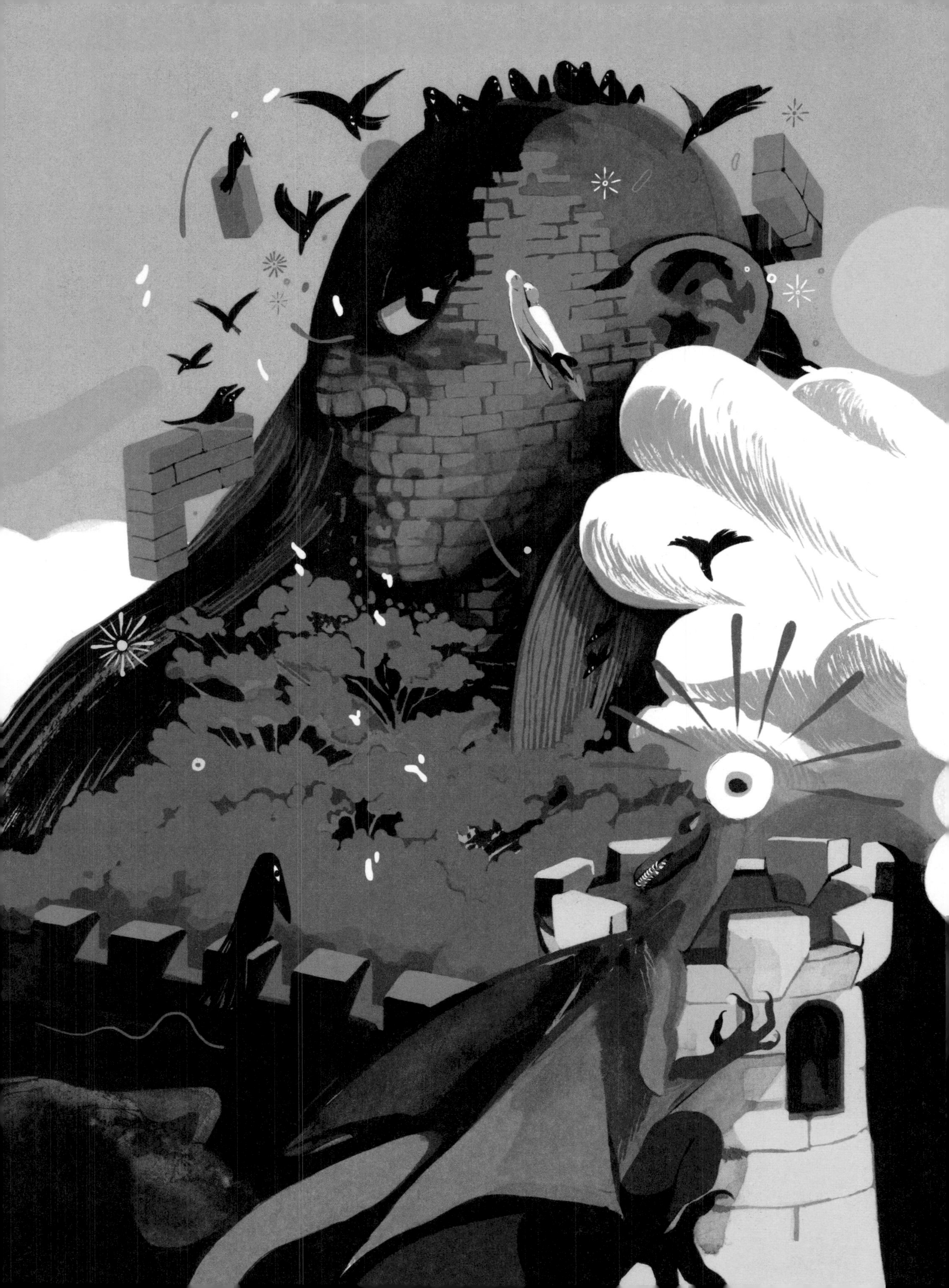

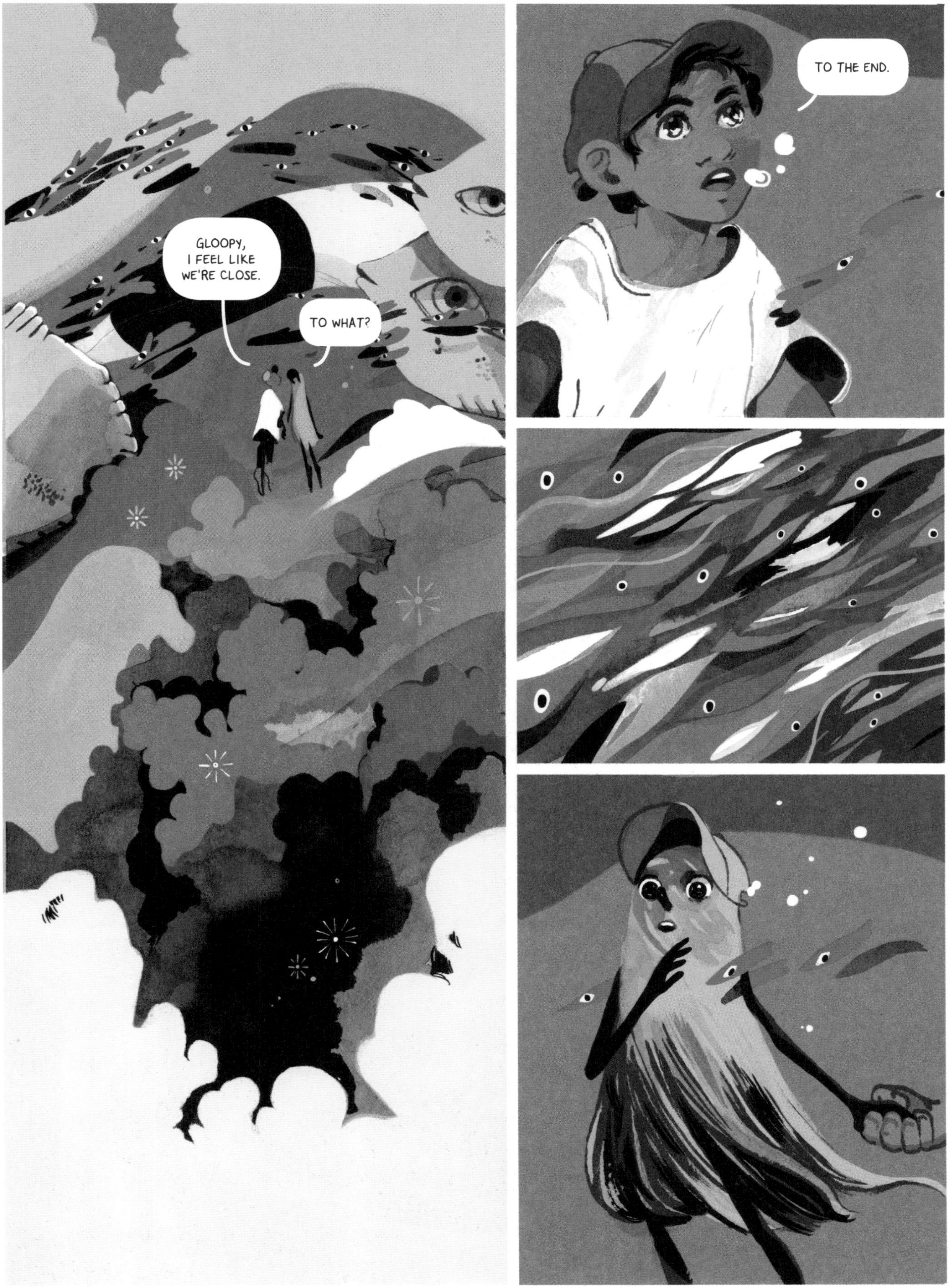
GLOOPY, I FEEL LIKE WE'RE CLOSE.
TO WHAT?
TO THE END.

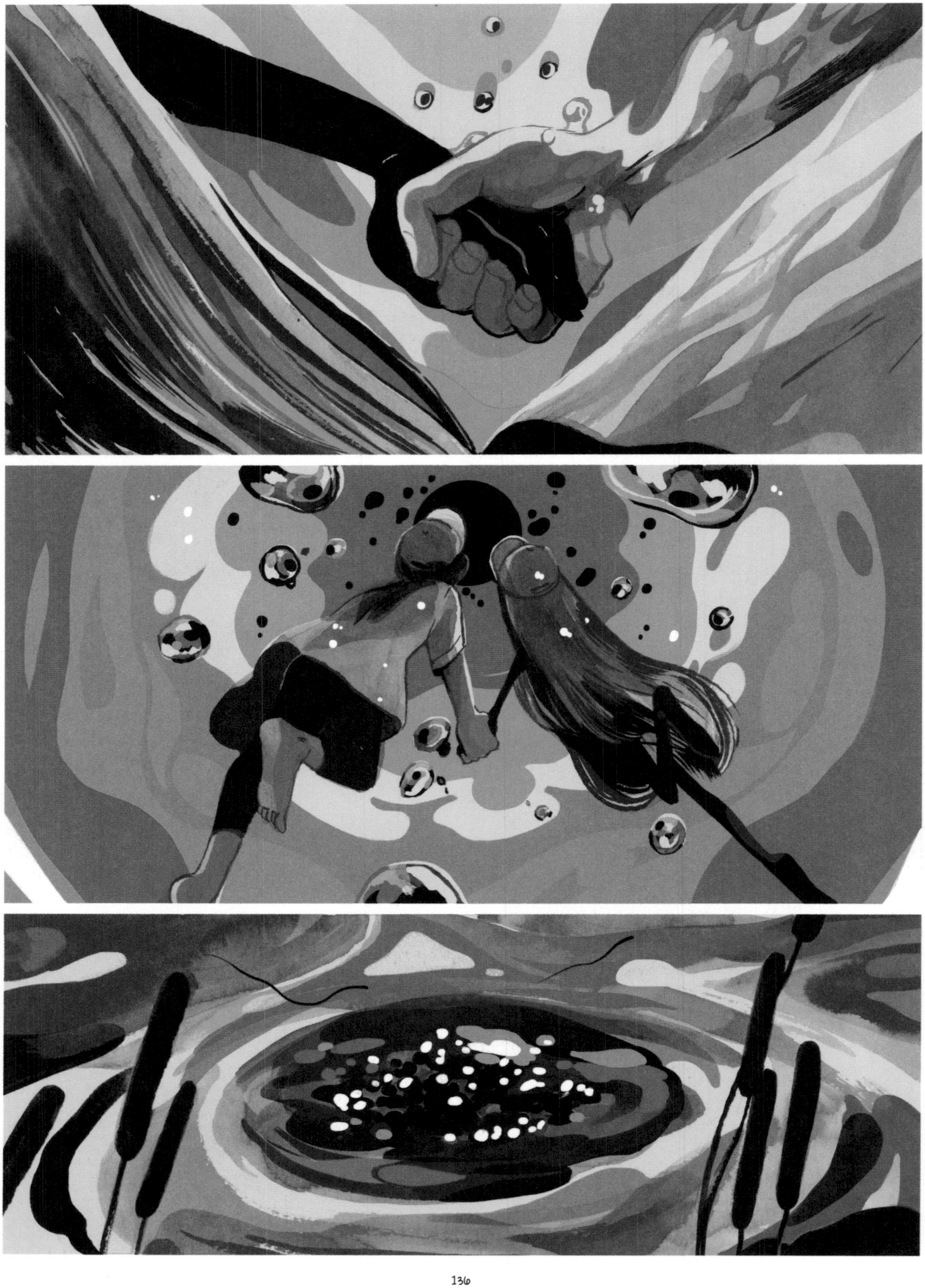

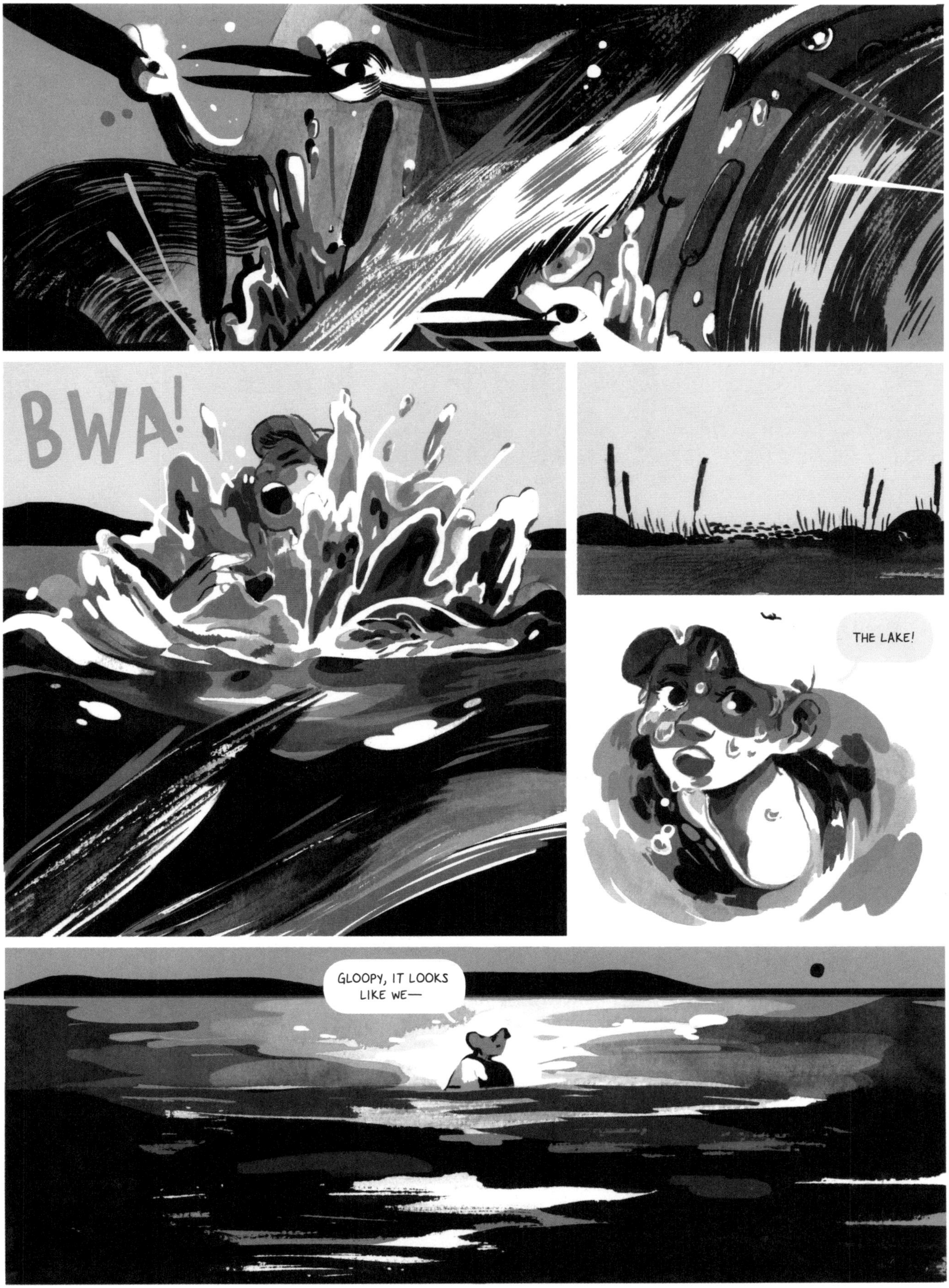
BWA!
THE LAKE!
GLOOPY, IT LOOKS LIKE WE—

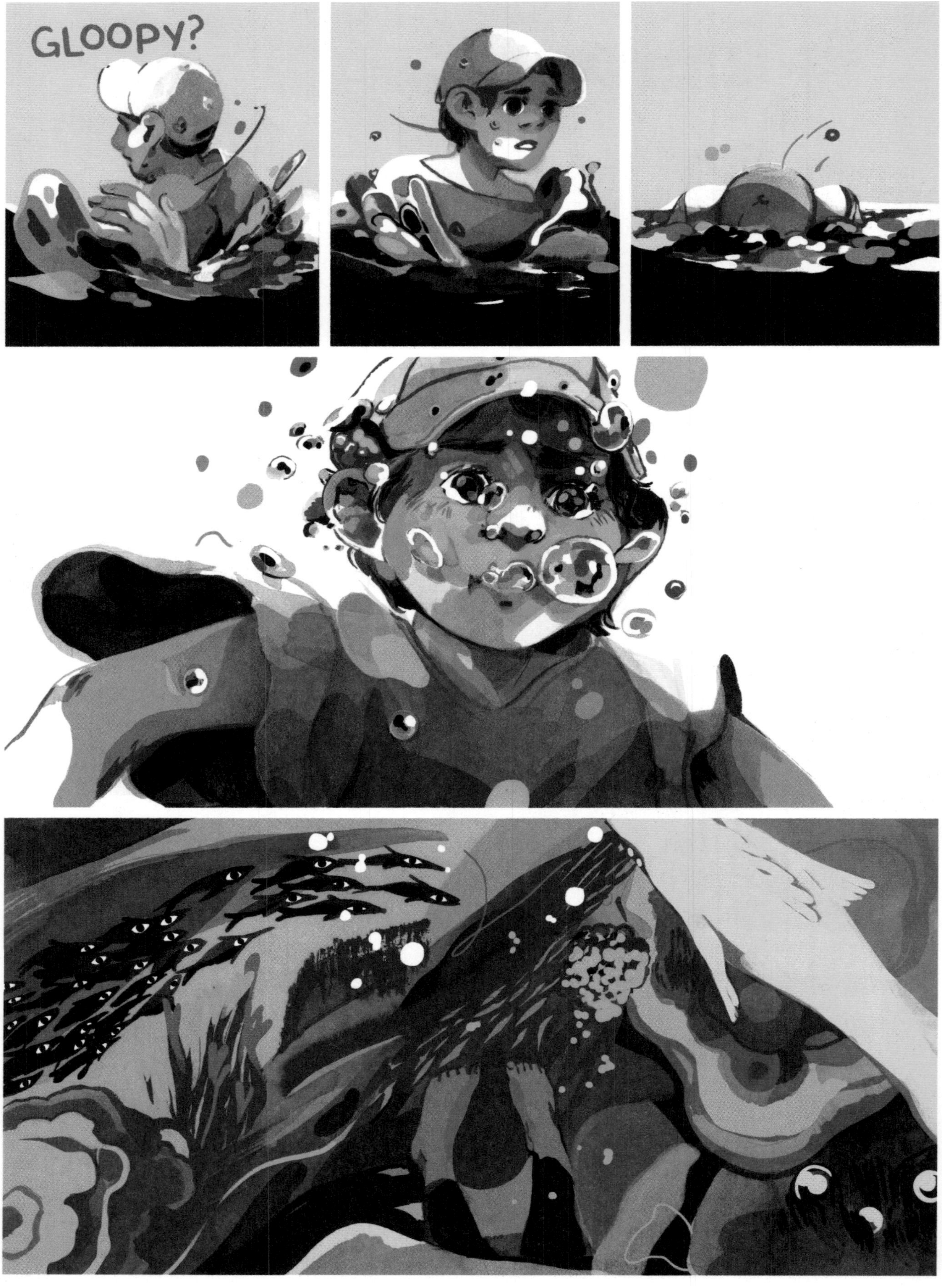
GLOOPY?

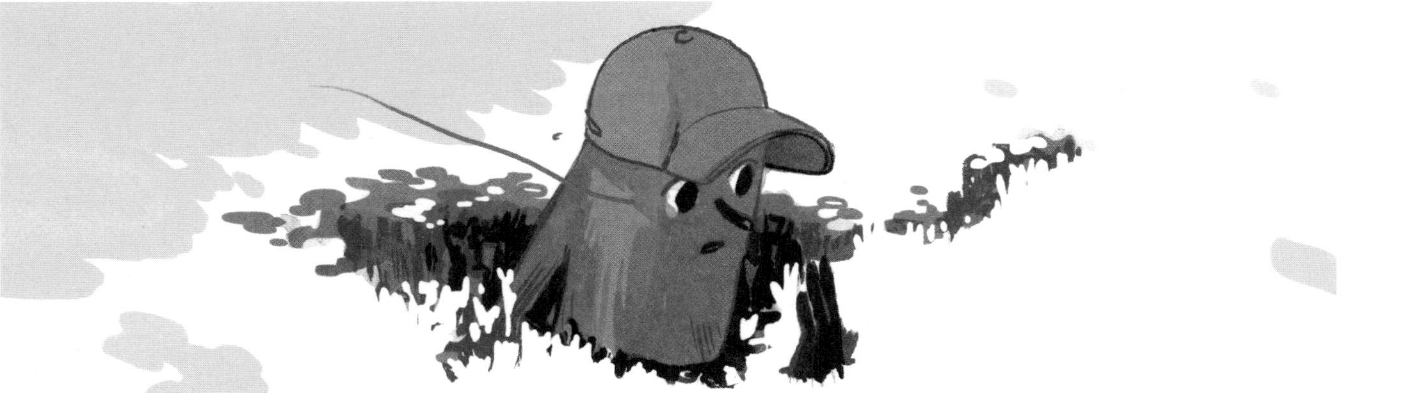

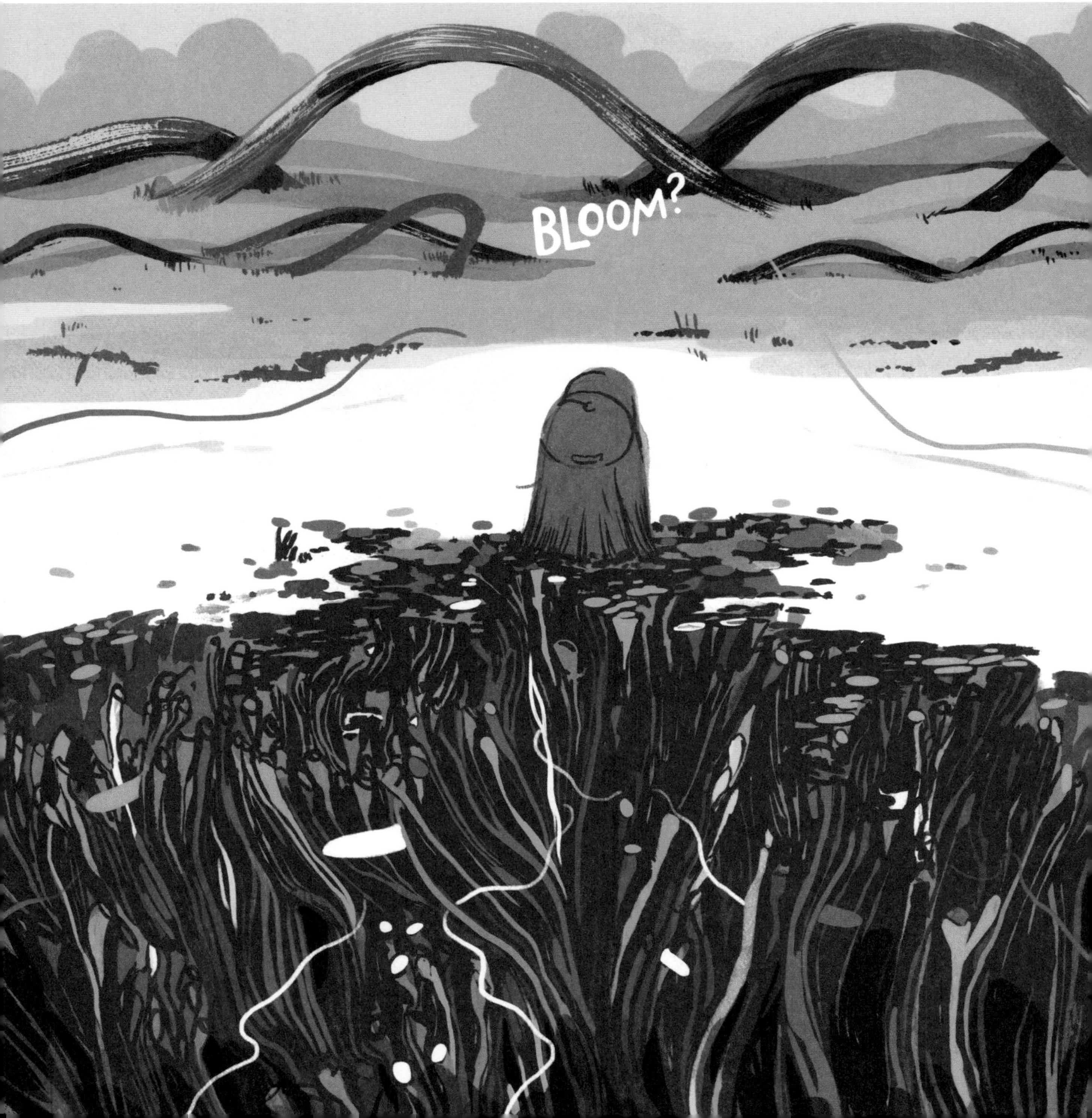
BLOOM?

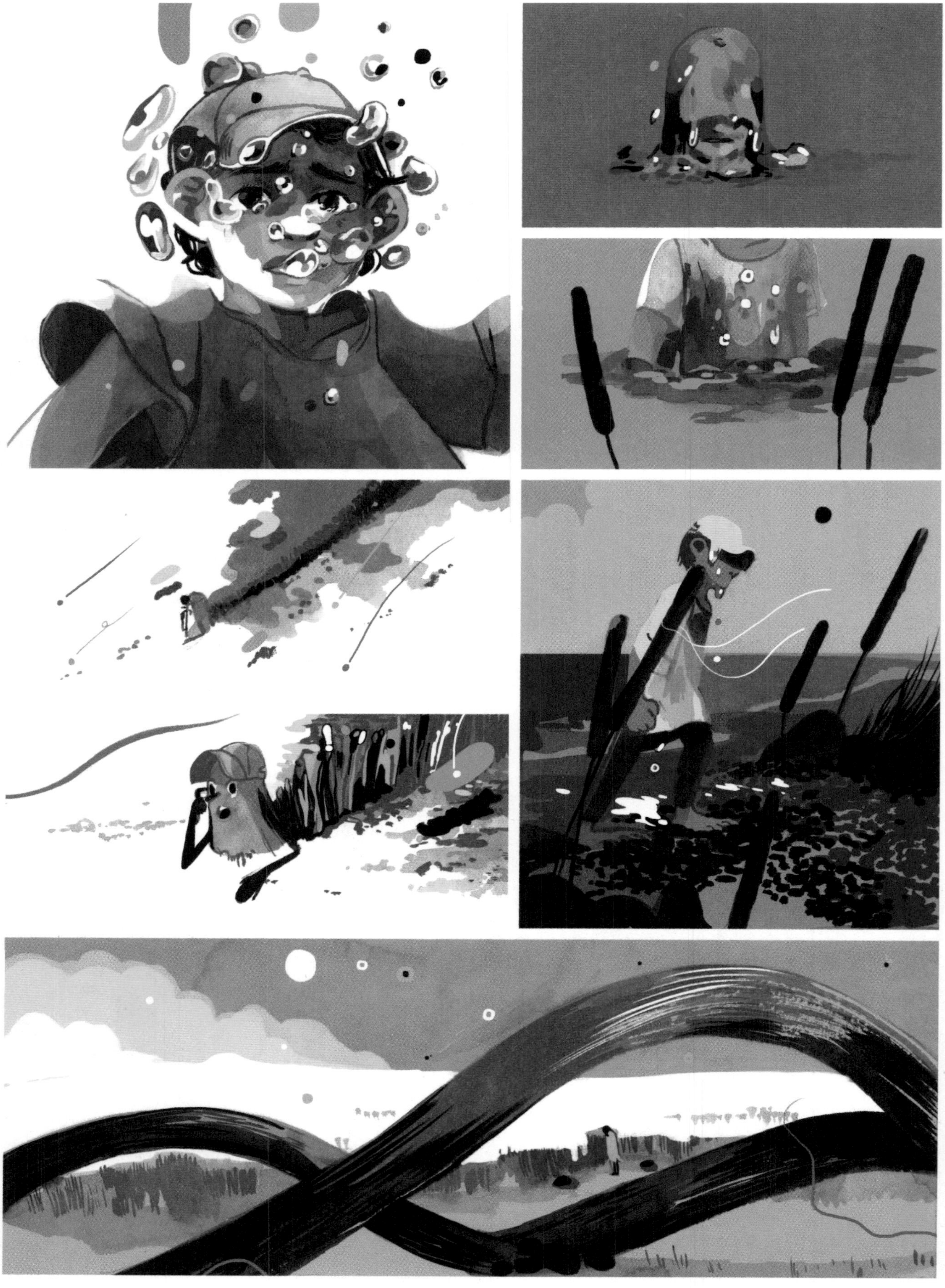

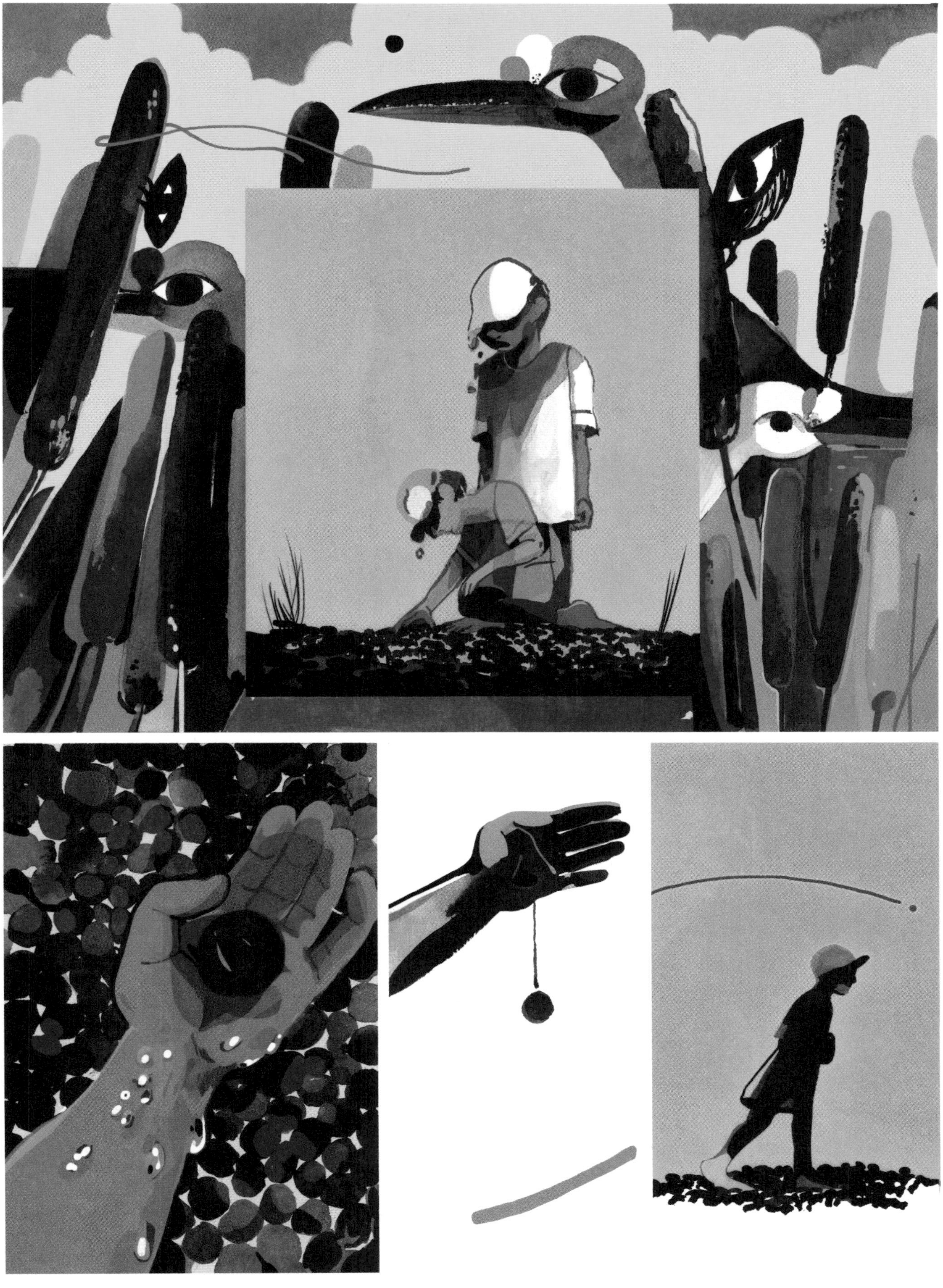

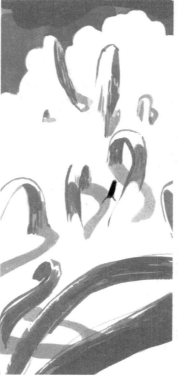
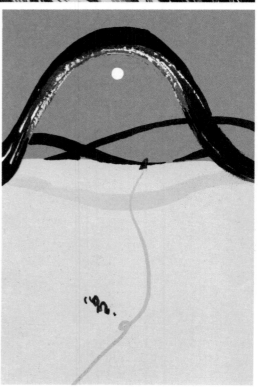

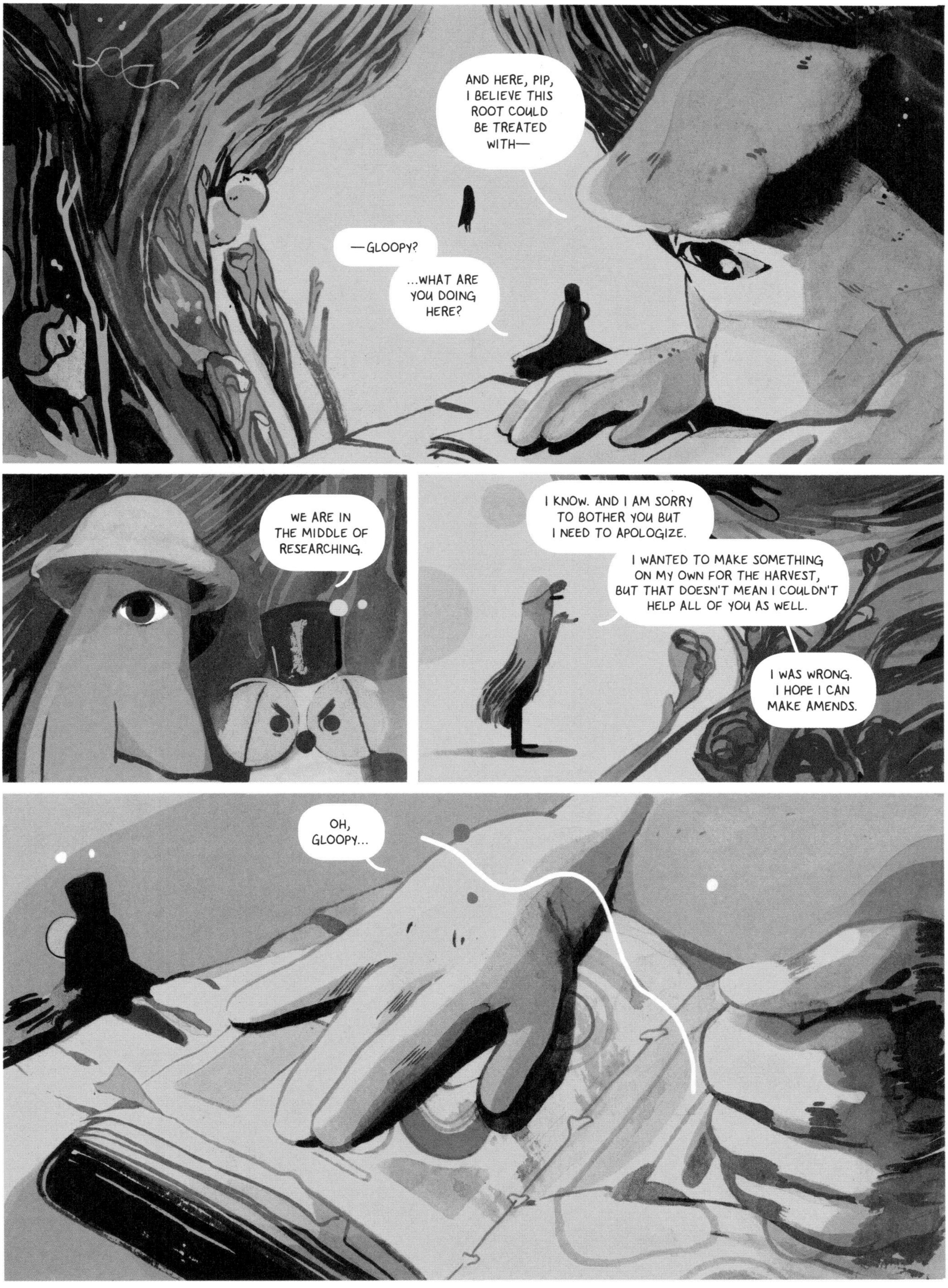
AND HERE, PIP, I BELIEVE THIS ROOT COULD BE TREATED WITH—
—GLOOPY?
...WHAT ARE YOU DOING HERE?
WE ARE IN THE MIDDLE OF RESEARCHING.
I KNOW. AND I AM SORRY TO BOTHER YOU BUT I NEED TO APOLOGIZE.
I WANTED TO MAKE SOMETHING ON MY OWN FOR THE HARVEST, BUT THAT DOESN'T MEAN I COULDN'T HELP ALL OF YOU AS WELL.
I WAS WRONG. I HOPE I CAN MAKE AMENDS.
OH, GLOOPY...

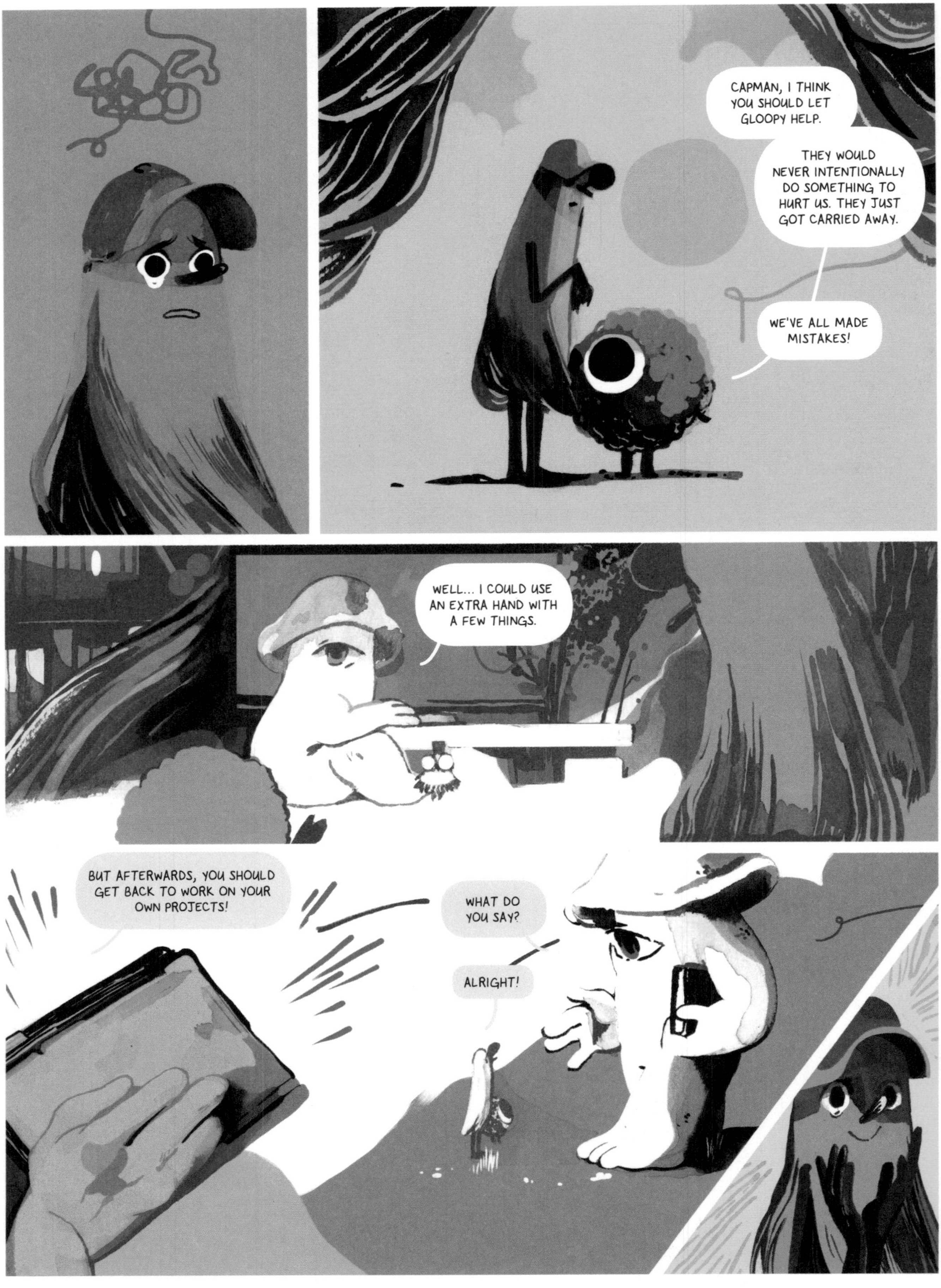
CAPMAN, I THINK YOU SHOULD LET GLOOPY HELP.
THEY WOULD NEVER INTENTIONALLY DO SOMETHING TO HURT US. THEY JUST GOT CARRIED AWAY.
WE'VE ALL MADE MISTAKES!
WELL... I COULD USE AN EXTRA HAND WITH A FEW THINGS.
BUT AFTERWARDS, YOU SHOULD GET BACK TO WORK ON YOUR OWN PROJECTS!
WHAT DO YOU SAY?
ALRIGHT!

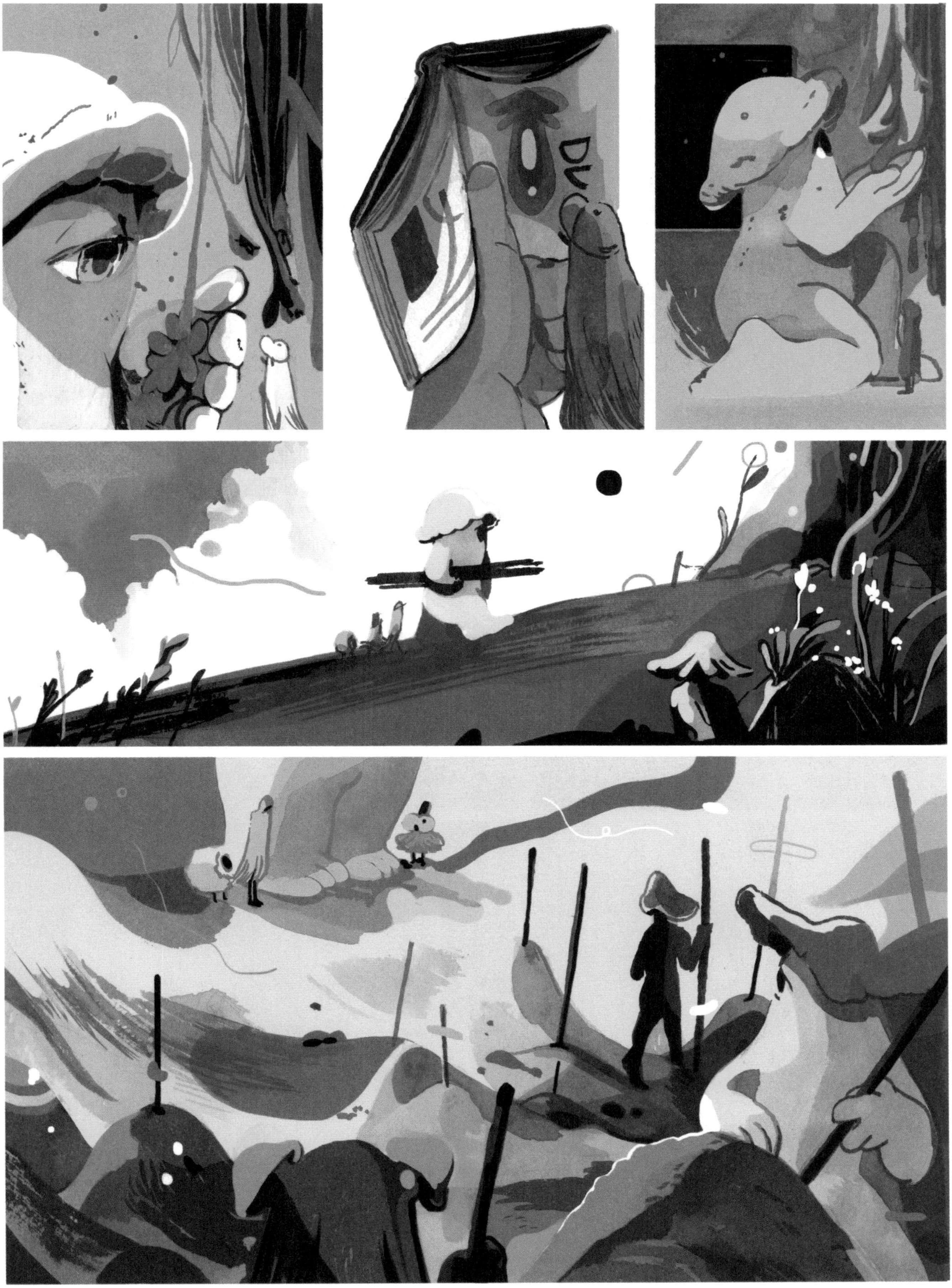

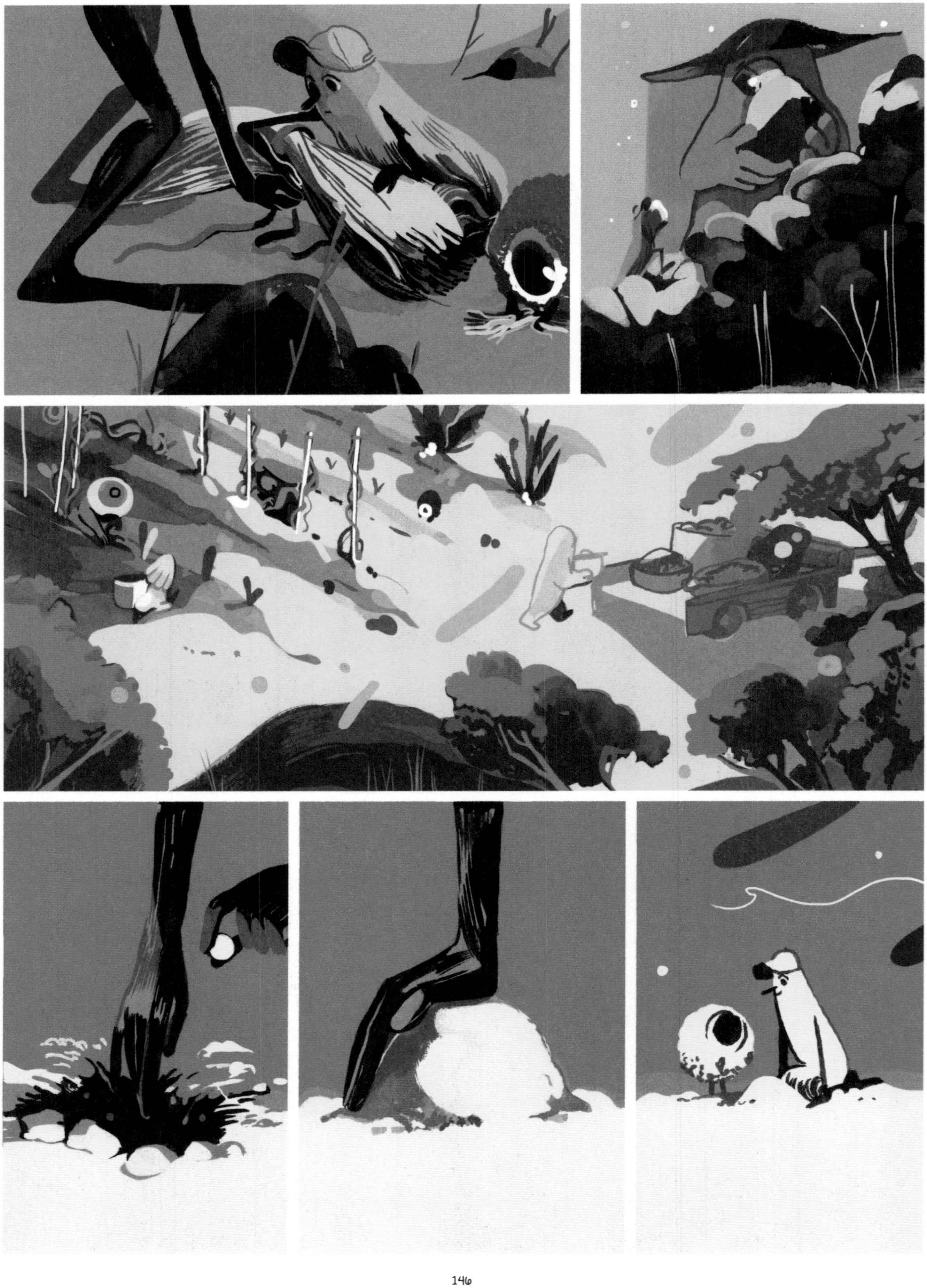

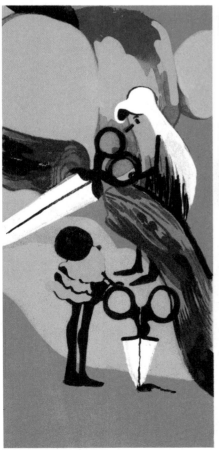

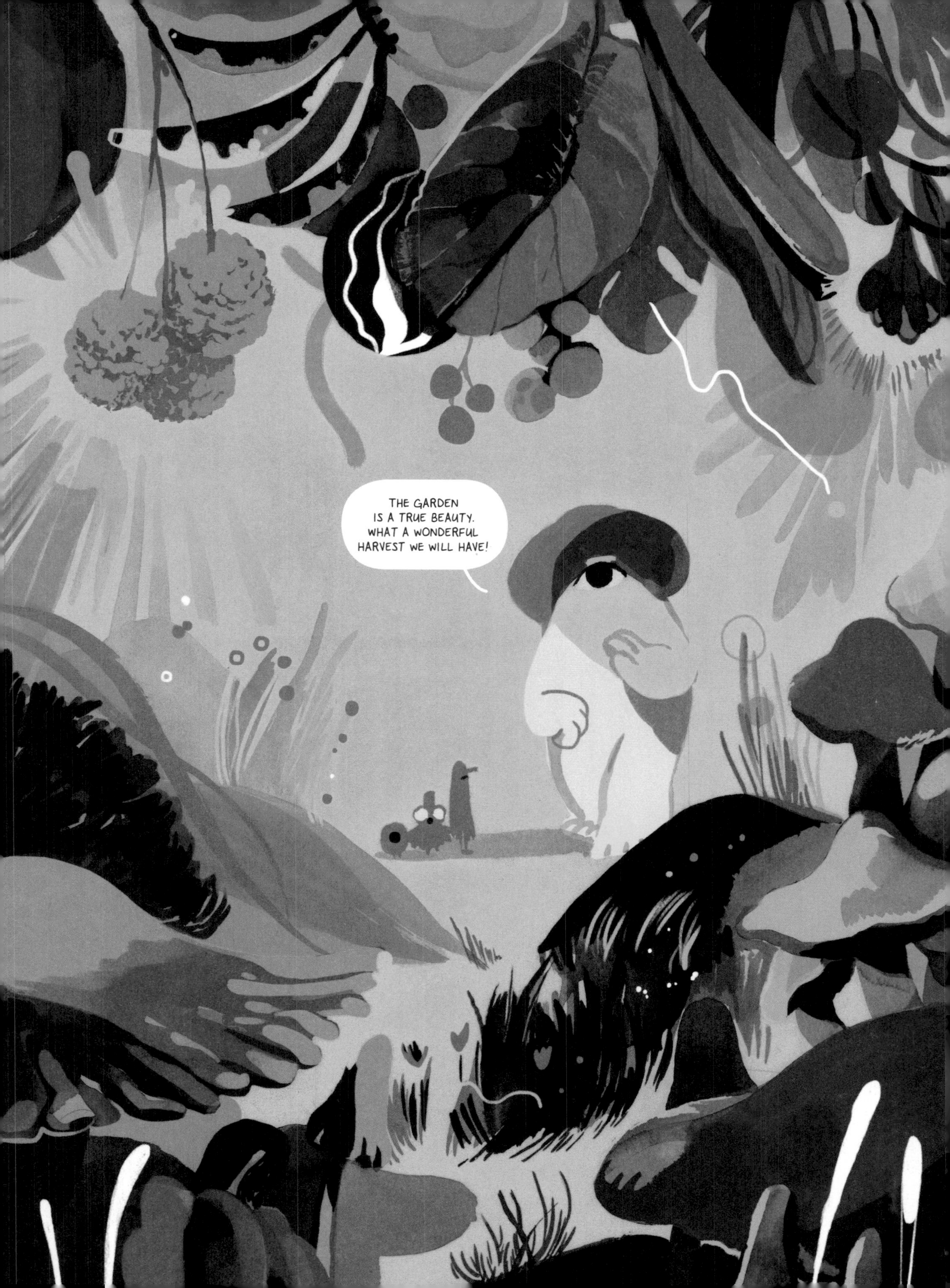
THE GARDEN IS A TRUE BEAUTY. WHAT A WONDERFUL HARVEST WE WILL HAVE!

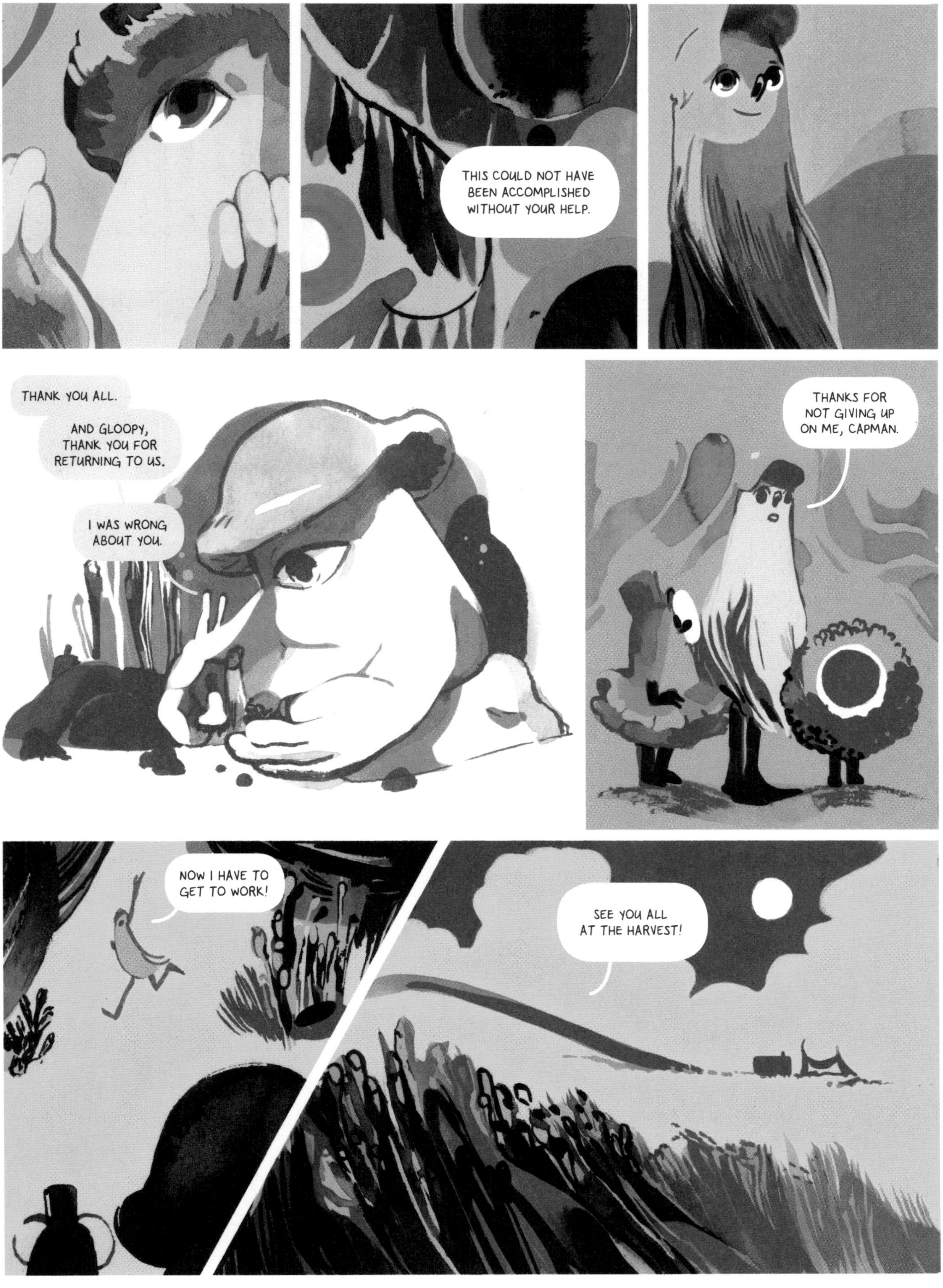
THIS COULD NOT HAVE BEEN ACCOMPLISHED WITHOUT YOUR HELP.
THANK YOU ALL.
AND GLOOPY, THANK YOU FOR RETURNING TO US.
I WAS WRONG ABOUT YOU.
THANKS FOR NOT GIVING UP ON ME, CAPMAN.
NOW I HAVE TO GET TO WORK!
SEE YOU ALL AT THE HARVEST!

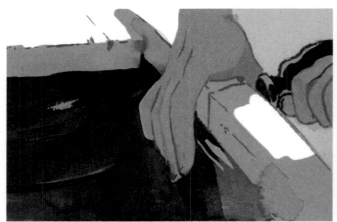

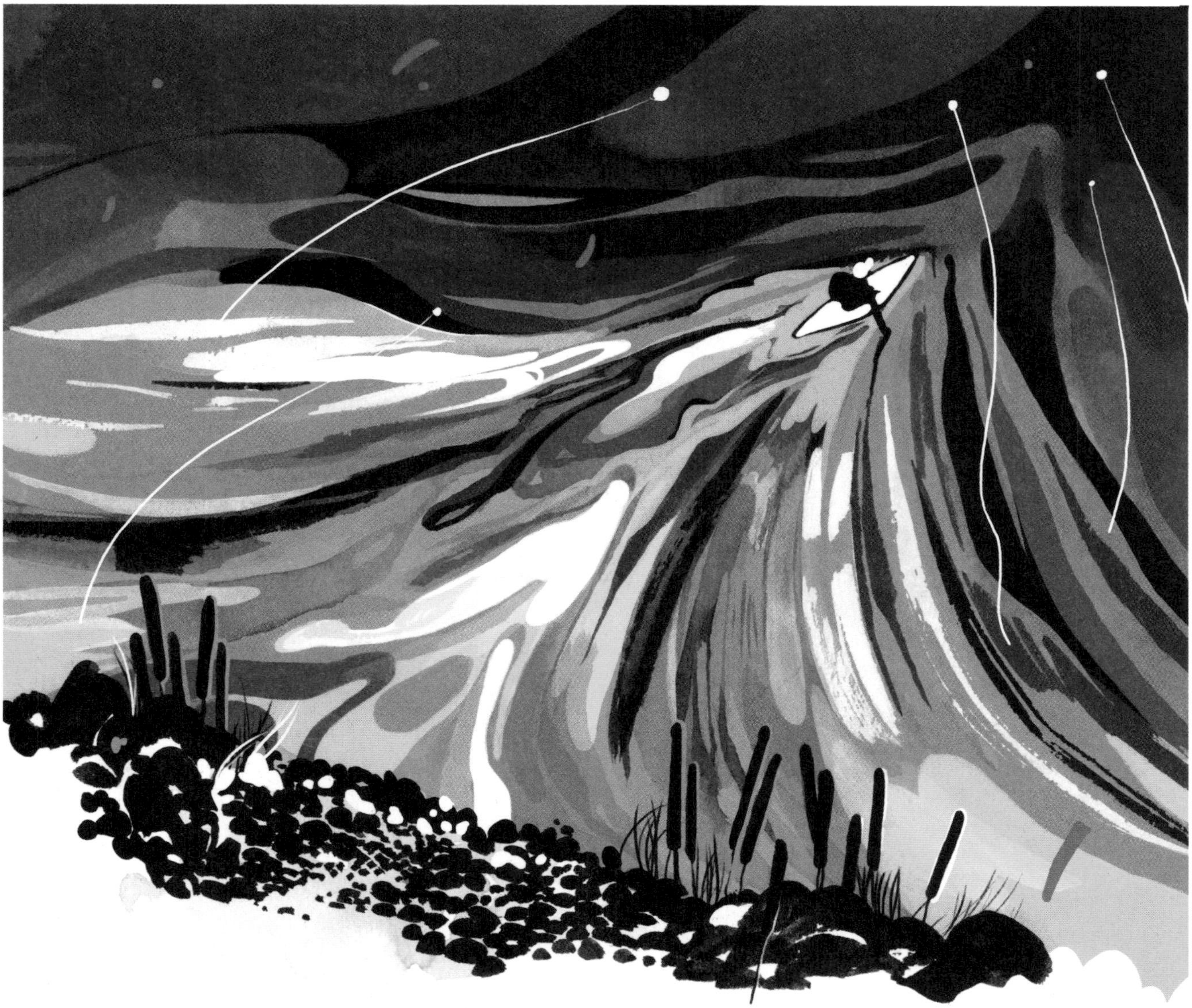

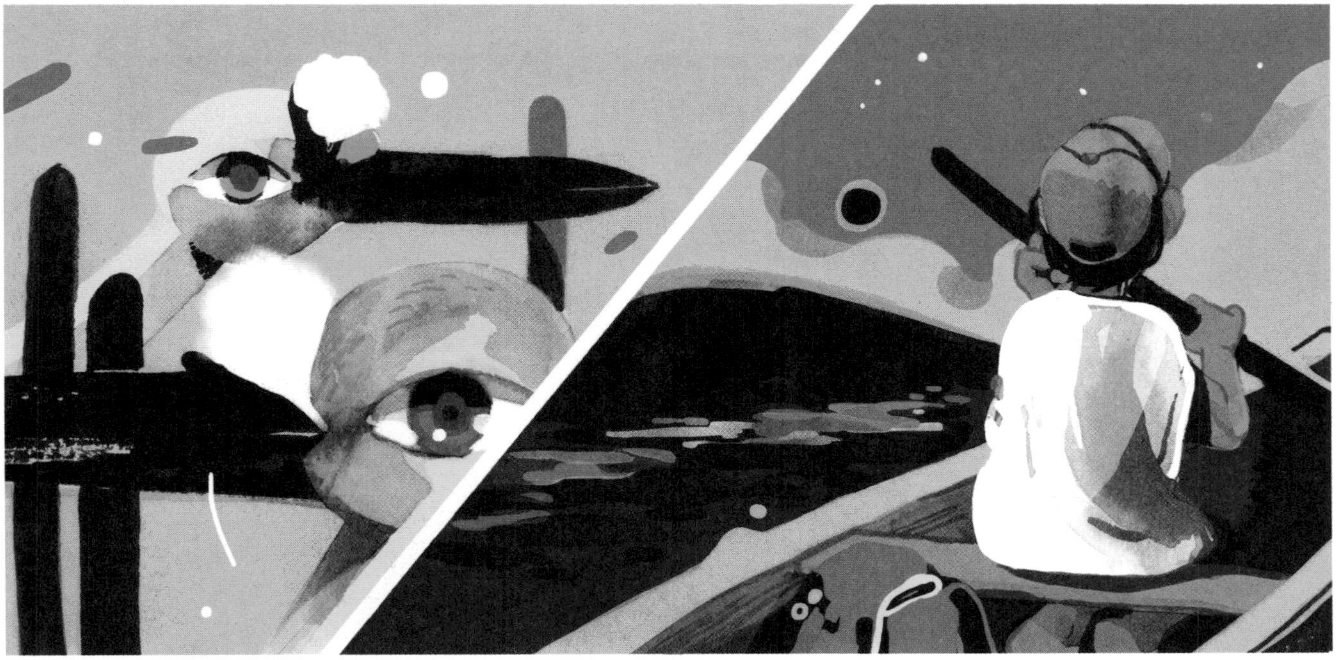

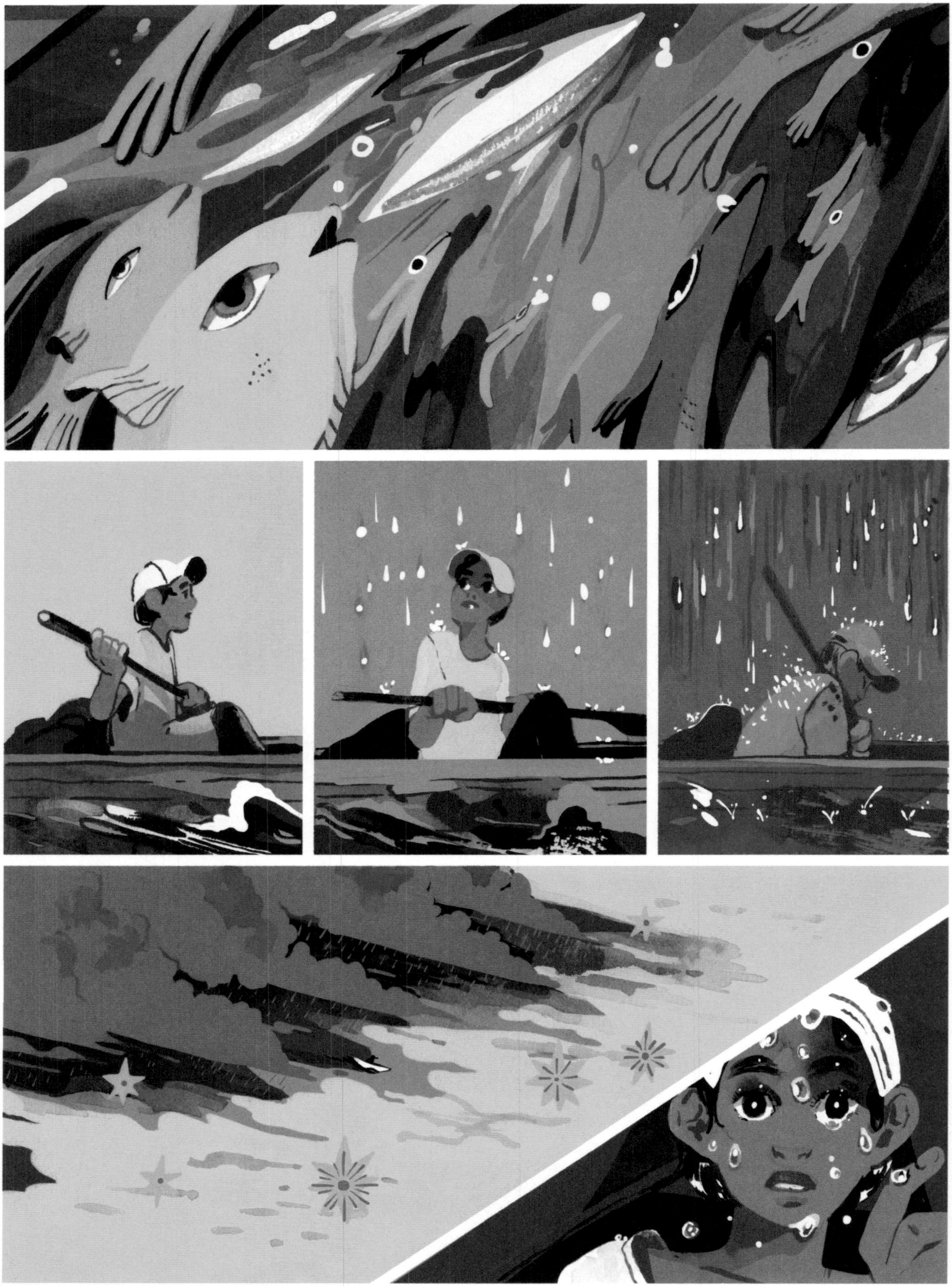

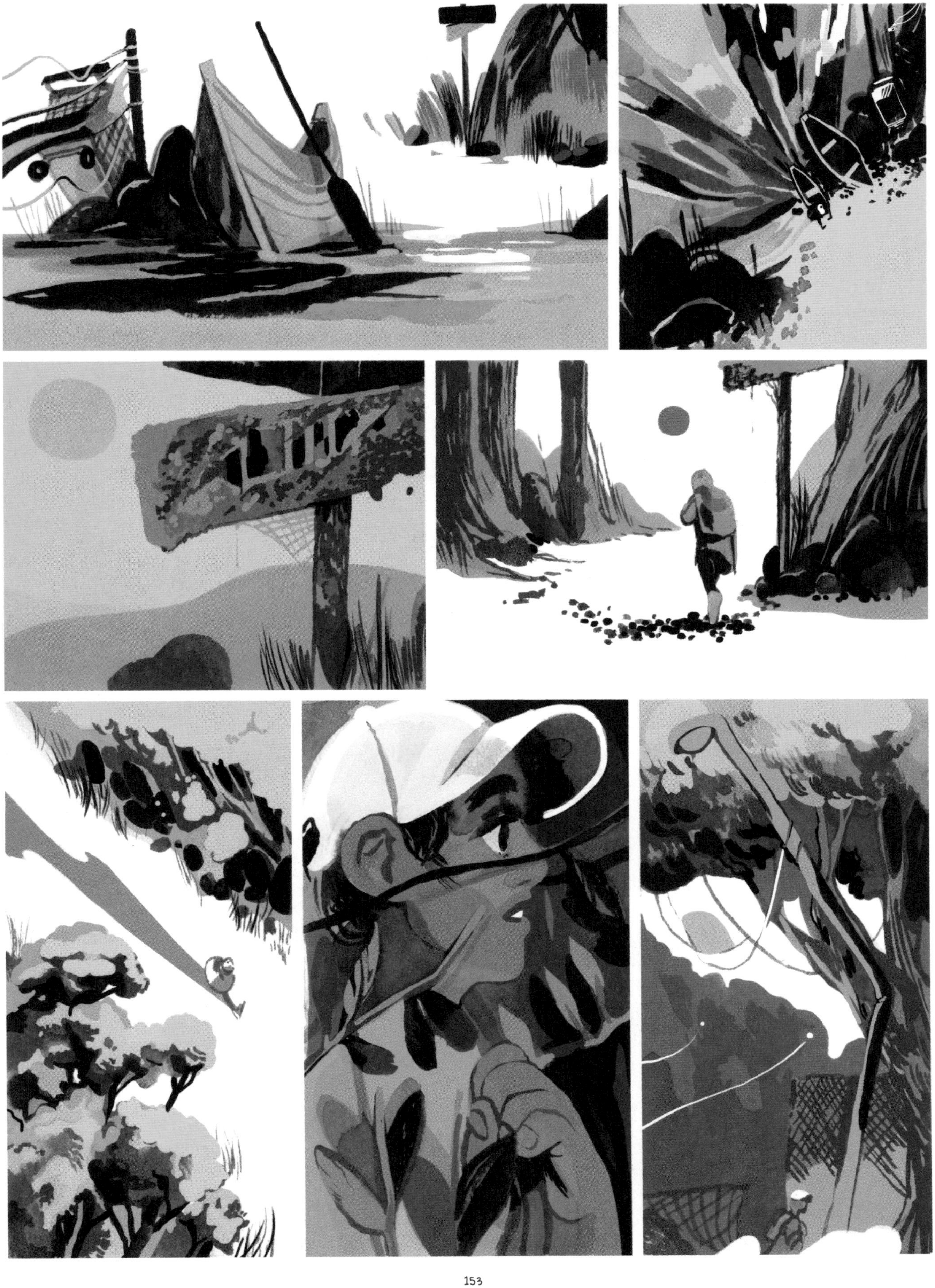

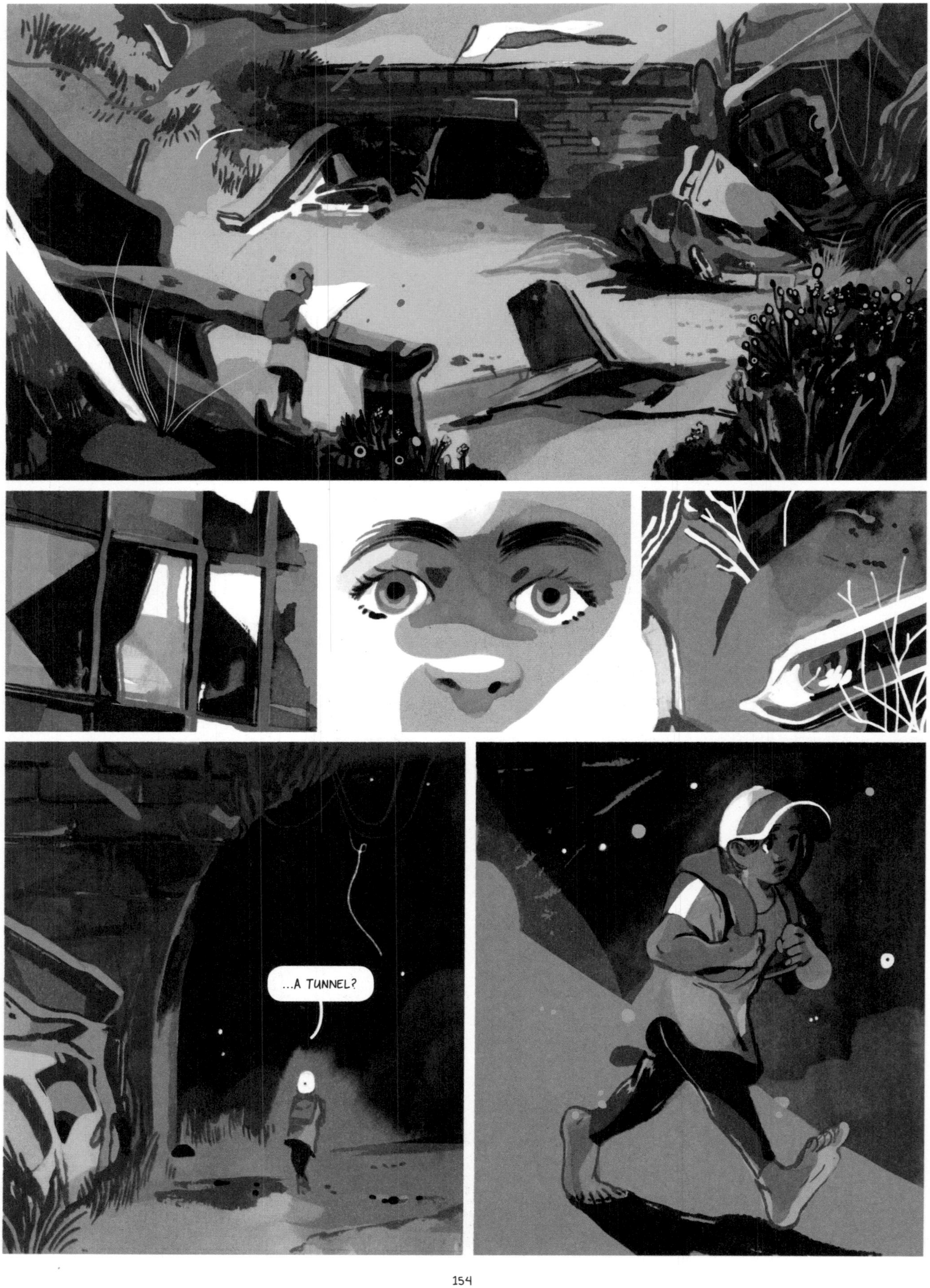
...A TUNNEL?

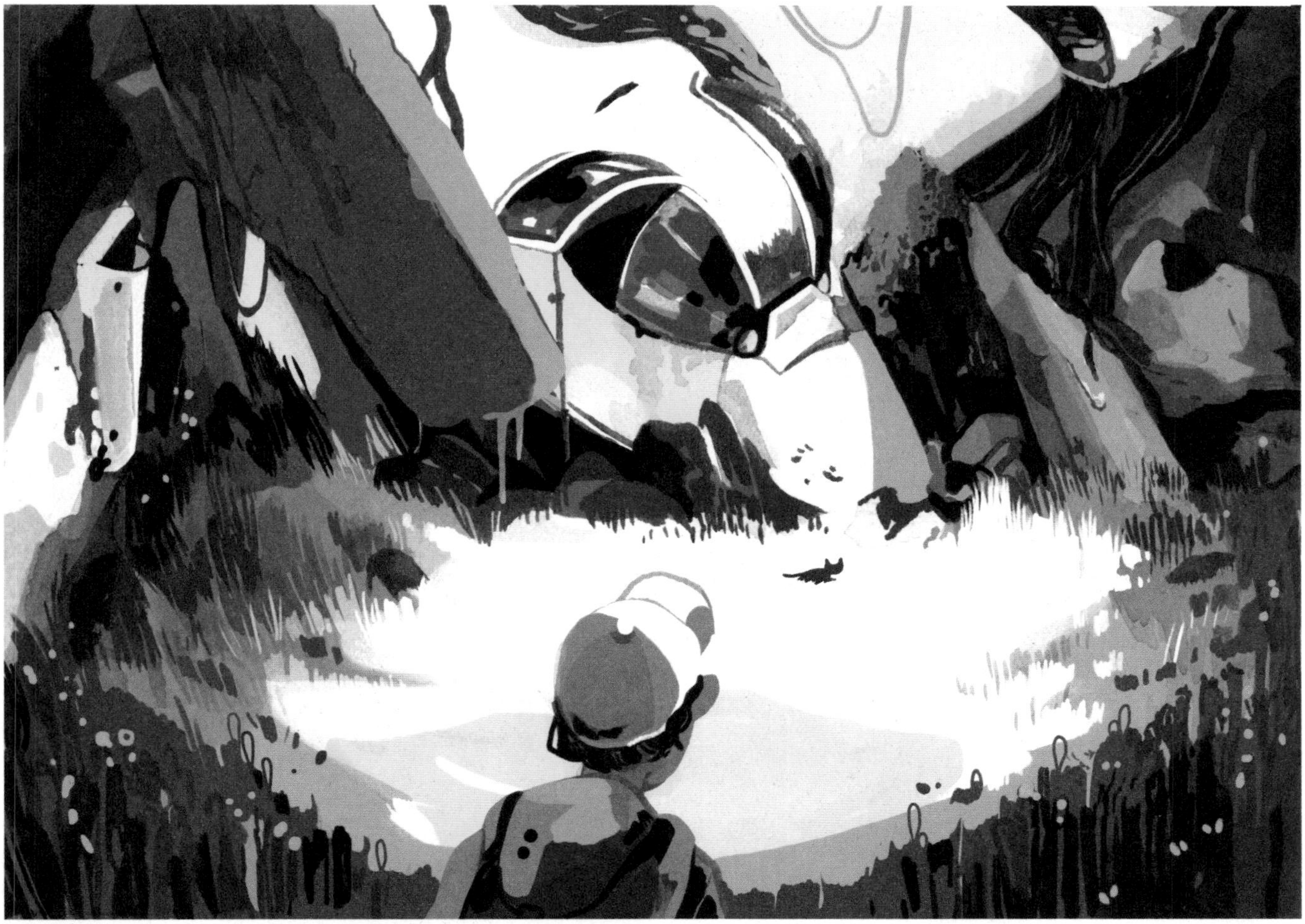
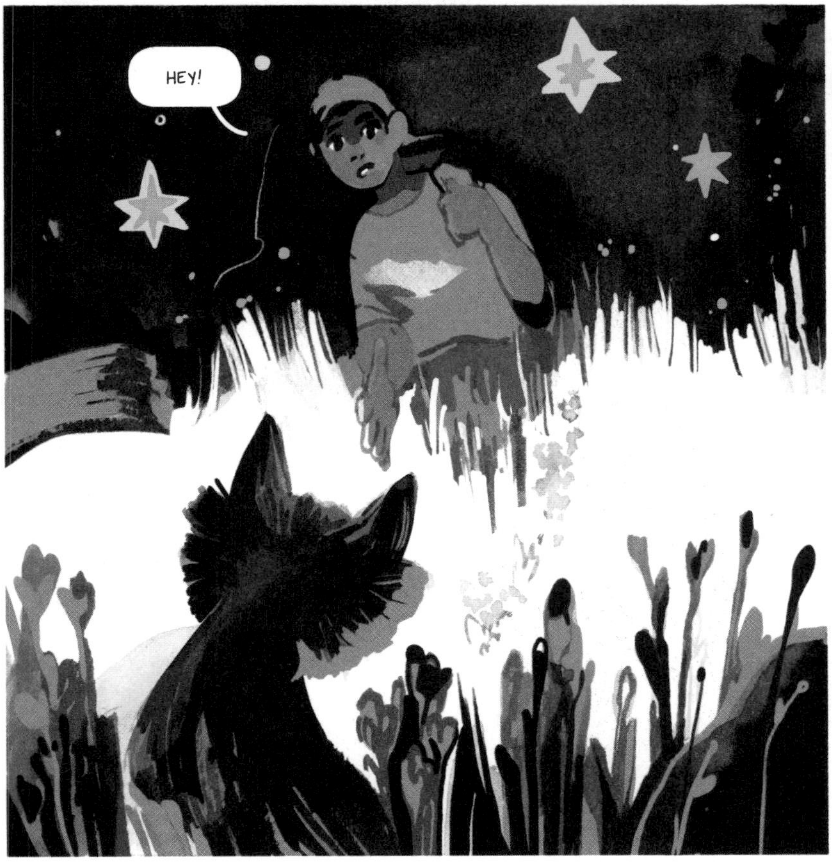
HEY!
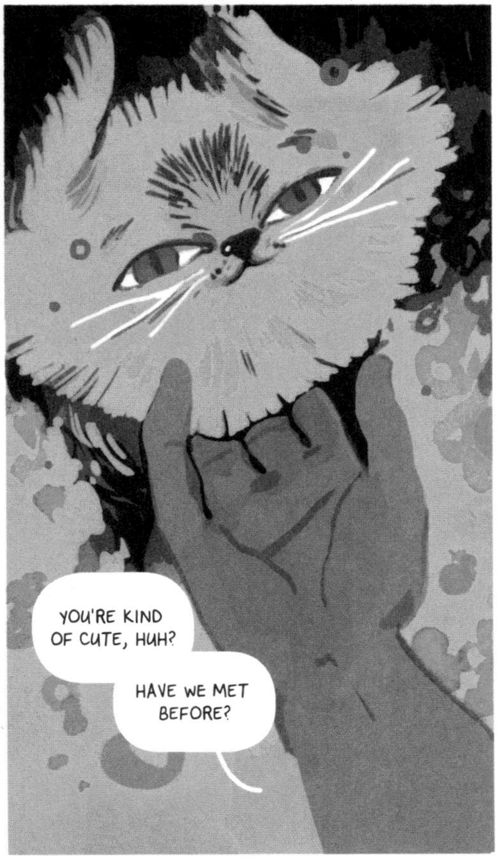
YOU'RE KIND OF CUTE, HUH?
HAVE WE MET BEFORE?

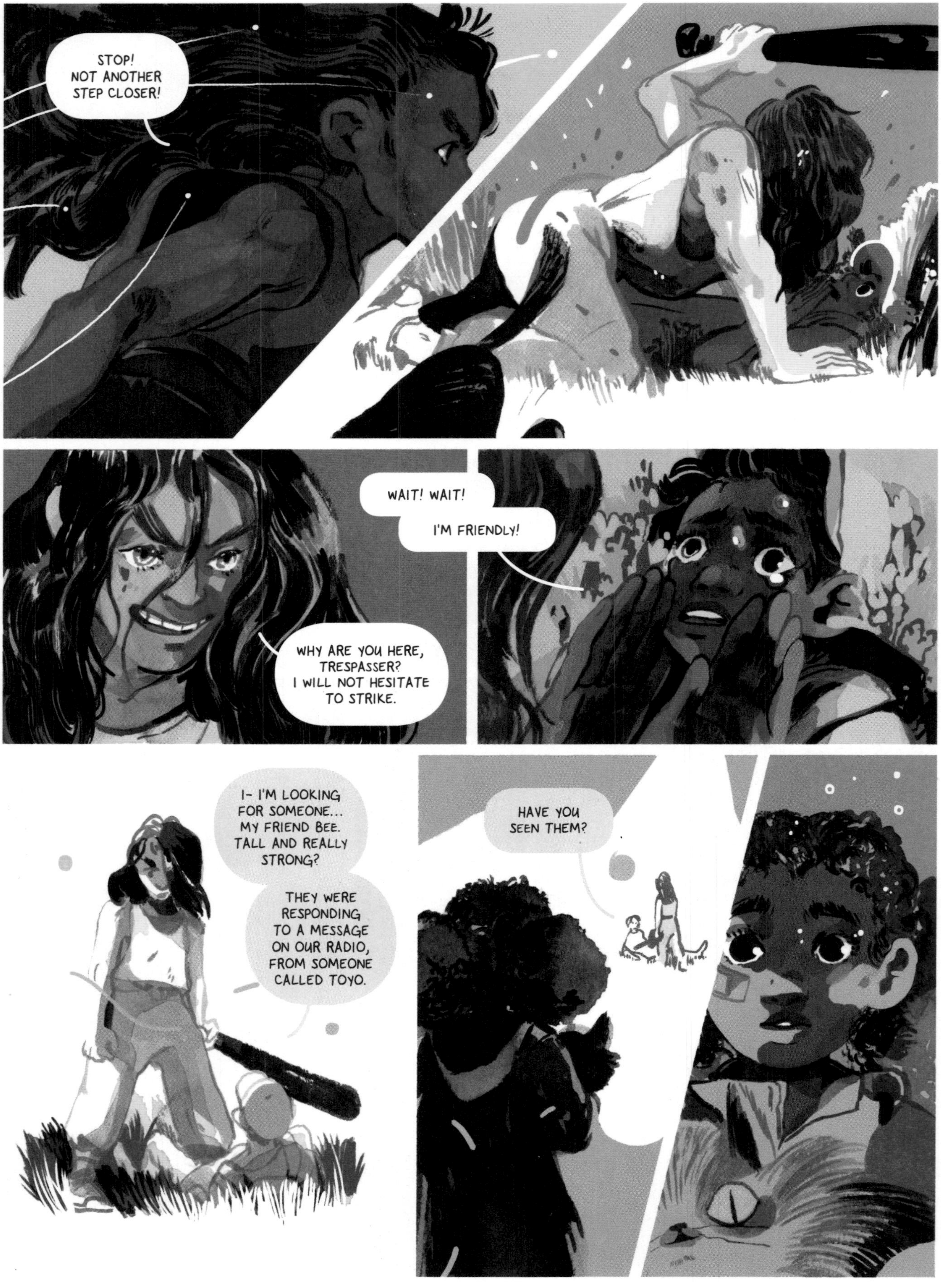
STOP! NOT ANOTHER STEP CLOSER!
WAIT! WAIT!
I'M FRIENDLY!
WHY ARE YOU HERE, TRESPASSER? I WILL NOT HESITATE TO STRIKE.
I- I'M LOOKING FOR SOMEONE... MY FRIEND BEE. TALL AND REALLY STRONG?
THEY WERE RESPONDING TO A MESSAGE ON OUR RADIO, FROM SOMEONE CALLED TOYO.
HAVE YOU SEEN THEM?

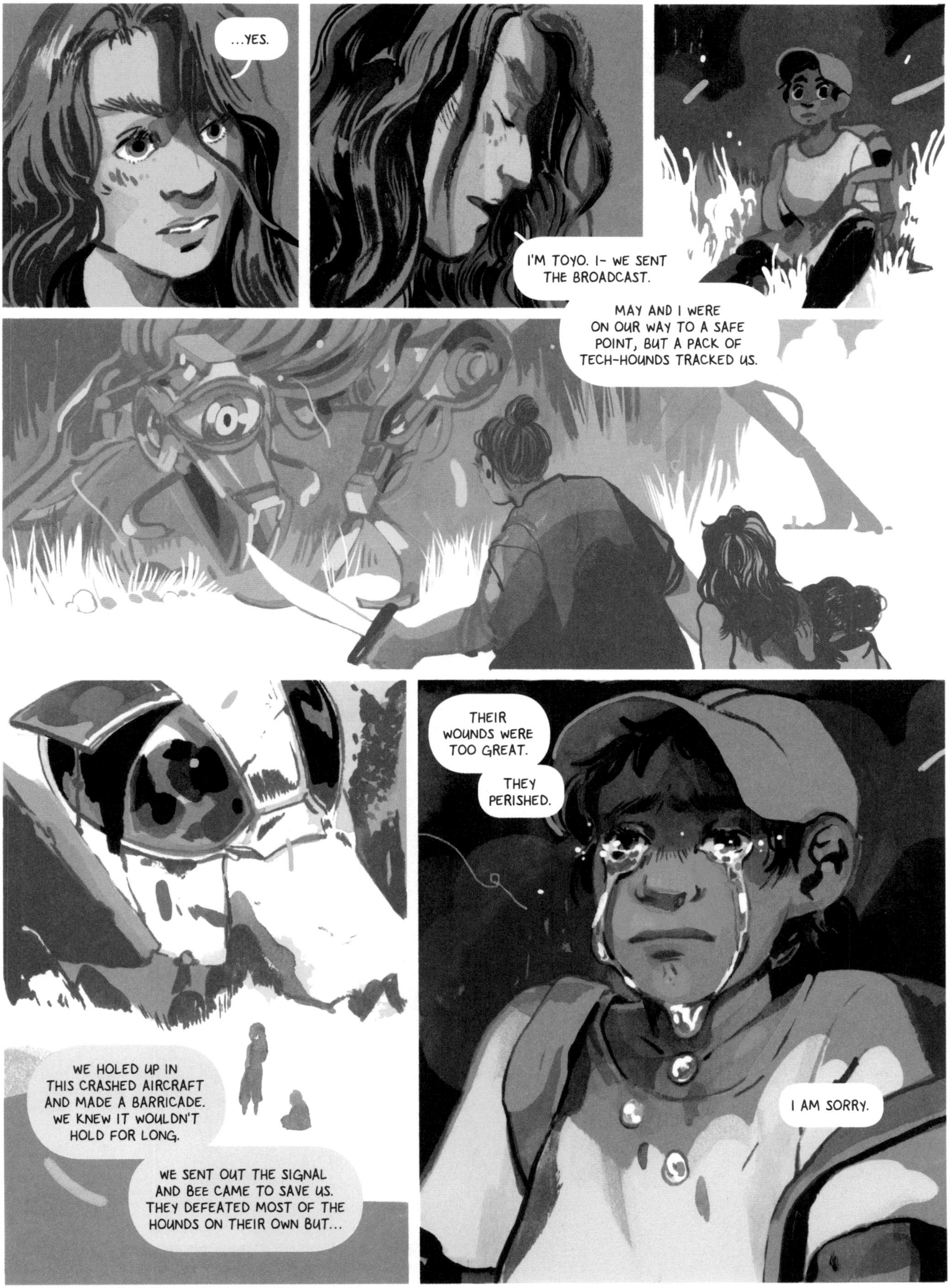
...YES.
I'M TOYO. I- WE SENT THE BROADCAST.
MAY AND I WERE ON OUR WAY TO A SAFE POINT, BUT A PACK OF TECH-HOUNDS TRACKED US.
WE HOLED UP IN THIS CRASHED AIRCRAFT AND MADE A BARRICADE. WE KNEW IT WOULDN'T HOLD FOR LONG.
WE SENT OUT THE SIGNAL AND BEE CAME TO SAVE US. THEY DEFEATED MOST OF THE HOUNDS ON THEIR OWN BUT...
THEIR WOUNDS WERE TOO GREAT.
THEY PERISHED.
I AM SORRY.

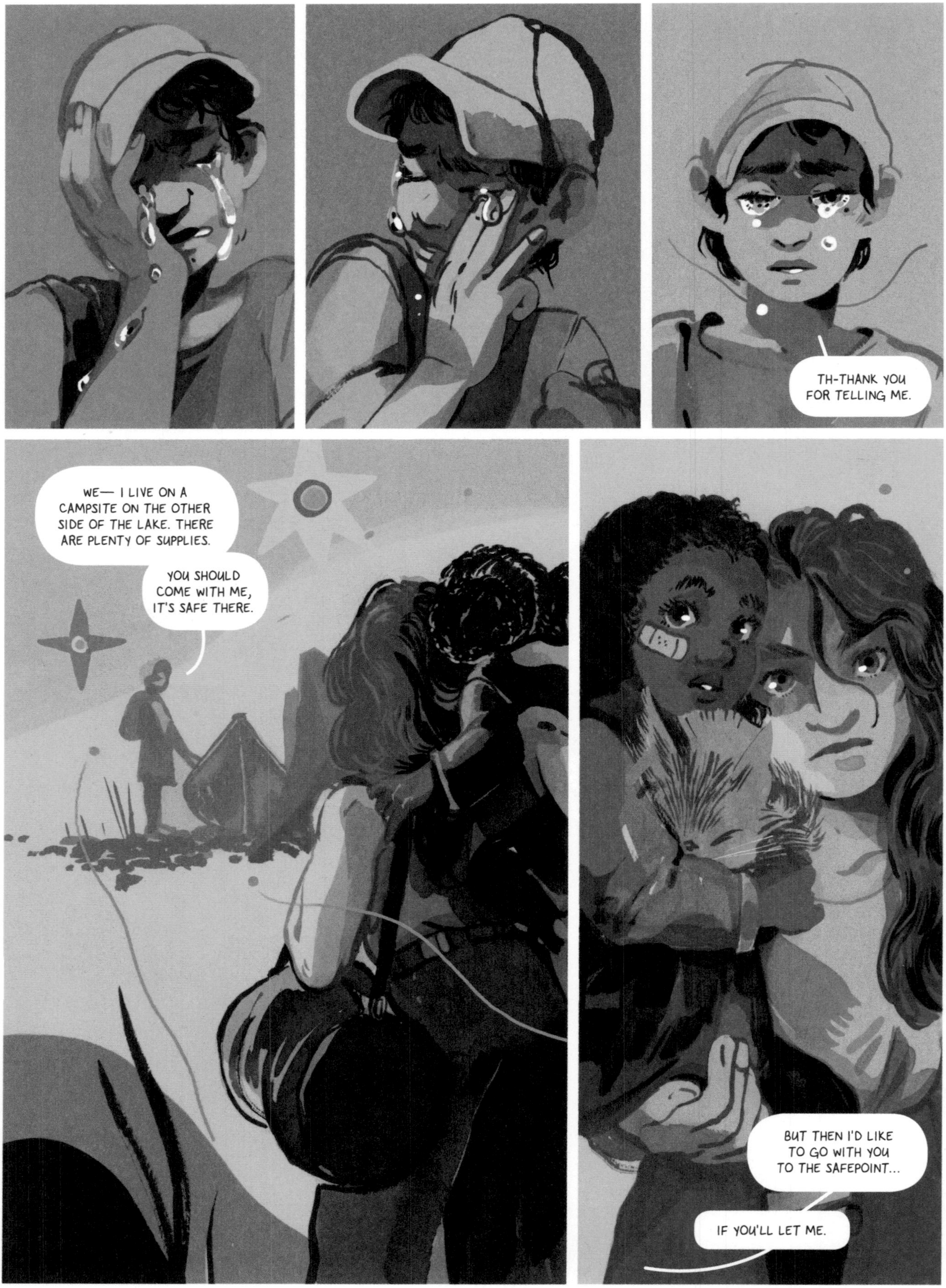
TH-THANK YOU FOR TELLING ME.
WE— I LIVE ON A CAMPSITE ON THE OTHER SIDE OF THE LAKE. THERE ARE PLENTY OF SUPPLIES.
YOU SHOULD COME WITH ME, IT'S SAFE THERE.
BUT THEN I'D LIKE TO GO WITH YOU TO THE SAFEPOINT...
IF YOU'LL LET ME.

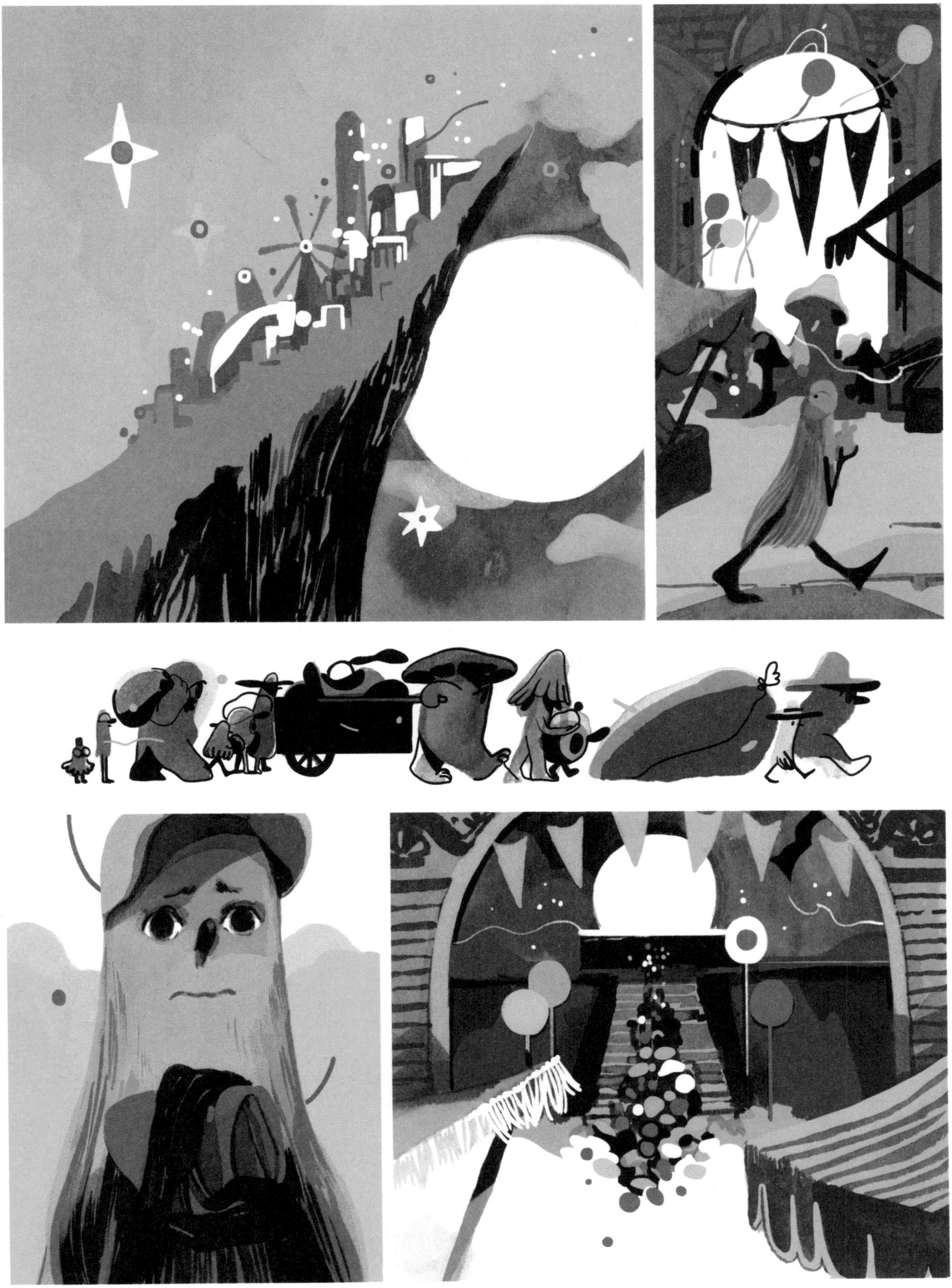

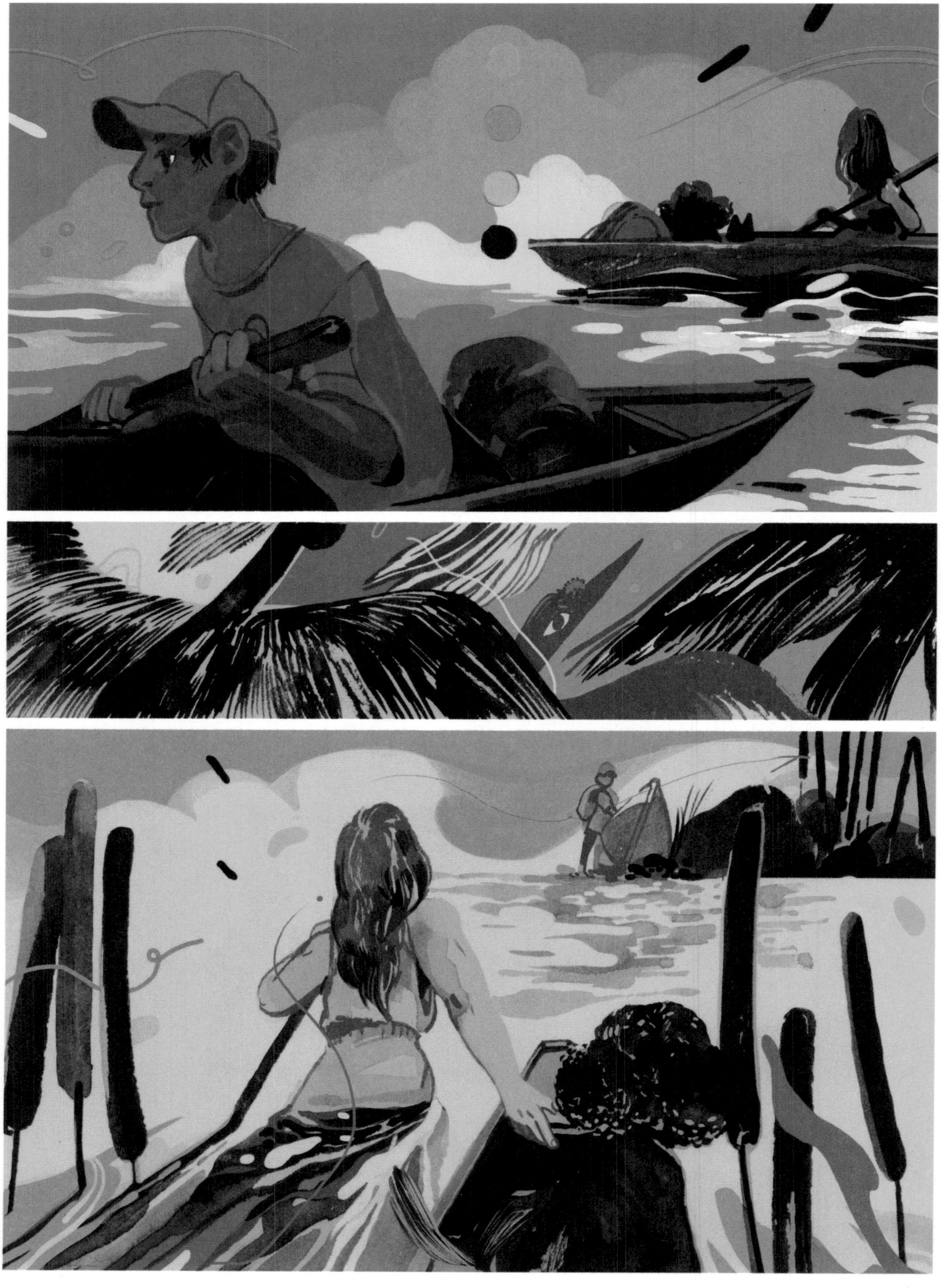

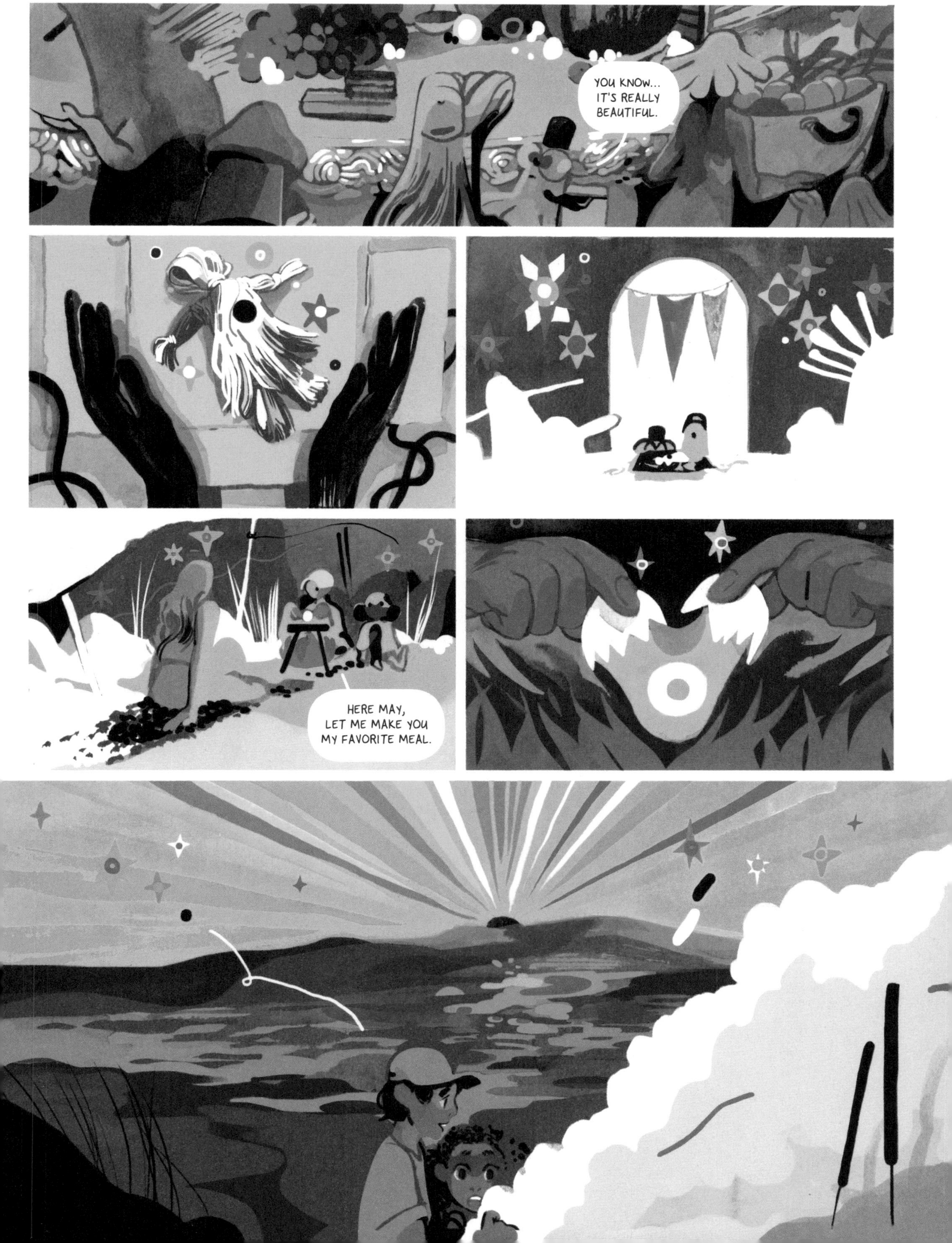
YOU KNOW... IT'S REALLY BEAUTIFUL.
HERE MAY, LET ME MAKE YOU MY FAVORITE MEAL.

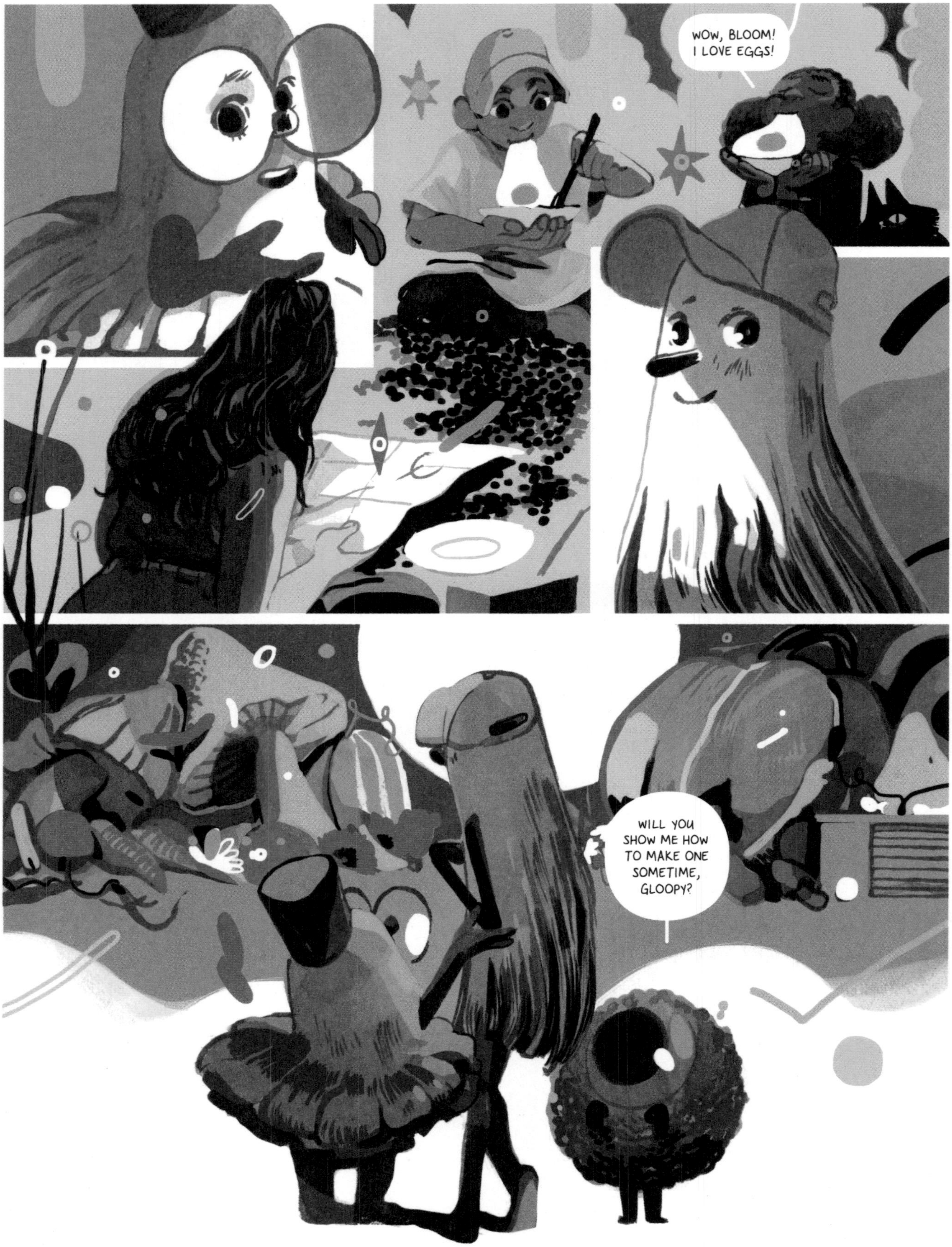
WOW, BLOOM! I LOVE EGGS!
WILL YOU SHOW ME HOW TO MAKE ONE SOMETIME, GLOOPY?

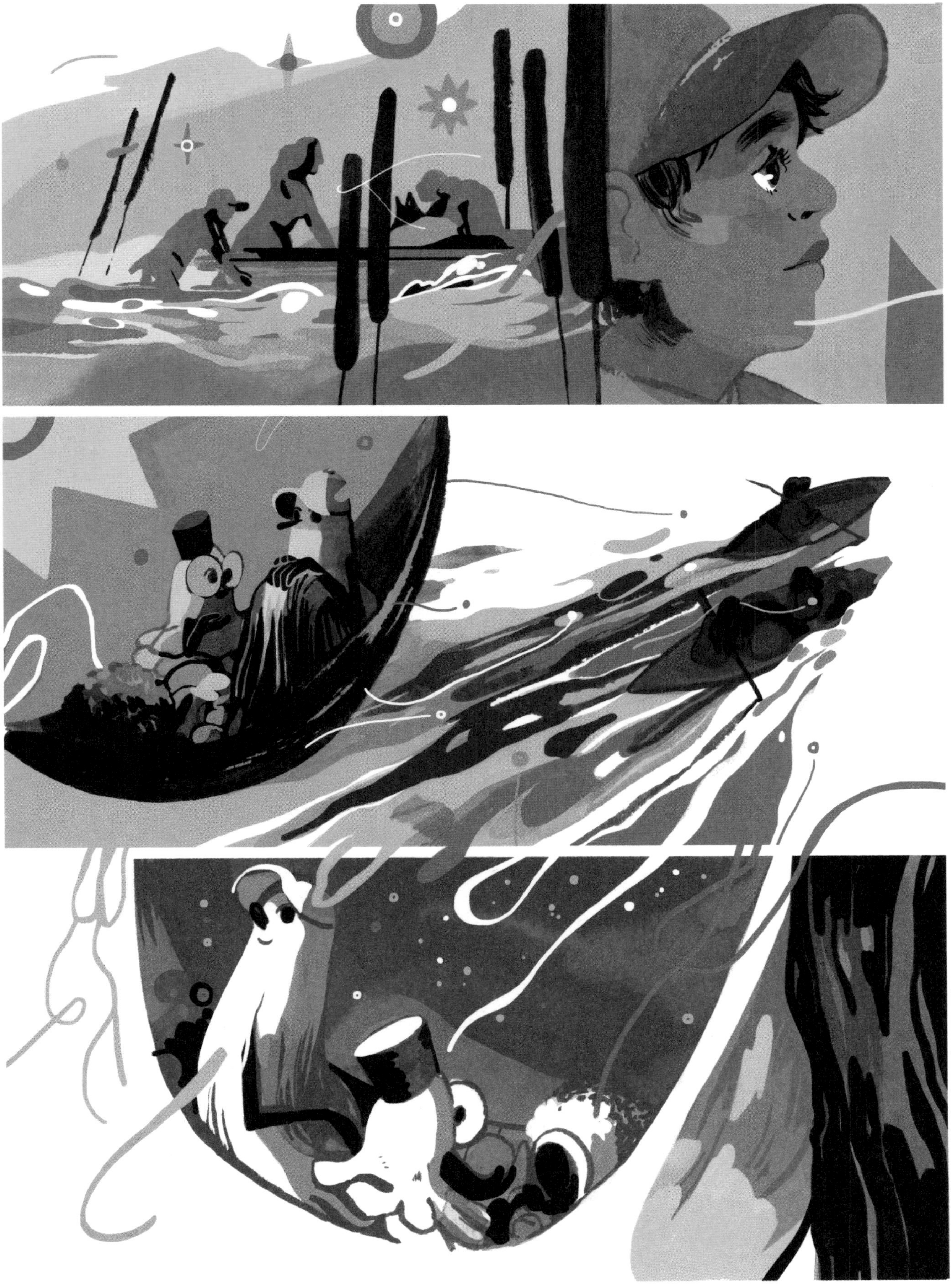

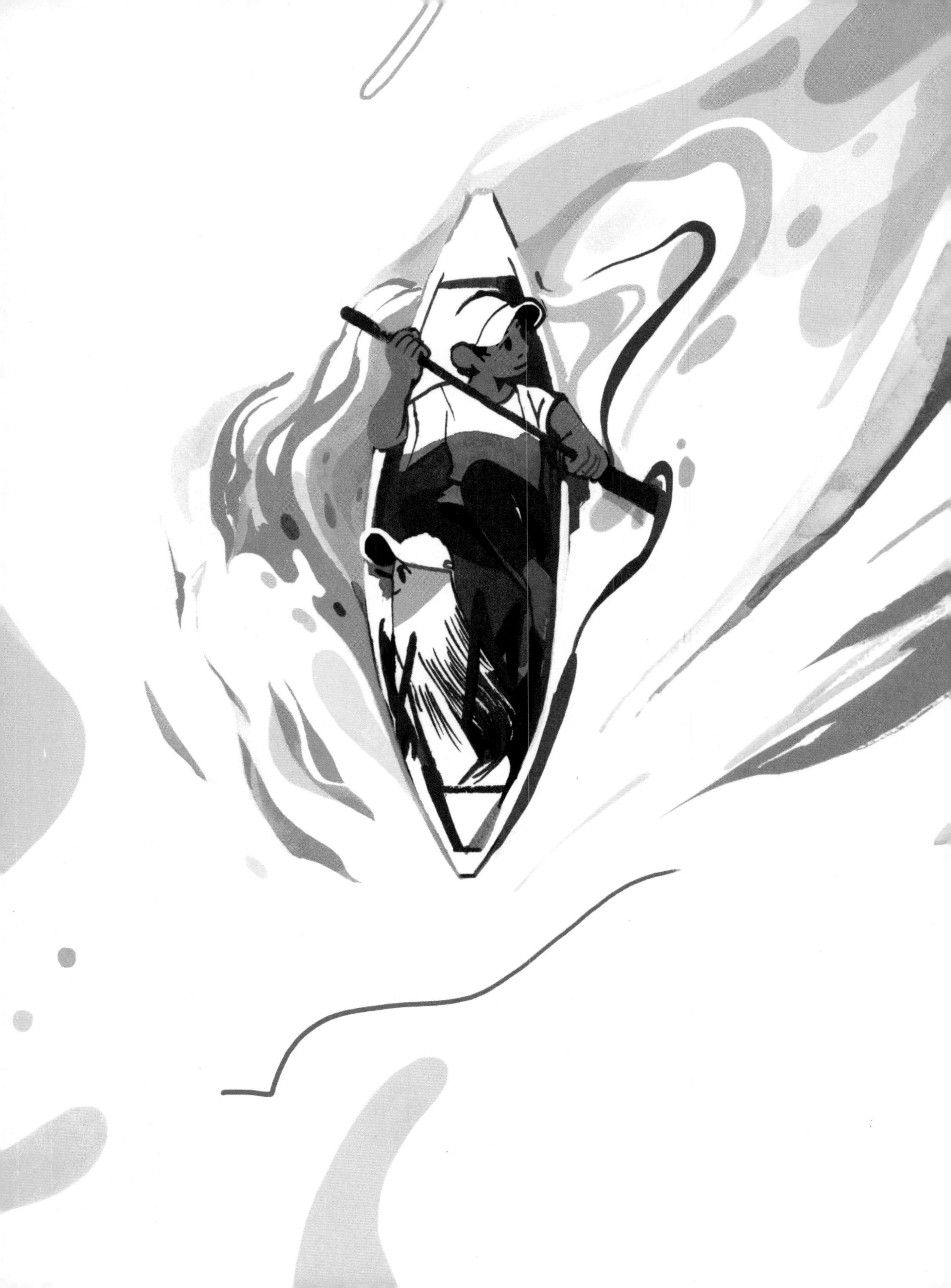

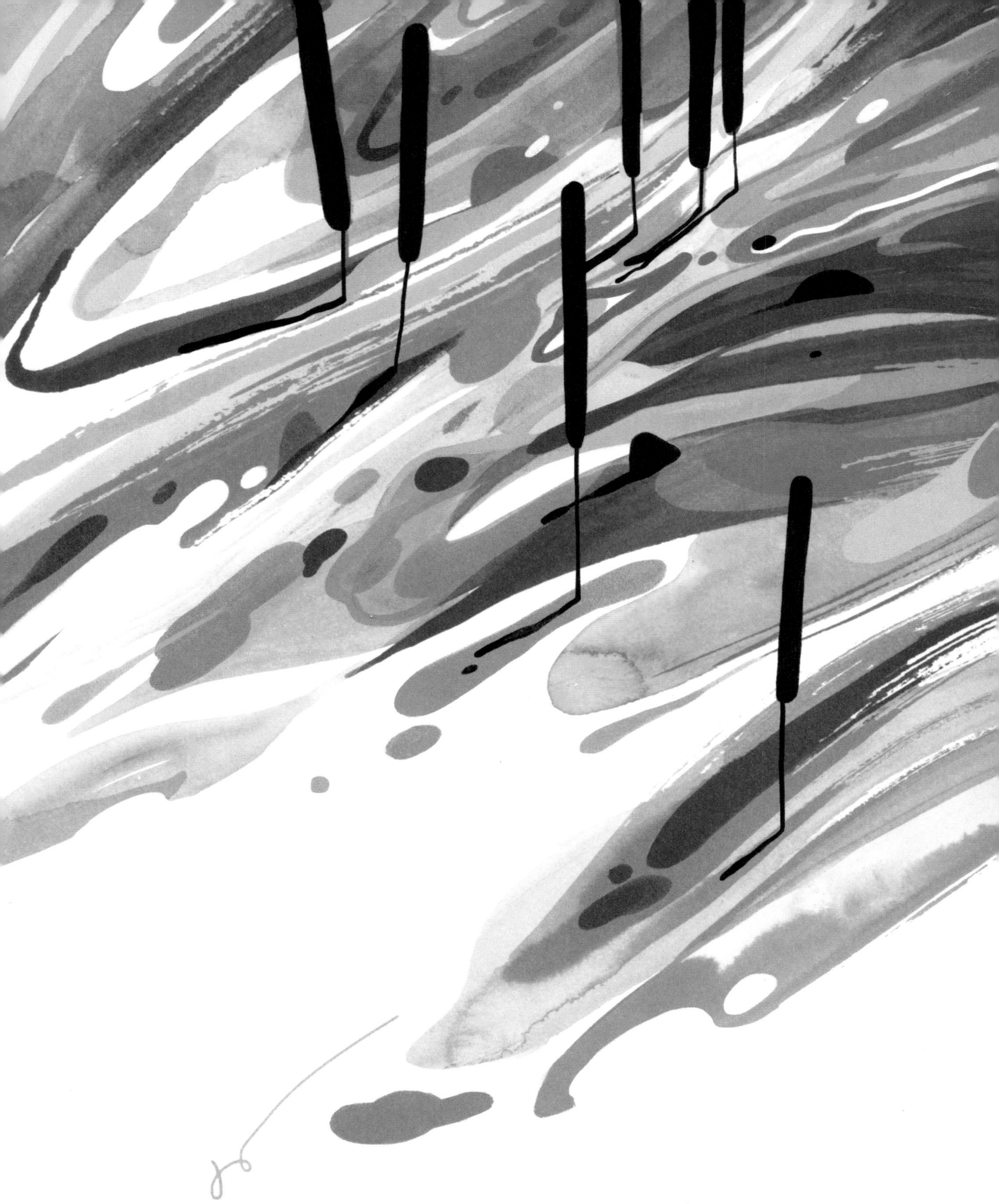

ABOUT THE AUTHOR

MOLLY MENDOZA IS AN AMERICAN ILLUSTRATOR AND
COMIC ARTIST WHO GRADUATED FROM PACIFIC NORTHWEST
COLLEGE OF ART. SHE HAS GONE ON TO DEVELOP A RICH
PERSONAL ART PRACTICE, SELF-PUBLISHING COMICS AS WELL
AS WORKING IN THE EDITORIAL WORLD. MOLLY HOPES
TO CONNECT HER VIEWERS TO THEIR DEEPEST FEELINGS
AND EMOTIONS THROUGH HER VISUALS AND STORIES.
SHE CURRENTLY LIVES IN PORTLAND, OREGON.